TITLES AVAILABLE IN THE BILL OF RIGHTS SERIES

THE FIRST AMENDMENT

*The Establishment of Religion Clause: Its Constitutional History
and the Contemporary Debate*
    Edited by Alan Brownstein

Freedom of the Press: Its Constitutional History and the Contemporary Debate
    Edited by Garrett Epps

*The Free Exercise of Religion Clause: Its Constitutional History
and the Contemporary Debate*
    Edited by Thomas C. Berg

Freedom of Speech: Its Constitutional History and the Contemporary Debate
    Edited by Vikram David Amar

*Freedom of Assembly and Petition: Its Constitutional History
and the Contemporary Debate*
    Edited by Margaret M. Russell

THE FOURTH AMENDMENT

Searches and Seizures: Its Constitutional History and the Contemporary Debate
    Edited by Cynthia Lee

BILL OF RIGHTS SERIES

Series Editor:
David B. Oppenheimer, *Clinical Professor of Law and Director of Professional Skills*
University of California, Berkeley, School of Law

Advisory Committee

"This is a highly useful edited compilation of some of the most important classic and recent articles published by some of the finest scholars of Fourth Amendment search-and-seizure law—a great overview of the history, present, and future of an amendment that is so important to the lives of American citizens."

—Joshua Dressler, Frank R. Strong Chair in Law,
Michael E. Moritz College of Law, Ohio State University;
coauthor of *Understanding Criminal Procedure* and
Criminal Procedure: Principles, Policies and Perspectives

THE FOURTH AMENDMENT
SEARCHES AND SEIZURES

THE FOURTH AMENDMENT
SEARCHES
AND SEIZURES

Its Constitutional History and the Contemporary Debate

EDITED BY CYNTHIA LEE

Prometheus Books
59 John Glenn Drive
Amherst, New York 14228-2119

Published 2011 by Prometheus Books

Background image Library of Congress/American Memory.
Cover design by Grace M. Conti-Zilsberger.

Inquiries should be addressed to
Prometheus Books
59 John Glenn Drive
Amherst, New York 14228–2119
VOICE: 716–691–0133
FAX: 716–691–0137
WWW.PROMETHEUSBOOKS.COM

15 14 13 12 11   5 4 3 2 1

Library of Congress Cataloging-in-Publication Data

Lee, Cynthia.
    The Fourth Amendment: searches and seizures : its constitutional history and the contemporary debate / [edited by] Cynthia Lee.
        p. cm. — (Bill of Rights series)
    Includes bibliographical references.
    ISBN 978–1–61614–180–6 (pbk.)
    1. Searches and seizures—United States—History. 2. United States. Constitution. 4th Amendment. I. Lee, Cynthia, 1961–

KF9630.F68 2010
345.73'0522—dc22

2010006932

Printed in the United States of America on acid-free paper

CONTENTS

8 CONTENTS

BILL OF RIGHTS
SERIES EDITOR'S PREFACE

Abortion; the death penalty; school prayer; the pledge of allegiance; torture; surveillance; tort reform; jury trials; preventative detention; firearm registration; censorship; privacy; police misconduct; birth control; school vouchers; prison crowding; taking property by public domain—these issues, torn from the headlines, cover many, if not most, of the major public disputes arising today, in the dawn of the twenty-first century. Yet they are resolved by our courts based on a document fewer than five hundred words long, drafted in the eighteenth century, and regarded by many at the time of its drafting as unnecessary. The Bill of Rights, the name we give the first ten amendments to the United States Constitution, is our basic source of law for resolving these issues. This series of books, of which this is volume 6, is intended to help us improve our understanding of the debates that gave rise to these rights, and of the continuing controversy about their meaning today.

When our Constitution was drafted, the framers were concerned with defining the structure and powers of our new federal government, and balancing its three branches. They didn't initially focus on the question of individual rights. The drafters organized the Constitution into seven sections, termed "Articles," each concerned with a specific area of federal authority. Article I sets forth the legislative powers of the Congress; Article II the executive powers of the president; Article III the judicial power of the federal courts. Article V governs the process for amending the Constitution. Article VI declares the supremacy of federal law on those subjects under federal jurisdiction, while Article VII provides the process for ratification. Only Article IV is concerned with individual rights, and only in a single sentence requiring states to give citizens of other states the same rights they provide to their own citizens. (Article IV also provides for the return of runaway slaves, a provision repealed in 1865 by the Thirteenth Amendment.)

When the Constitutional Convention completed its work, in 1787, it sent the Constitution to the states for adoption. The opponents of ratification, known as the "Anti-Federalists" because they opposed the strong federal government envisioned in the Constitution, argued that without a Bill of Rights the federal government would be a danger to liberty. The "Federalists," principally Alexander Hamilton, James Madison, and John Jay, responded in a series of anonymous newspaper articles now known as the "Federalist Papers." The Federalists initially argued that there was no need for a federal Bill of Rights, because most states (seven) had a state Bill of Rights, and because the proposed Constitution limited the power of the federal government to only those areas specifically enumerated, leaving all remaining powers to the states or the people. But in time, Madison would become the great proponent and drafter of the Bill of Rights.

The proposed Constitution was sent to the states for ratification on September 17, 1787. Delaware was the first state to assent, followed rapidly by Pennsylvania, New Jersey, Georgia, and Connecticut. But when the Massachusetts Legislature met in January 1788 to debate ratification, several vocal members took up the objection that without a Bill of Rights the proposed Constitution endangered individual liberty. A compromise was brokered, with the Federalists agreeing to support amending the Constitution to add a Bill of Rights following ratification. The Anti-Federalists, led by John Adams and John Hancock, agreed, and Massachusetts ratified. When Maryland, South Carolina, and New Hampshire followed, the requisite nine states had signed on. Virginia and New York quickly followed, with North Carolina ratifying in 1789, and Rhode Island in 1790. In addition to Massachusetts's, the New Hampshire, Virginia, and New York ratifying conventions conditioned their acceptance on the understanding that a Bill of Rights would be added.

The first Congress met in New York in March 1789, and among its first acts began debating and drafting the Bill of Rights. Federalist Congressman

James Madison took responsibility for drafting the bill, having by then concluded that it would strengthen the legitimacy of the new government. He relied heavily on the state constitutions, especially the Virginia Declaration of Rights, in setting out those individual rights that should be protected from federal interference.

Madison steered seventeen proposed amendments through the House, of which the Senate agreed to twelve. On September 2, 1789, President Washington sent them to the states for ratification. Of the twelve, two, concerning congressional representation and congressional pay, failed to achieve ratification by over three-quarters of the states (the congressional pay amendment was finally ratified in 1992). The remaining ten were ratified and, with the vote of Virginia, on December 15, 1791, became the first ten amendments to the Constitution, or the "Bill of Rights."

The Bill of Rights as originally adopted only applied to the federal government. Its purpose was to restrict Congress from interfering with rights reserved to the people. Thus, under the First Amendment the Congress could not establish a national religion, but the states could establish state support for selected religions, as seven states to some extent did (Connecticut, Georgia, Maryland, Massachusetts, New Hampshire, South Carolina, and Vermont). Madison had proposed that the states also be bound by the Bill of Rights, and the House agreed, but the Senate rejected the proposal.

Although the Declaration of Independence provided that "We hold these truths to be self-evident, that all men are created equal," the Constitution and the Bill of Rights are conspicuously silent on the question of equality, because the agreement that made the Constitution possible was the North/South compromise permitting the continuation of slavery. Thus, today's issues like affirmative action, race and sex discrimination, school segregation, and same-sex marriage cannot be resolved through application of the Bill of Rights. This omission of a guarantee of equality led to the Civil War, and in turn to the post–Civil War Fourteenth Amendment that made the newly freed slaves US and state citizens and prohibited the states from denying equal protection of the laws or due process of law to any citizen. In light of this amendment, the Supreme Court began developing the "incorporation doctrine," holding that the Fourteenth Amendment extended the Bill of Rights so that it applied to all government action. By applying the Bill of Rights so expansively, the legal and social landscape of America was fundamentally changed.

In the aftermath of the Civil War, as the Supreme Court slowly began applying the Bill of Rights to state and local governments through the Four-teenth Amendment, the debates of 1787–91 became more and more im-portant to modern life. Could a high school principal begin a graduation ceremony by asking a minister (or a student leader) to say a prayer? Could a state require a girl under sixteen to secure her parent's permission to have an abortion? Could a prison warden deny a pain medication to a prisoner between midnight and 7:00 a.m.? Could a college president censor an article in a student newspaper? These questions required the courts to examine the debates of the eighteenth century to determine what the framers intended when they drafted the Bill of Rights (and raised the related question, hotly disputed, of whether the intent of the framers was even relevant, or whether a "living" Constitution required solely contemporary, not historical, analysis).

Hence this series. Our intent is to select the very best essays from law and history and the most important judicial opinions, and to edit them so that the leading views of what the framers intended, and of how we should interpret the Bill of Rights today, are made accessible to today's reader. If you find yourself passionately agreeing with some of the views expressed, angrily dis-agreeing with others, and appreciating how the essays selected have examined these questions with depth and lucidity, we will have succeeded.

David B. Oppenheimer
Clinical Professor of Law and Director of Professional Skills
University of California, Berkeley, School of Law

INTRODUCTION

Cynthia Lee

The right of the people to be secure in their persons, houses, papers, and effects, against unreasonable searches and seizures, shall not be violated, and no Warrants shall issue, but upon probable cause, supported by Oath or affirmation, and particularly describing the place to be searched, and the persons or things to be seized.

The Fourth Amendment is one of the most important provisions of the Bill of Rights. Its interpretation governs whether public high school officials can strip-search a teenage student without a warrant or probable cause, whether candidates for political office can be forced to submit to drug testing, whether government officials can require subway riders to submit to random searches of backpacks and purses, and whether police officers can search the contents of a homeowner's trash. The Fourth Amendment controls whether a police officer can pull over a motorist and search his car. It also dictates when an officer can stop and frisk an individual on the street.

For years, legal scholars and the Justices on the Supreme Court have debated the meaning of the words in the Fourth Amendment. From this debate, two competing interpretations of the Fourth Amendment have emerged: (1) the Warrant Preference view and (2) the Separate Clauses (or Reasonableness) view. Supporters of the Warrant Preference view interpret the Fourth Amendment as requiring police to obtain a warrant based on probable cause before conducting a search, unless an exception to the warrant requirement applies. Because a search warrant must be issued by a neutral and detached magistrate prior to the search, this view of the Fourth Amendment addresses the concern that governmental officials not have unfettered discretion to search. Supporters of the Separate Clauses model read the Fourth Amendment as divided into two separate clauses. In their view, the first clause ("The right of the people to be secure in their persons, houses, papers, and effects, against unreasonable searches and seizures, shall not be violated") requires that searches and seizures not be unreasonable. The second clause ("and no Warrants shall issue, but upon probable cause...") specifies the requirements that must be met for a warrant to be valid. To proponents of the Separate Clauses view, the Fourth Amendment requires only that searches and seizures be reasonable. If a warrant is sought, then the second clause of the amendment requires that the warrant be based on probable cause, be supported by oath or affirmation, and particularly describe the place to be searched and the person or things to be seized.

For much of the twentieth century, a majority of the Supreme Court embraced the Warrant Preference view. In case after case, the Court would expound on the importance of having a neutral and detached judicial officer, as opposed to a police officer, make the determination as to whether there was probable cause to search. An extensive Fourth Amendment jurisprudence was developed by the Court, emphasizing the importance of requiring police to seek warrants prior to engaging in searches of private property. At the same time that the Court was expressing a preference for warrants, it was also recognizing numerous exceptions to the warrant requirement—situations when the police do not have to obtain a warrant based on probable cause prior to searching. For example, police do not need a warrant to engage in searches incident to a lawful custodial arrest, automobile searches, consent searches, administrative searches, border searches, and inventory searches. The number of exceptions to the warrant requirement has grown so much over the years that some have lamented that the exceptions have all but swallowed the rule.

More recently, the Separate Clauses view has taken on a more prominent role in the Supreme Court's Fourth Amendment jurisprudence, with various Justices opining in various contexts that reasonableness is all the Fourth Amendment requires. In determining whether a search or seizure is reasonable, courts must balance the government's interest in crime control against the individual's interest in privacy. Balancing tests and reasonableness standards offer the advantage of flexibility but provide little in the way of guidance to police officers and citizens. What may seem reasonable to one person may appear completely unreasonable to another.

Perhaps the Court's current embrace of reasonableness is simply a reflection of the fact that reasonableness standards already pervade the Fourth Amendment landscape. To determine whether a search within the meaning of the Fourth Amendment has taken place, the Court asks whether the defendant had a *reasonable* expectation of privacy. To determine whether a person has been seized within the meaning of the Fourth Amendment, the Court asks whether a *reasonable* person in the defendant's shoes would have felt free to leave or terminate the encounter with the police. Police officers need probable cause to arrest an individual. This means the police must have *reasonable* grounds to believe that a crime has been committed and that the arrestee committed it. Police officers need probable cause to search. In other words, they need *reasonable* grounds to believe evidence of a crime will be found in the place to be searched. To stop an individual on the street, an officer needs *reasonable* suspicion that the person is engaging in criminal activity. To frisk that individual, the officer needs *reasonable* suspicion that he is armed and dangerous.

The debate over the meaning of the Fourth Amendment has taken on particular significance today in light of fears of another terrorist attack like the September 11, 2001, attacks on the World Trade Center and the Pentagon. Such fears may have encouraged Congress in 2001 to hastily pass legislation granting government officials increased power to engage in searches and seizures without prior judicial approval. Another concern is the proliferation of new technologies that enable the government to collect information without physical intervention. Such advances in technology have resulted in increasing surveillance by both government and private actors.

This volume is divided into three parts. Part I provides historical background on the Fourth Amendment. Chapter 1 features excerpts from the leading scholarly articles providing support for both sides of the debate over the meaning of the Fourth Amendment. It also addresses the relevance of history to today's Court. Part II focuses on the doctrinal underpinnings of the Fourth Amendment today, providing both description and critique of the U.S. Supreme Court's current search and seizure jurisprudence. Chapter 2 explores the history and meaning of the reasonable expectation of privacy test, also known as the *Katz* test, which governs whether governmental activity constitutes a "search" within the meaning of the Fourth Amendment. Chapter 3 critically examines the Court's various tests for a "seizure" of the person.

Chapter 4 focuses on *Terry v. Ohio*, the case that approved the police practice of stopping and frisking individuals on less than probable cause. Chapter 5 explores the subject of racial profiling. Chapter 6 examines the exclusionary rule, the primary remedy for a Fourth Amendment violation. Part III examines the future of the Fourth Amendment in light of new and emerging technologies and fears of another terrorist attack. Whether and how the Court should deal with the advent of new technologies that implicate Fourth Amendment interests is the subject of chapter 7. Chapter 8 illustrates the various ways in which the government has used the so-called War on Terror to intrude on the privacy interests of American citizens. The excerpts in chapter 9 offer different perspectives on what should be done to improve the Court's Fourth Amendment jurisprudence. Detailed summaries of the individual excerpts within each chapter are provided at the beginning of each chapter rather than in this introduction.

This volume includes both classic articles written by well-known legal academics as well as more recent writings by junior scholars and practitioners. I endeavored to choose works that were clearly written, and I edited these selections so they would be accessible to lay readers. Indeed, the forty-three works chosen for inclusion within were heavily edited. Therefore, interested readers are encouraged to consult the original works in their entirety. Except for correcting obvious spelling, grammatical, and typographical errors, I tried to leave all word choices, including capitalization, as they appeared in the original texts.

Some of the articles featured in this volume were chosen for inclusion because of their unique insight or perspective regarding an important Supreme Court decision. For example, chapter 2 starts with an excerpt from Peter Winn's article "*Katz* and the Origins of the 'Reasonable Expectation of Privacy' Test." In this article, Winn discusses the behind-the-scenes story of how the test expressed in Justice Harlan's concurrence in *Katz v. United States* became the test now used for determining whether a search within the meaning of the Fourth Amendment has taken place. Chapter 3 features Devon Carbado's critical race theory critique of *Florida v. Bostick*, the case in which the Supreme Court modified the traditional test for a seizure of the person. Chapter 3 also includes an excerpt by Janice Nadler, who applies insights from social psychology to critique *United States v. Drayton*, another Supreme Court case discussing the requirements for a Fourth Amendment seizure of the person. Chapter 4 includes an excerpt by Earl C. Dudley, the law clerk who worked for Chief Justice Earl Warren on *Terry v. Ohio*. Dudley provides insight into the political pressures that likely influenced the Court when it decided this case. Chapter 6 includes an excerpt by law professor David Moran who argued the case of *Hudson v. Michigan* before the Supreme Court and lost. The Court in that case held that the exclusionary rule does not apply to violations of the knock-and-announce requirement. Chapter 8 features an excerpt by Arnold Loewy, which includes a narrative by Dudley Hiibel, the man at the center of *Hiibel v. Sixth Judicial Circuit*, a 2004 Supreme Court decision that held that the state can punish a person for refusing to identify himself, even if that person is guilty of no other crime. These and other articles in this volume help bring to life the concerns that animate many Fourth Amendment cases.

The body of Fourth Amendment law and related commentary is complex, ever-changing, and growing. This book is my attempt to distill a huge area of the law into one concise, readable volume. Because of space limitations, I was not able to feature many of the excellent articles written on the Fourth Amendment, nor was I able to delve into all the subject areas relevant to this topic. After the manuscript for this book was submitted in September 2009, I found several articles I would have included had I discovered them earlier. For example, I would have included Ric Simmons's article "Searching for Terrorists: Why 'Public Safety' Is Not a Special Need" in chapter 8, and Jed Rubenfeld's "The End of Privacy" in chapter 9.

This book would not have been possible without the help of numerous individuals. I would like to thank the following George Washington University law students who assisted me in the production of this book: Peter Feldman, Evan Deichert, Matthew Korn, Lauren Schmidt, Audrey Stanley, Corrina Sowden, Jane Kim, and Tamara Rubb. A special thanks to Corrina Sowden, who was in charge of collecting the copyright permissions and making sure the excerpts were reproduced exactly as they appeared in the original. I also want to thank Daniel Solove, Orin Kerr, Andrew Taslitz, David Harris, Charles Craver, and John Castiglione, who provided me with helpful advice on the book proposal, contract, and/or book outline. Finally, I wish to thank Leslie Duche, my administrative assistant; Jason Hawkins, my library liaison; and Dean Frederick Lawrence of The George Washington University Law School.

Part I
HISTORICAL BACKGROUND

Chapter 1

WHAT CAN HISTORY TEACH US ABOUT THE MEANING OF THE FOURTH AMENDMENT?

INTRODUCTION

The fundamental debate over the words in the Fourth Amendment involves the question of whether the Fourth Amendment expresses a preference for warrants (the Warrant Preference view) or merely requires that searches and seizures not be unreasonable (the Separate Clauses, or Reasonableness, view of the Fourth Amendment). The bulk of this chapter focuses on this debate.

In "Fourth Amendment First Principles," Akhil Amar suggests that, contrary to what much of the US Supreme Court's Fourth Amendment jurisprudence suggests, the Fourth Amendment does not require warrants, probable cause, or the exclusion of evidence. Instead, Amar claims, all the Fourth Amendment requires is that searches and seizures be reasonable. Amar uses the text of the Fourth Amendment, as well as its history, to support his position.

Thomas Y. Davies argues that the historical evidence does not support Amar's claim. In "Recovering the Original Fourth Amendment," Davies accuses Amar of distorting history by interpreting the Framers' distrust of general warrants as a broader disapproval of warrants in general. Davies demonstrates that the Framers favored the use of specific warrants over warrantless intrusions.

William J. Cuddihy takes issue with both Amar and Davies. In his book *The*

Fourth Amendment: Origins and Original Meaning 602–1791, Cuddihy argues that both Amar and Davies have misread or ignored the available historical evidence. Cuddihy charges Amar with ignoring the fact that warrants were quite central to searches and seizures in both England and the colonies. Cuddihy accuses Davies of being too constrained in his understanding of what the Framers meant by *unreasonable* searches and seizures. Under Davies's reading of the Fourth Amendment, an unreasonable search was a search executed with a general warrant. Cuddihy argues that in addition to searches executed with a general warrant, the Framers also considered unreasonable warrantless searches, searches at nighttime, and searches where the government officials failed to knock and announce prior to entry.

Unlike Amar, Davies, and Cuddihy, who look to history to understand the meaning of the Fourth Amendment, Carol S. Steiker argues that our understanding of the Fourth Amendment must change over time to accommodate circumstances that may not have been present at the time the Bill of Rights was drafted. In "Second Thoughts about First Principles," Steiker notes two important changes between colonial times and the present that must inform our current understanding of the Fourth Amendment: (1) the development of an armed, quasi-military professional police force, and (2) the intensification of interracial conflict.

In "Perspectives on the Fourth Amendment," an article that has been described as "the mother of all fourth amendment articles,"* Anthony G. Amsterdam argues that neither the language nor the history of the Fourth Amendment help illuminate its meaning. If anything, Amsterdam posits, the available history suggests that a search is unreasonable unless authorized by a warrant. Like Steiker, Amsterdam sees the Fourth Amendment as part of a living Constitution.

In the final excerpt in this chapter, "The Fourth Amendment and Common Law," David A. Sklansky examines the relevance of history to judicial rulings on the Fourth Amendment today. Sklansky critiques the modern Court's embrace of history as a guide to interpreting the Fourth Amendment. Increasingly, the Court has started asking whether a particular governmental action was regarded as an unlawful search or seizure under the common law at the time the Fourth Amendment was framed in order to decide whether that action implicates the Fourth Amendment.

---

*Silas J. Wasserstrom and Christine L. Snyder, eds., *A Criminal Procedure Anthology* (Cincinnati: Anderson Publishing, 1996), p. 77.

Sklansky argues that the Court's "new Fourth Amendment originalism" is inconsistent with the text of the Fourth Amendment, which on its face prohibits searches and seizures that are unreasonable, not searches and seizures that were illegal at common law. He also argues that having judges rely on history in interpreting the Fourth Amendment is not likely to provide helpful guidance to lawyers and litigants because eighteenth-century common law was wildly indeterminate. Sklansky also notes that limiting the Fourth Amendment inquiry to eighteenth-century rules of search and seizure, which systematically codified class privilege, could result in inattention to issues of race, class, and gender.

FOURTH AMENDMENT FIRST PRINCIPLES

AKHIL REED AMAR

The Fourth Amendment today is an embarrassment. Much of what the Supreme Court has said in the last half century—that the Amendment generally calls for warrants and probable cause for all searches and seizures, and exclusion of illegally obtained evidence—is initially plausible but ultimately misguided. As a matter of text, history, and plain old common sense, these three pillars of modern Fourth Amendment case law are hard to support; in fact, today's Supreme Court does not really support them. Except when it does. Warrants are not required—unless they are. All searches and seizures must be grounded in probable cause—but not on Tuesdays. And unlawfully seized evidence must be excluded whenever five votes say so. Meanwhile, sensible rules that the Amendment clearly does lay down or presuppose—that all searches and seizures must be reasonable, that warrants (and only warrants) always require probable cause, and that the officialdom should be held liable for unreasonable searches and seizures—are ignored by the Justices. Sometimes. The result is a vast jumble of judicial pronouncements that is not merely complex and contradictory, but often perverse. Criminals go free, while honest citizens are intruded upon in outrageous ways with little or no real remedy. If there are good reasons for these and countless other odd results, the Court has not provided them.

*   *   *

There is a better way to think about the Fourth Amendment—by returning to its first principles. We need to read the Amendment's words and take them seriously: they do not require warrants, probable cause, or exclusion of evidence, but they do require that all searches and seizures be reasonable.

*   *   *

I. THE MESS: A CRITIQUE

The words of the Fourth Amendment really do mean what they say. They do not require warrants, even presumptively, for searches and seizures. They do not require probable cause for all searches and seizures without warrants. They do not require—or even invite—exclusions of evidence, contraband, or stolen goods. All this is relatively obvious if only we read the Amendment's words carefully and take them seriously:

> The right of the people to be secure in their persons, houses, papers, and effects, against unreasonable searches and seizures, shall not be violated, and no Warrants shall issue, but upon probable cause, supported by Oath or affirmation, and particularly describing the place to be searched, and the persons or things to be seized.

A. WARRANT REQUIREMENT?

The modern Supreme Court has claimed on countless occasions that there is a warrant requirement in the Fourth Amendment. There are two variants of the warrant requirement argument—a strict (per se) variant that insists that searches and seizures always require warrants, and a looser (modified) variant that concedes the need to craft various common-sense exceptions to a strict warrant rule. Both variants fail.

    1. The Per Se Approach.—The first (per se) variant interpolates but never-

theless purports to stay true to the text. The Amendment contains two discrete commands—first, all searches and seizures must be reasonable; second,
warrants authorizing various searches and seizures must be limited (by probable cause, particular description, and so on). What is the relationship
between these two commands? The per se approach reasons as follows: Obviously, the first and second commands are yoked by an implicit third that no
searches and seizures may take place except pursuant to a warrant. Although
not expressing the point in so many words, the Amendment plainly presumes
that warrantless searches and seizures are per se unreasonable.

*   *   *

[Amar discusses a number of well-established exceptions to the warrant
requirement, which he argues prove that the Fourth Amendment does not
require warrants].

2. *The Modified Per Se Approach.*—At this point, a supporter of the so-called
warrant requirement is probably tempted to concede some exceptions and
modify the per se claim: warrantless searches and seizures are per se unreasonable, save for a limited number of well-defined historical and commonsensical exceptions.

This modification is clever, but the concessions give up the game. The per
se argument is no longer the textual argument it claimed to be; it no longer
merely specifies an implicit logical relationship between the reasonableness
command and the Warrant Clause. To read in a warrant requirement that is
not in the text—and then to read in various non-textual exceptions to that so-
called requirement—is not to read the Fourth Amendment at all. It is to
rewrite it. What's more, in conceding that, above and beyond historical exceptions, common sense dictates various additional exceptions to the so-called
warrant requirement, the modification seems to concede that the ultimate
touchstone of the Amendment is not warrants, but reasonableness.

*   *   *

3. *The Per Se Unreasonableness of Broad Warrants.*—If all this is so, why has the
Court continued to pay lip service to the so-called warrant requirement?
What *is* the purpose of the Warrant Clause, and how does it relate to the more
general command of reasonableness?

*   *   *

Begin with the doubly flawed logic driving the warrant requirement. Consider the person who issues the warrant. In England, certain Crown *executive* officials regularly exercised this warrant power. We need only recall the facts of the 1763 English case, *Wilkes v. Wood*, whose plot and cast of characters were familiar to every schoolboy in America, and whose lessons the Fourth Amendment was undeniably designed to embody. *Wilkes . . .* was *the* paradigm search and seizure case for Americans. Indeed, it was probably the most famous case in late eighteenth-century America, period. In *Wilkes*, a sweeping warrant had been issued by a Crown officer, Secretary of State Lord Halifax. In colonial America, Crown executive officials, including royal Governors, also claimed authority to issue warrants. Well into the twentieth century, states vested warrant-issuing authority in justices of the peace—even when such justices also served as prosecutors—and today, states confer warrant authority on clerks and "magistrates" who are neither lawyers nor judges and who at times look rather like police chiefs.

Even when a judge issued a warrant, revolutionary Americans greeted the event with foreboding. Prior to the Revolution, American judges lacked the independence from the Crown that their British brothers had won after the Glorious Revolution. Sitting at the pleasure of the monarch, the King's judicial magistrates in America were at times hard to distinguish from His executive magistrates—especially when a single Crown lackey wore several hats, as often occurred. Nor did the foreboding disappear after the Revolution, when American judges won a measure of institutional independence from the executive branch. Even an Article III judge, after all, had been appointed by the President, looked to the President for possible promotion to a higher court, and drew his salary from the government payroll. What's more, such a judge was an official of the central government—perhaps not so imperial as his Crown-directed colonial predecessors, but suspicious nonetheless. Would the handful of elite federal judges truly be able to empathize with the concerns of ordinary folk? And a single bad apple could spoil the bunch; if even one federal judge was a lord or a lackey, executive officials shopping for easy warrants would know where to go. Far more trustworthy were twelve men, good and true, on a local jury, independent of the government, sympathetic to the legitimate concerns of fellow citizens, too numerous to be corrupted, and whose vigilance could not easily be evaded by governmental judge-shopping.

Consider next the process by which warrants issued in eighteenth-century America. This, too, was hardly likely to inspire enthusiasm for a blanket warrant requirement. The typical search warrant for stolen goods or contraband was issued at the request of an accuser or the government, ex parte, with no notice or opportunity to be heard afforded the target.

*   *   *

What would happen if no warrant issued? Here we come to the second big error in the doubly flawed logic driving the warrant requirement. Warrantless intrusions were hardly immune from judicial review in the early years of the Republic. Rather, any official who searched or seized could be sued by the citizen target in an ordinary trespass suit—with both parties represented at trial and a jury deciding between the government and the citizen. If the jury deemed the search or seizure unreasonable—and reasonableness was a classic jury question—the citizen plaintiff would win and the official would be obliged to pay (often heavy) damages. Any federal defense that the official might try to claim would collapse, trumped by the finding that the federal action was unreasonable, and thus unconstitutional under the Fourth Amendment, and thus no defense at all.

Fearing this, federal officials would try to get ex parte warrants whenever they could, for a lawful warrant would provide—indeed, was designed to provide—an absolute defense in any subsequent trespass suit. Warrants then, were friends of the searcher, not the searched....

Now we can see why the Fourth Amendment text most emphatically did not require warrants—why, indeed, its reference to warrants is so plainly negative: "*no* Warrants shall issue, but...." The Warrant Clause says only when warrants may not issue, not when they may, or must. Even if all the minimum prerequisites spelled out in the Warrant Clause are met, a warrant is still unlawful, and may not issue, if the underlying search or seizure it would authorize would be unreasonable.

The history of the federal Bill of Rights powerfully supports this textual analysis. In every state constitution prior to the federal Bill, "the warrant is treated as an enemy, not a friend." No state convention proposes a warrant requirement for the federal Bill of Rights. And in early drafts of the federal Fourth, it is the loose warrant, not the warrantless intrusion, that is explicitly labeled "unreasonable."

*   *   *

RECOVERING THE ORIGINAL FOURTH AMENDMENT

Thomas Y. Davies

*　　*　　*

For most of this century, the Supreme Court has endorsed what is now called the "warrant-preference" construction of Fourth Amendment reasonableness, in which the use of a valid warrant—or at least compliance with the warrant standard of probable cause—is the salient factor in assessing the reasonableness of a search or seizure. The warrant-preference construction is favored by advocates of civil liberties because it enhances the potential for judicial supervision of police conduct.

*　　*　　*

For several decades, the Supreme Court has been shifting away from the warrant-preference construction and toward what is now called the "generalized-reasonableness" construction, in which the value of the warrant is discounted and the constitutionality of a search or seizure is determined simply by making a relativistic assessment of the appropriateness of police conduct in light of the totality of the circumstances. The generalized-reasonableness construction is favored by law and order advocates because it tends to allow greater leeway for police aggressively to enforce the law.

*   *   *

Professor Akhil Amar has produced a series of articles constituting the most ambitious attempt to craft a textual and historical case for the generalized-reasonableness construction. Amar has followed [Professor Telford] Taylor's lead in attacking the conventional understanding that the Framers valued the warrant as a protection against arbitrary intrusions, and in insisting that any warrant requirement is contrary to the Framers' intention. However, he has departed from Taylor's position that the Framers were simply unconcerned with warrantless intrusions and instead has asserted that the Framers intended for a reasonableness standard to be the *essence* of the Fourth Amendment. Thus, Amar has asserted that the first clause of the text should be understood as a "Reasonableness Clause" that articulates a freestanding reasonableness standard. He has also insisted that the Framers intended for reasonableness to be the "global" standard by which all government searches or seizures should be judged. In his reading, the warrant standards in the second clause were meant only to discourage the use of warrants.

Amar's attack is novel because, in addition to repeating Taylor's claim that the Framers viewed the warrant as "an enemy," he has attempted to provide a historical explanation for that hostility. Specifically, he has asserted that the Framers were hostile toward the use of warrants because a warrant provided an officer with an "absolute defense" against trespass liability. Thus, if an officer used a warrant to make an arrest or search, the victim was prevented from obtaining a jury's assessment, in a subsequent trespass suit, of whether the search or seizure was actually reasonable (and thus lawful). In contrast, Amar suggests that the Framers approved of warrantless searches and arrests because no legal bar prevented a jury from subsequently assessing the reasonableness of those intrusions.

*   *   *

...Amar has addressed only selective aspects of the history to muster support for his normative proposals for revising search and seizure doctrine. Thus, if one examines Taylor's and Amar's accounts closely, one finds that each offered little evidence for their central historical claims—that the Framers broadly approved of warrantless intrusions and that the Framers viewed "the warrant" as "an enemy." Moreover, both ignored salient features of the history that are not easily reconciled with their claims.

1. THE FRAMERS' ATTITUDE TOWARD WARRANTLESS INTRUSIONS

*   *   *

The historical evidence indicates that the Framers preferred use of specific warrants rather than warrantless intrusions. The Framers sought to *prevent* unjustified searches and arrests from occurring, not merely to provide an after-the-fact remedy for unjustified intrusions. For example, the complaints they voiced about searches concerned the breach of the security of the house....

The historical evidence also demonstrates that the Framers believed that the orderly and formal processes associated with specific warrants, including the judicial assessment of whether there was adequate cause for the intrusion, provided the best means of preventing violations of the security of person or house. In particular, the Framers thought that magistrates were more capable than ordinary officers of making sound decisions as to whether a search was justified.

*   *   *

The common-law tradition viewed any form of discretionary authority with unease—but delegation of discretionary authority to ordinary, "petty," or "subordinate" officers was anathema to framing-era lawyers. Contrary to Amar's claims, framing-era common law never permitted a warrantless officer to justify an arrest or search according to any standard as loose or flexible as "reasonableness." Instead,... the common law imposed rigid limits on the *ex officio* authority of ordinary officers. For example, under framing-era common law, an officer could *not* even justify a warrantless arrest by showing "probable cause" to believe an offense had been committed (let alone by a loose "reasonableness" standard); rather, a framing-era peace officer (like a private person) could justify a warrantless arrest only by proving [a] "felony in fact" (that is, that a felony had *actually* been committed).

*   *   *

The repeated objections to allowing "subordinate" officers to exercise discretionary search or arrest authority cannot be explained away simply as a concern with the "immunizing" effect that a general warrant might have had if allowed. Rather, the nature of the complaints that were actually made about general warrants—that it would be "extremely hard" to leave the decision to intrude to an ordinary officer, that it would not be "fit" to have ordinary officers decide whom to arrest or where to search—demonstrate a deep-rooted distrust and even disdain for the judgment of ordinary officers. Given that distrust, it is wholly implausible that the Framers would have approved of broad use of warrantless intrusions, because such intrusions would necessarily have rested solely on the officers' own judgment....

2. THE FRAMERS' ATTITUDE TOWARD SPECIFIC WARRANTS

No one questions that the Framers despised and sought to ban general warrants. The modern doctrinal debate has been about whether use of *specific warrants*—warrants that comply with the constitutional standards—should be required or at least preferred over warrantless intrusions. Thus the significant historical inquiry is about the Framers' view of specific warrants....

...Amar has repeatedly made the generic-sounding claim that the Framers viewed "judges and warrants" as "heavies," and has also asserted that their disapproval was "not merely of general warrants, but of ... *all* search warrants." Thus, his statements also connote that historical hostility toward use of "warrants" had been diffuse, and had reached specific as well as general warrants. However, neither Taylor nor Amar has made out a persuasive historical case that the Framers felt any generic hostility toward all "warrants."

*   *   *

...Amar has held out some post-framing statements as evidence of hostility toward "all search warrants"—however, the complaints he cited were actually about house searches which could be made only under warrant authority, not complaints about specific warrants as such. None of the complaints he cited indicated a preference that house searches be made without warrant, or even that house searches be allowed without warrants. In addition, Taylor and Amar overlooked direct evidence that the Framers approved of specific warrants.

*   *   *

Amar's claim that the Framers viewed "judges and warrants" as "heavies" because they feared the "immunizing" effect of a "warrant" also lacks historical support. The Framers did not express any general antagonism toward judges regarding search matters....

In addition, the "immunizing" claim that Amar makes so much of is more in the nature of a hypothesis than a historical observation: it is *not* evident in historical statements. For example, Amar cited ten sources to document a supposed "linkage" between the Framers' concerns about "warrants" and about preserving jury trials in civil trespass cases. However, those sources expressed concern only that "*general warrants*" might be made legal—not concern regarding the "immunizing" effect of specific warrants. Amar has never identified a single historical complaint about the "immunizing" effect of a specific warrant. In addition, Amar's renditions of the effect a "warrant" had on trespass liability have been oversimplified and incomplete. Because a general warrant was clearly deemed illegal by the framing era, it did not protect either the issuing magistrate or the executing officer against trespass liability. Only a legal (that is, specific) warrant indemnified the officer against trespass liability.

*   *   *

Moreover, a valid warrant's indemnification of the executing officer did not "preclud[e]" the victim of an unjustified intrusion from obtaining legal recourse, as Amar has asserted. Rather, Amar overlooked an aspect of common law that has disappeared from modern doctrine but was well known at the time of the framing: the *complainant* who swore out a valid search warrant was subject to trespass liability if the search proved fruitless (and that rule also applied to officers who acted as complainants). Common law assigned trespass liability for inappropriate searches under warrants where it belonged—on the complainant who initiated the search rather than on the executing officer who only did his duty.

Most importantly, Amar's insistence on the "immunizing" effect of a valid warrant has deflected attention away from the more salient concern noted above: like modern courts, the Framers understood that the magistrate's review of the factual allegations offered as cause for a search could *prevent* an unjustified invasion of a house. Like modern judges, the Framers understood that no post-search remedy could adequately restore the breached security of the house. They valued the specific warrant, in large part, because the magistrate's judgment offered the best available protection against too-hasty invasions of houses. They did not perceive any post-intrusion remedy as an adequate substitute for *preventing* unjustified intrusions.

At bottom,...Amar's claims that the Framers feared "the warrant" only blurred the Framers' focused fear of general warrants into a diffuse-sounding disapproval of all warrants. But the history, like the texts, contradicts that overgeneralized disapproval of "warrants."

*   *   *

[In the excerpted article, Davies also argues that the Fourth Amendment was originally intended only to ban general warrants, not to create any broad "reasonableness" standard applicable to warrantless arrests or searches. Davies posits that "unreasonable searches and seizures" was simply a pejorative label for general warrant searches or arrests. Recently, Davies has also argued that the Framers assumed a criminal warrant was required for a search or arrest in a house because Sir Edward Coke had asserted as much in his then-famous interpretation of the "law of the land" chapter of Magna Carta. Moreover, because Coke also asserted that the "due process of law" required by Magna Carta mandated compliance with accusatory common-law arrest standards (which were more rigorous than modern probable cause), Davies argues that the Framers actually intended for the Fifth Amendment (not Fourth) to preserve those standards. See Thomas Y. Davies, "Correcting Search-and-Seizure History: Now-Forgotten Common-Law Warrantless Arrest Standards and the Original Understanding of 'Due Process of Law,'" *Mississippi Law Journal* 77, no. 1 (2007).]

THE FOURTH AMENDMENT:
ORIGINS AND ORIGINAL MEANING 602–1791

WILLIAM J. CUDDIHY

Much of current scholarship on Fourth Amendment originalism aligns with the opposing paradigms of two law professors, Akhil Reed Amar of Yale and Thomas Davies of the University of Tennessee.... In Amar's formulation, "general reasonableness" supersedes the warrant requirement as the amendment's nucleus. At the opposite interpretative extreme, Professor Davies would dilate the warrant clause as the amendment's foundation, constricting "unreasonable searches and seizures" to little more than the lone category of general warrants.

I. THE AMAR PARADIGM

Legal history substantiates Amar's hostility to the warrant preference up to a point. Warrantless procedures were the orthodox methods of search, seizure, and arrest in the Saxon and medieval infancy of those methods. The Normans inherited warrantless motifs of contraband recovery that were already centuries-old by the conquest, and the earliest customs, vagrancy, and guild laws, as well as the old hue and cry for fugitives and debt-recovery actions, remained overwhelmingly warrant-free throughout the Angevin, Plantagenet, Lancastrian, and Tudor periods.

Warrantless procedures retained numerous footholds in seventeenth- and eighteenth-century British laws regarding the hearth, land, and excise taxes, the guilds, bankruptcy, landlord-tenant disputes, and counterfeiting. These procedures also pervaded colonial laws regarding Sabbatarian observance, slave patrols, and the South's "tobacco" legislation.

Nevertheless, warrantless searches diminished rapidly after the English Reformation. From the origin of the Stuart Dynasty, 1603, James I and Charles I issued proclamations resembling general search warrants to find and detain Crown enemies. Also in that year, 1603, the king ordered his Council of the North to issue warrants "for the search of any houses or places" suspected to conceal Catholic priests. Thus, even in the early seventeenth century, general warrants were already encroaching into the entrenched jurisdictional territory of their warrantless predecessors, and doing so, moreover, for religious and political purposes of paramount significance to Reformation society....

By 1763, general warrants to censor the British press were so common that their champions published an anthology of them dating back a century. The diversity of colonial warrants rivaled or exceeded that of Britain. Colonists literally used them for the abc's of law enforcement, for everything from the abandonment of spouses to bastardy to measuring corn supplies.

Thus far, all examples in this odyssey to warrants were general, but the eighteenth century not only accelerated the transition but also spawned a component trend toward the specific warrant as well. By 1760, as the diverse multitude of warrants in the legal literature also implied, most categories of British law had already transitioned, one by one, from warrantless searches to warrants as the foremost Crown technique of entry, search, and seizure. This warrant odyssey involved three stages that commenced with general, warrantless searches, yielded to general warrants, and terminated with specific warrants.

The colonists repeated the warrant odyssey in the same sequence as the mother country but they started about a half century later and introduced regional variations.

*   *   *

Although specific warrants had originated as isolated enclaves in the intricate edifice of general warrants around 1607, by 1791 the proportions had inverted, leaving both warrantless intrusions on land and general warrants as islands in a sea of specific warrants. The problem with this evidence in regard to Amar is not just that he ignores it, but also that it overwhelms contrary data. In disparaging warrants, Amar disregards centuries of their proliferating centrality to evolving procedures of search and seizure....

This conclusion does not operate without paradox. No legislation or case law at any level or of any jurisdiction announced the orthodoxy of warrants over alternative methods. Nor did the state constitutions do so, or any speaker at the Continental Congress, the Constitutional Convention, the ratifying conventions, the Congress, or the eighteenth-century federal or state judiciaries. Contemporary correspondence, pamphlets, and newspapers are likewise silent. Before 1800, the "warrant preference" enjoys not one sanction in "black letter law."

Nevertheless, warrants enjoyed the overriding mandate of established usage. The dispersed origins of the warrant preference enhanced its orthodoxy because they had furnished not one example of it but thousands. Precedents for the warrant had multiplied not only for two centuries but concurrently across the ever-widening spectrum of its applications.

*   *   *

II. THE DAVIES PARADIGM

To Davies, the amendment's language and immediate predecessors are the cornerstones of its architecture. In the constitutional parlance of 1776–91, Davies notes that the pivotal phrase, "unreasonable searches and seizures," originated late in the game, in the Massachusetts Constitution of 1780, and was conspicuously absent from seven of the nine state constitutions of the era. Citing a fictional episode in which a silent stable watchdog cued Sherlock Holmes that the theft of a horse indicated an "inside job," Davies theorizes that

> People rarely write down what they do not think; hence, unexpected silences
> in historical statements indicate aspects of contemporary thought without
> analogs in historical thought. One can learn a good deal about what the
> Framers did not think about search and seizure by tracing modern concepts

backwards in time—and finding they sometimes disappear from the historical record.... Dogs that do not bark in the night are essential guides to the past.

Davies concludes that the silence of most state constitutions regarding "unreasonable searches and seizures" implied the deliberate "[a]bsence of a [b]road [r]easonableness [s]tandard in Framing-Era [l]aw" and proscribed only the general warrant as an unreasonable process.

"Unreasonable" search begins somewhat earlier than the Davies chronology. In 1447, leaders of the London Company of Tailors protested that officials of the Drapers' Company had searched their houses "with outen matier [i.e., matter] or cause reasonable." Virginia's legislature of 1738 forbade "unreasonable seizures and distresses." Otherwise, however, Davies is correct in asserting that the historical record before 1780 rarely yoked searches and seizures with the adjectives "reasonable" or "unreasonable."

*   *   *

To Davies, "unreasonable searches and seizures" embrace little more than the declarations of the 81 members of the First Congress who framed the amendment and its immediate antecedents employing the identical phraseology. Davies excludes, side-tracks, and otherwise minimizes unarticulated but palpable assumptions, documentation incompatible with his thesis, and most of the legacy of search and seizure before 1780. The reader is left with historical meaning without 99 percent of the history that vests meaning.

*   *   *

Reading legal precedent forwards from 692 yields not only a different perspective than reading them backwards from 1791 but also a different outcome. The Congressional protests of 1774 were probably published over seventy times, in every American colony, and were even available in German and French translation. The propagation of these congressional protests in pamphlets and newspapers was the most extensive dissemination of opinion ever involving search and seizure on the American continent before the amendment's framing. By providing a consensus against promiscuous, warrantless house searches that preceded national existence, they had already established a constitutional mandate against those searches before Adams, in 1780, furnished a terminology in the word "unreasonable." The problem, then, is not that the warrantless dog didn't bark but that Davies did not register the pitch at which it did so.

A different foundation, that of unspoken assumption, had also established the unconstitutionality of nocturnal searches. Although Americans often denounced general warrants and warrantless, door-to-door searches in the 1770s and 1780s, they said nothing regarding nocturnal entrance of their dwellings, either for or against. Nonetheless, the statutes that they enacted on the subject, both federal and state, palpably assumed the unconstitutionality of nocturnal entrance into the domicile in the decade before the amendment's framing. No state permitted such entrance; Delaware ignored it; the rest voted against it by assumption, yielding, in effect, a *de facto* 12-0-1 mandate against the entry of dwellings after the sun set.

*   *   *

SECOND THOUGHTS ABOUT FIRST PRINCIPLES

Carol S. Steiker

*   *   *

...[C]ritics of modern Fourth Amendment law have questioned whether the Constitution necessitates the price that society currently pays in the name of Fourth Amendment freedoms. Many of these critics have charged that the Warren Court's expansive interpretations of the Fourth Amendment in the 1960s smacked of "politics" rather than constitutional "principle." The post–Warren Court years have witnessed increasingly urgent attempts to resolve the issue of what is "really in" the Fourth Amendment by reference to some authoritative method of interpretation that transcends politics. Some judges and scholars have maintained that reference to the "intent of the Framers" is just such a method and have attempted to use it both to rationalize and to cabin modern applications of the Fourth Amendment.

Professor Amar's thoughtful and provocative essay begins by invoking this strand of Fourth Amendment "intentionalism" or "originalism" in order to question the mainstays of the Warren Court's expansive Fourth Amendment jurisprudence—the warrant requirement, the probable cause requirement, and the exclusionary rule. According to Professor Amar, the modern Supreme Court flies in the face of pre-ratification history when it connects the "reasonableness" clause of the Fourth Amendment to the Warrant Clause by imposing (at least on occasion) a "warrant requirement" or a "probable cause requirement." Arguing that the famous colonial-era case of *Wilkes v. Wood* taught "lessons" that "the Fourth Amendment was designed to embody," Professor Amar contends that the Framers' fear of general warrants led them to limit the warrant rather than to exalt it (or the warrant-related "probable cause" requirement) as the touchstone of "reasonable" searches and seizures....

A common reaction to invocations of intentionalist authority is to fight fire with fire. Judges and scholars who support some type of warrant requirement—or "warrant preference"—and the exclusionary rule have invoked the same sort of historical evidence on *their* side....

I find this sort of debate puzzling and ultimately not particularly helpful in arriving at "first principles" of Fourth Amendment interpretation. My puzzlement may stem partly from the much-discussed difficulties of forming any clear picture of what the "Framers" (or do we mean "ratifiers"?) can be said to have "intended" (or should we say "expected"?) about the Constitution. But only partly. Even if I were convinced that one could derive plausible versions of the Framers' intentions by viewing the Constitution's text in historical context, I would question the programmatic implications of those intentions. Why? First, almost no one, and certainly not Professor Amar, believes that we should be bound for all time by the specific intentions or expectations of the Framers about, say, precisely what kinds of searches are "reasonable" ones or precisely what sorts of remedies are required for violations of the Fourth Amendment. At some point, all but the most absolutist originalists formulate notions of the Framers' intent at some higher level of abstraction, a move that necessarily renders less significant even highly persuasive historical claims about more specific intentions. Moreover, the Fourth Amendment, more than many other parts of the Constitution, appears to require a fairly high level of abstraction of purpose; its use of the term "reasonable" (actually, "unreasonable") positively invites constructions that change with changing circumstances.

If we accept this proposition—that the construction of the Fourth Amendment's "reasonableness" clause should properly change over time to accommodate constitutional purposes more general than the Framers' specific intentions—Professor Amar's focus on colonial history to support a disjunctive reading of the "reasonableness" clause and the Warrant Clause and to attack the exclusionary rule seems short-sighted. Such a focus ignores at least two crucial changes between colonial times and the present that must inform our current readings of the Fourth Amendment as a whole. First, at the time of the drafting and ratifying of the Fourth Amendment, nothing even remotely resembling modern law enforcement existed. The invention in the nineteenth century of armed, quasi-military, professional police forces, whose form, function, and daily presence differ dramatically from that of the colonial constabulary, requires that modern-day judges and scholars rethink both the relationship between "reasonableness" and "warrants" and the nature of Fourth Amendment remedies. Second, the intensification of inter-racial conflict in our society during the Civil War and Reconstruction, and the myriad ways in which this conflict has intersected with law enforcement, likewise necessitate new constructions of the Fourth Amendment. It is no accident that the modern pillars of Fourth Amendment law attacked by Professor Amar were significantly fortified during the 1960s at the same time that the Supreme Court and the rest of the country began to address systematically our legacy of racial discrimination.

*   *   *

B. CHANGED CIRCUMSTANCES

1. *Professional Police.*—....

Our twentieth-century police and even our contemporary sense of "policing" would be utterly foreign to our colonial forebears. Law enforcement in colonial times was, as legal historian Lawrence Friedman tells us, "a business of amateurs." Public order was maintained by a loose system of sheriffs, constables, and night watchmen. Most counties had a sheriff, appointed by the governor of the colony as the chief law enforcement officer, in charge not only of jails and prisoners, but of jury selection as well. But sheriffs had no professional law enforcement staffs under their direction. Instead, ordinary citizens who were employed in other trades or professions as their means of livelihood took turns serving as constables during the day or watchmen during the night.

*   *   *

Given their amateur personnel and "narrow compass" of duty, it is not surprising that the colonial institutions of the constabulary and the watch were extremely ineffectual in combating any serious threats to public security. Constables often proved "no match for the lowlifes they wanted to arrest" and not infrequently fell victim to resistance and assault; even more frequently, they fell asleep on the job. Throughout the colonial period "[t]here was a constant chorus of complaints about the constables and watchmen."

*   *   *

All of this changed dramatically in the nineteenth century. The explosive growth in both the density and diversity of America's urban population, the wave of riots that swept through a number of Northern cities in the 1830s and 1840s, and the effort in many Southern cities and towns to control first the slave population and then the freed black population after the Civil War all contributed to the development of modern police forces—one of the "major social inventions" of the nineteenth century. The new police forces differed in their personnel, function, and organization from the rapidly obsolete institutions of the constabulary and the watch; these differences created the potential for unprecedented incursions upon individual liberties.

First, consider the staffing, training, and equipping of the new police forces. Unlike the part-time and often unpaid constabulary and watch, the new police were full-time, salaried men. In addition, they often had some training in the form of military-style drilling or the issuance of police department rule books. In place of the bell with which the colonial constable had rung the hours of the night watch, the new police officers began to receive uniforms, horses, and eventually guns. They were subject to the supervision of a hierarchical and bureaucratic system that developed into "a recognizable police superstructure." These new modes of staffing and organizing police forces separated the new police officers from the community in a way that part-time watchman service never did; the police developed not only their own "superstructure" but their own *culture* as well[.]

*   *   *

Police brutality, like police corruption, emerged in the nineteenth century as a consequence of the creation of the new police.

*　*　*

The sort of "excesses" to which the police have regularly resorted both on the street and in the stationhouse—beatings, torture, false arrests, the third-degree, and the like—are well documented. Although there may be some reason to think that these practices have become less common today, the recent experiences of Rodney King in Los Angeles and Malice Green in Detroit suggest that the threat of police brutality remains a pressing concern, particularly for members of minority groups.

*　*　*

The metamorphosis of the colonial constabulary and watch into the recognizable precursors of modern-day law enforcement illustrates the ways in which the invention of the police created new threats to liberty. Our colonial forebears could not have predicted the sheer numbers of law enforcement agents at work today, the breadth of their operational mandate, or their pervasive authoritarian presence. They could not have imagined that the informal structures of constabulary and watch would be transformed into a bureaucracy isolated from and frequently beyond the control of local communities. They had no experience with the kind of institutionalized corruption or shocking brutality that are among the most common complaints about law enforcement today.

*　*　*

2. *Racial Divisions.*—Although Professor Amar does not acknowledge that the invention of professional police forces might change the calculus of Fourth Amendment "reasonableness," he *does* suggest that the racial impact of police practices should weigh in the balance to determine the constitutional "reasonableness" of such practices. Indeed, he "applaud[s] ... recent efforts to restore race to a central place in the Fourth Amendment discourse." What Professor Amar fails to explore, however, are the *connections* between our country's history of racial discrimination in law enforcement and the creation of the modern pillars of Fourth Amendment law that he would dismantle. The efforts of twentieth-century judges to forge new connections in the Fourth Amendment between "reasonableness" and warrants and to create a Fourth Amendment remedy of evidentiary exclusion have been linked,

both chronologically and ideologically, to attempts to address the larger problem of racial injustice.

The racial diversity and divisions that characterize twentieth-century American society were unimagined by, and indeed unimaginable to, our eighteenth-century forebears. To the Framers, the "race problem" of the day was the controversy over the continued existence of the slave trade; that debate did not extend to the issue of securing the "blessings of liberty" for blacks or other racial minorities. It was not generally questioned that "the People" of "We the People" were free white men. The Framers never envisioned a society in which blacks and other racial minorities would constitute such a large portion of the general population, or a society in which they would be declared equal under law to white men. Nor could the Framers have foreseen the ways in which the struggle to implement formal equality would create deep and bitter divisions. Finally, the Framers could not have predicted how industrialization and urbanization would exacerbate the problems of racial animus by creating concentrated black communities in close proximity to often hostile white communities. This novel trio—racial diversity, division, and density—captures the most significant ways in which race relations in the twentieth century diverge from those of the eighteenth century.

Few dispute that America's history of racial division has played a large role in the development of modern law-enforcement practices. The influence of race on the structure of law enforcement dates back at least to the creation of the first modern police forces. The military style of the new police—their uniforms, arms, and military drilling—first appeared in the early nineteenth-century "slave patrols" organized by many Southern cities to police their slave populations. Moreover, the rapid spread of modern police forces in the South during Reconstruction was due largely to the desire to control the "vagabond freed element" pouring off the formerly slave-holding plantations and into the cities. As a result, the new police in the South, and to a lesser degree in the North as well, treated blacks and black communities with extraordinary harshness, while often ignoring, and sometimes actively encouraging, illegal white-on-black violence. This tolerance of and participation in white racial violence by organized police forces continued throughout the post–Civil War period and well into the twentieth century.

Although the heyday of lynch-mob violence has passed, racial discrimination in law enforcement remains a major problem today. First, racial hatred is far from eradicated in our society, and the police are hardly immune from racist feelings. There are no doubt frequent occurrences of police over-reaching and brutality motivated by racial hatred, pure and simple, although such motivation is generally difficult to prove. Second, and even more deeply entrenched, is the widespread use by police of race as a proxy for criminality. From the very inception of modern preventative law enforcement, police offi-cers have used social standing, as evidenced by appearance, as an indicator of dangerousness. There is widespread consensus among contemporary scholars that this practice continues today, with race still playing a large role in police determinations of dangerousness. Thus, blacks found walking in white neigh-borhoods, traveling on interstate buses, or committing minor traffic offenses are much more likely to be stopped, searched, and subjected to brutal treat-ment than similarly situated white people. Moreover, prevalent racial segre-gation in housing allows for more aggressive and intrusive policing of black and other minority neighborhoods than of white or mixed communities:

> Across the nation, blacks—and some Latinos—complain that their neighbor-hoods are barricaded, that roadblocks are set up for identification checks, that they are rousted from their apartments without warrants, that police target them with "stop on sight" policies and that they are disproportionately arrested in "sweep" operations for minor misdemeanors and traffic violations....

In short, if the modern police in general can be compared to a standing army, with all of the danger to liberty that such a military presence entails, the modern police in minority communities can be compared to an army of occu-pation, with all of the additional antagonism and brutality that such an analogy implies. This is exactly the image conjured up by James Baldwin in writing about the policing of black urban ghettos: "[The policeman] moves through Harlem, therefore, like an occupying soldier in a bitterly hostile country; which is precisely what, and where he is, and is the reason he walks in twos and threes."

Racial discrimination in law enforcement has not escaped the Supreme Court's notice. Indeed, in the last half century or so—the same period iden-tified by Professor Amar as the time of the creation of the modern pillars of Fourth Amendment law—the Court's criminal procedure cases have fre-quently presented some of the most appalling racially discriminatory abuses of police power imaginable. I contend that this coincidence of the Court's growing awareness of racial discrimination in law enforcement and its creation of modern Fourth Amendment law is hardly accidental. Rather, this chronological connection suggests that the Court's modern focus on warrants, probable cause, and the exclusionary rule was in some significant sense a response to the problems of racial discrimination that it and the nation as a whole were forced to confront forthrightly in the middle of this century.

*   *   *

PERSPECTIVES ON THE FOURTH AMENDMENT

Anthony G. Amsterdam

*   *   *

The third and fourth problems in developing a satisfactory general theory of the fourth amendment's scope can be stated in one sentence. Its language is no help and neither is its history.

I hardly need justify the first half of that sentence. As applied to law enforcement activities, the terms "searches," "seizures," "persons," "houses," "papers" and "effects" could not be more capacious or less enlightening. The plain meaning of the English language would surely not be affronted if every police activity that involves seeking out crime or evidence of crime were held to be a search. When the policeman shines his flashlight in the parked car or listens at the tenement door, what else is he doing than searching? When he climbs up a telephone pole and peers beneath a second-story window shade, what on earth is he doing up that pole but searching? What is a police spy used for, but to search out suspected wrongdoing that would otherwise evade the scrutiny of the authorities? Unless history restricts the amplitude of language, no police investigative activity can escape the fourth amendment's grasp.

To Mr. Justice Frankfurter we owe the observation, and the firmest insistence on the principle, that "the meaning of the Fourth Amendment must be distilled from contemporaneous history." But Justice Frankfurter looked to the history for a specific purpose, with a keen awareness of its limitations for other purposes. As he saw it—and as I see it—that history teaches three great lessons.

The first is that the amendment is not "a kind of nuisance, a serious impediment in the war against crime" or "an outworn bit of Eighteenth Century romantic rationalism but an indispensable need for a democratic society." The second is that the amendment's basic concern is to protect the people "against search and seizure by the police, except under the closest judicial safeguards." "[W]arrants lacking strict particularity as to location to be searched or articles to be seized were deemed obnoxious" because of the root principle stated by Lord Mansfield: that "[i]t is not fit, that the receiving or judging of the information should be left to the discretion of the officer. The magistrate ought to judge; and should give certain directions to the officer." The power asserted by the English messengers and colonial customs officers and condemned by history was "a discretionary power . . . to search wherever their suspicions may chance to fall," "a power that places the liberty of every man in the hands of every petty officer."

The third lesson is that the principal check designed against the arbitrary discretion of executive officers to search and seize was the requirement of a "search warrant exacting in its foundation and limited in scope"; and consequently that "history decidedly does not leave the phrase 'unreasonable searches and seizures' at large," but places upon it the "gloss . . . that a search is 'unreasonable' unless a warrant authorizes it, barring only exceptions justified by absolute necessity." . . . Justice Frankfurter drew from history only the conclusion that the fourth amendment did not license judges to sustain warrantless searches as "reasonable" under a vague and amorphous concept of general reasonableness that ignored the warrant clause. He did not suggest that anything in the history confined the scope of what were to be held "searches and seizures." To the contrary, he . . . echoed Mr. Justice Brandeis' dissenting views in *Olmstead* that the fourth amendment broadly protected the "right to be let alone."

So Mr. Justice Frankfurter, who more than any other of the Justices sought the fourth amendment's meaning in its history, found there no limitation of its sweeping term "searches and seizures," nor of the "persons, houses, papers, and effects" that the amendment protects. Ought we nonetheless to do so? We are necessarily brought back to the first of the large questions that I raised yesterday: whether the specific historical experiences that preceded the adoption of the amendment—the conflicts over trespassory ransackings under general warrants in England and writs of assistance in the colonies—ought to be taken as the measure of the evils that the fourth amendment curbs? Or should we say at least that practices such as eavesdropping and the use of spies, known at the time of those conflicts but not implicated in them, should be held beyond the reach of the amendment?

I think the answer must be no to both forms of the question. I cannot find in the background of the amendment any justification for limiting its reach to the particular "mischief which gave it birth." Nor do I think that provisions of the Bill of Rights, or the fourth amendment in particular, should be read as containing implied negative covenants running with the Bill.

First, it is important to distinguish—as Justice Frankfurter did—between the use of background history to establish that the framers of the Bill of Rights meant to limit or forbid a particular evil, and the use of background history to support the negative inference that they did not. Even the former use of background history encounters the objection that it treats the framers as a collection of bodies having but one head; it assumes that from their common "living experience" they drew but one conclusion. As soon as the question becomes one of generalizing beyond a particular evil, this hypostatic conception of "the framers" becomes still more dubious; for generalization requires reference to the reasons for a prescription, and a variety of minds may agree upon a common prescription for a variety of reasons. When, in addition, the generalization is negative, the usefulness of seeking to construct the common thought of that variety of minds called "the framers" asymptotically approaches zero. The agreement of many minds upon the decision to disapprove particular practices does not signify the least agreement to approve other practices not upon the agenda.

Indisputably the "searches and seizures" on the agenda at the time the fourth amendment was written were the rummagings of the English messengers and colonial customs officers. We can reconstruct with some fair confidence what "the framers" thought of those. It is illusory to suppose that we can know what they thought of anything else. Nothing else was then in controversy.

*   *   *

What we do know, because the language of the fourth amendment says so, is that the framers were disposed to generalize to some extent beyond the evils of the immediate past. No other view is possible in light of the double-barreled construction of the amendment. The second clause, requiring probable cause and particularity in the issuance of warrants, was alone quite sufficient to forbid the general warrants and the writs of assistance that had been the exclusive focus of the pre-constitutional history. But the framers went further. They added—not to diminish, as Justice Frankfurter reminds us, but to expand the warrant clause—a wide provision that the people should be secure in their persons, houses, papers, and effects against unreasonable searches and seizures. Of course it is impossible to say from this what the axis or the principle of generalization was. Conceivably, "searches and seizures" might have meant warrantless ones having the same physical characteristics as those experienced under general warrants. But there is no evidence to support that conclusion, and I see no reason to draw it. Nor do I see a reason to conclude that the framers intended the fourth amendment, any more than the rest of the Bill of Rights or the Constitution, to state a principle like the dwarf in Gunter Grass' *Tin Drum*, who suddenly and perversely decided to stop growing because growth was what grownups expected of him.

Growth is what statesmen expect of a Constitution. Those who wrote and ratified the Bill of Rights had been through a revolution and knew that times change. They were embarked on a perilous course toward an uncertain future and had no comfortable assurance what lay ahead. To suppose they meant to preserve to their posterity by guarantees of liberty written with the broadest latitude nothing more than hedges against the recurrence of particular forms of evils suffered at the hands of a monarchy beyond the seas seems to me implausible in the extreme.... The revolutionary statesmen were plainly and deeply concerned with losing liberty. That is what the Bill of Rights is all about.

I myself would go a trifle further than this truism. My own view of the "Spirit of the Constitution" is not that far removed from Charles Beard's. But I think that another spirit, sometimes warring, sometimes interweaving with the first, compelled the Constitution's early amendment by the Bill of Rights. To be sure, the framers appreciated the need for a powerful central government. But they also feared what a powerful central government might bring, not only to the jeopardy of the states but to the terror of the individual. When

I myself look back into that variegated political landscape which no observer can avoid suffusing with the color of his own concerns, the hues that gleam most keenly to my eye are the hues of an intense sense of danger of oppression of the individual.

I find that sense of danger all the more striking because so many of us in this country today have lost it. It is largely left to "those accused of crime" and to the dwellers of the ghettos and the barrios of this land to view the policeman as "an occupying soldier in a bitterly hostile country." For the rest of us, the image of the policeman is the friendly face of the school crossing guard. From childhood we are reared to see government and law and law enforcement as benign. They pose no threat to us. But the authors of the Bill of Rights had known oppressive government. I believe they meant to erect every safeguard against it. I believe they meant to guarantee to their survivors the right to live as free from every interference of government agents as our condition would permit. And, to this end, it seems to me that the guarantee against unreasonable "searches and seizures" was written and should be read to assure that any and every form of such interference is at least regulated by fundamental law so that it may be "restrained within proper bounds."

*   *   *

THE FOURTH AMENDMENT AND COMMON LAW

David A. Sklansky

*   *   *

Famously short on specifics, the opening clause of the Fourth Amendment guarantees "[t]he right of the people to be secure in their persons, houses, papers, and effects, against unreasonable searches and seizures." For most of the past half-century, the interpretation of this guarantee has had little to do with its origins. To identify "searches and seizures" governed by the Amendment, the Supreme Court since *Katz v. United States* has asked whether a particular investigative technique invades an "expectation of privacy...that society is prepared to recognize as 'reasonable'"—a standard that pointedly directs attention to the present, not to the past. In determining whether a search or seizure is "unreasonable" and hence forbidden, the Court since *Terry v. Ohio* has balanced the need for the intrusion against the burdens it imposes—an explicitly functional test, requiring no historical inquiry. Fittingly, the Court's reasoning in *Katz* and *Terry* itself focused on the realities of modern law enforcement rather than the eighteenth-century origins of the Fourth Amendment.

*   *   *

In tying search-and-seizure law to the present rather than the past, the modern Court was in rare agreement with its critics. Peter Arenella voiced the consensus of a generation of criminal procedure scholars when he blamed the "intractable uncertainties in the text and historical record" of the Fourth Amendment for the Court's marked disinterest in the "Framers' intent." Anthony Amsterdam was blunter, but no further from the mainstream, when he concluded in his acclaimed lectures on the Fourth Amendment that "[i]ts language is no help and neither is its history."

Within the past decade, though, the academic tide has turned. History, as one leading scholar has noted, "is becoming the dominant subject matter" of Fourth Amendment studies, and of writings on criminal procedure more broadly. Some part of this development must be laid at the feet of Akhil Amar, whose provocative call for returning search-and-seizure law to "first principles" has generated its own subgenre of responses and counterresponses. A smaller portion of the credit or blame may be due William Cuddihy, whose doctoral dissertation Justice O'Connor has rightly praised as "one of the most exhaustive analyses of the original meaning of the Fourth Amendment ever undertaken." Whatever the causes, today much of the academy views history as "crucial to an understanding of the Fourth Amendment," and even a scholar as unsympathetic to Amar's project as Carol Steiker faults Amsterdam's lectures for their "virtual dismissal of the role of text and history in constitutional interpretation."

So perhaps it is unsurprising that the Supreme Court itself recently has turned back to history for guidance in interpreting the Fourth Amendment.... The Court...has made the principal criterion for identifying violations of the Fourth Amendment "whether a particular governmental action...was regarded as an unlawful search or seizure under the common law when the Amendment was framed."

Novelty aside, this is a curious reading in at least two respects. First, the Fourth Amendment on its face says nothing about common law, but bans all unreasonable searches and seizures, whether or not they were legal before the Amendment was adopted. Second, the chief proponent of the Court's new understanding of the Fourth Amendment has been Justice Scalia, who is also its most vocal advocate of giving constitutional and statutory provisions their "plain meaning."

*   *   *

...Justice Scalia's commitment to eighteenth-century common law as the measure of Fourth Amendment protection [is reflected] in...his concurrence in *Minnesota v. Dickerson*. The defendant in *Dickerson* had been stopped for brief questioning and frisked for weapons under the rule of *Terry v. Ohio*. After satisfying himself that the defendant was unarmed, the officer nonetheless continued his tactile inspection of the defendant's clothing, eventually recovering a lump of crack cocaine. Reasoning much as it had in *Arizona v. Hicks*, the Court found the additional search unlawful without a warrant. Justice Scalia joined the Court's opinion but wrote separately to voice reservations about even the frisk permitted by *Terry*.

The purpose of the Fourth Amendment, Scalia declared, was "to preserve that degree of respect for the privacy of persons and the inviolability of their property that existed when the provision was adopted." He therefore had little use for the analysis in *Terry*, because the Court had "made no serious attempt to determine compliance with traditional standards," but instead simply had asked what "was 'reasonable' by current estimations"—applying what Scalia derided as "the original-meaning-is-irrelevant, good-policy-is-constitutional-law school of jurisprudence." Still, Scalia thought that brief investigatory detentions of the kind approved in *Terry* probably were consistent with the common law, because "it had long been considered reasonable to detain suspicious persons for the purpose of demanding that they give an account of themselves." He was less sure about frisks for weapons, because when "the detention did not rise to the level of a full-blown arrest (and was not supported by the degree of cause needful for that purpose), there appears to be no clear support at common law for physically searching the suspect." What is more, Scalia "frankly doubt[ed]...whether the fiercely proud men who adopted our Fourth Amendment would have allowed themselves to be subjected, on mere *suspicion* of being armed and dangerous, to such indignity"—although he also noted that subsequent developments in firearms technology may have altered what is "reasonable."

As in *McLaughlin* and *Acevedo*, Scalia wrote only for himself in *Dickerson*.

And even Professor Amar, who applauded Justice Scalia's opinion in *Acevedo*, was given pause by the concurrence in *Dickerson*, which Amar thought flirted with a "'frozen in amber' approach to Fourth Amendment reasonableness." Within two years, however, there were signs of sympathy elsewhere on the Court for Scalia's interpretive method. The evidence came in *Wilson v. Arkansas*, in which Justice Thomas wrote for a unanimous court. The holding was almost humdrum: a search of a home can be rendered "unreasonable" for purposes of the Fourth Amendment if the officers fail to knock and to announce their presence before entering—unless, under the circumstances, it is reasonable to dispense with the warning. What was noteworthy about the opinion was its reasoning. To support the Court's conclusion that "the reasonableness of a search of a dwelling may depend in part on whether law enforcement officers announced their presence and authority prior to entering," Justice Thomas reviewed common-law decisions dating from the early seventeenth century up through the 1800s. Ignoring *Terry* and *Katz*—indeed, ignoring almost all search-and-seizure decisions from the second half of the twentieth century—Justice Thomas suggested that in determining the scope of the Fourth Amendment "we have looked to the traditional protections against unreasonable searches and seizures afforded by the common law at the time of the framing." To be sure, "the underlying command of the Fourth Amendment is always that searches and seizures be reasonable," but "our effort to give content to this term may be guided by the meaning ascribed to it by the Framers of the Amendment." Remarkably, no member of the Court objected to the importance Justice Thomas gave common law in assessing the constitutionality of searches and seizures.

*   *   *

The full Court had hinted at sympathy for Scalia's new Fourth Amendment originalism in *Wilson v. Arkansas*, and finally embraced it in *Wyoming v. Houghton*. The question in *Houghton* was whether a warrantless search of an automobile based on probable cause could include a search of a passenger's purse; the Court ruled that it could. That result followed easily enough from *Acevedo*, but Justice Scalia, writing for a majority of six, took the opportunity to sweep more broadly. In applying the Fourth Amendment, he explained, the Court asks first whether the challenged conduct "was regarded as an unlawful search or seizure under the common law when the Amendment was framed."

Only if "that inquiry yields no answer" will the Court assess the search or seizure "under traditional standards of reasonableness," balancing the intrusion on privacy against the promotion of legitimate government interests. This was a good deal more emphatic than the suggestion in *Wilson v. Arkansas* that eighteenth-century understandings "may" give content to the Fourth Amendment, and it drew an objection from Justice Stevens: "To my knowledge, we have never restricted ourselves to a two-step Fourth Amendment approach wherein the privacy and governmental interests at stake must be considered only if 18th-century common law 'yields no answer.'" But only Justice Souter and Justice Ginsburg joined his dissent.

Strictly speaking, no "18th-century common law" was found applicable by the Court in *Houghton*. Instead the majority relied on federal legislation in the late-eighteenth century authorizing warrantless inspections of ships by customs officers with probable cause to suspect the presence of contraband. The Court had cited this same legislation when first authorizing warrantless searches of automobiles based on probable cause, and later when extending that authorization to include containers found in automobiles. As in those earlier decisions, the majority in *Houghton* inferred from the Founding-era legislation that "the Framers" would have thought the challenged search "reasonable."

In the weeks following *Houghton*, the Court twice reaffirmed its commitment to the interpretive method announced in that case. Writing for a majority of seven in *Florida v. White*, Justice Thomas again invoked the 1790s legislation, this time to uphold warrantless *seizures* of automobiles based on probable cause to believe they are forfeitable as contraband, and he reiterated that "[i]n deciding whether a challenged governmental action violates the [Fourth] Amendment, we have taken care to inquire whether the action was regarded as an unlawful search and seizure when the Amendment was framed." The justices made the same point implicitly in *Wilson v. Layne*, when they read the Fourth Amendment to forbid as unreasonable most media "ride-alongs" on arrests in private homes. Writing on this point for a unanimous Court, Chief Justice Rehnquist found it helpful to begin his analysis with platitudes from William Blackstone's *Commentaries* about the sanctity of the home, and with the 1604 decision in *Semayne's Case*, the source of the maxim that "the house of every one is to him as his castle and fortress." Even when no pre-enactment authorities were remotely on point, the Court suggested, the common law remained the ultimate touchstone of Fourth Amendment reasonableness.

*   *   *

Together with its prolonged gestation, the novelty of the new Fourth Amendment originalism suggests it is a development worthy of attention. We do not deal here with a verbal formula chosen carelessly or even casually. We have instead a doctrine developed and promoted over a period of years by a justice particularly attentive to linguistic nuances, and then explicitly embraced by the Court.

*   *   *

What is harder to tell with certainty is how much it will matter. The principal difficulty here could be called the problem of sincerity: is the Court genuinely conforming its view of reasonableness to eighteenth-century understandings, or is it manipulating eighteenth-century understandings to fit its own view of reasonableness?

*   *   *

... Because Scalia's originalism has never driven him to interpret the Fourth Amendment in a manner that seems contrary to his own preferences, the question lingers whether the originalism has any cash value. In Louis Michael Seidman's words, originalism does "independent work" only when it "requires judges to reach results that they would not reach using some other theory." By this standard, it is unclear whether the new Fourth Amendment originalism has ever done any "independent work," either for Scalia or for the Court. So is it worth worrying about?

It is, for two reasons. First, whatever its limitations as *theory*, the new Fourth Amendment originalism has distinct strengths as *rhetoric*. Even in cases where it does not affect results, it can help to legitimize them. All varieties of constitutional originalism do this, by attributing outcomes not to unelected judges but to the collective determination of an older and particularly revered generation. But the new Fourth Amendment originalism goes one better, by appealing not just to the wisdom of the Framers, but to the wisdom of the ages....

Second, over the long term the new Fourth Amendment originalism could well have substantive consequences. I argue below that "the common law" will rarely if ever provide a determinate answer to modern search-and-seizure questions. But the rhetoric of the new Fourth Amendment originalism legitimizes some outcomes more easily than others and is relatively uncongenial to certain broad uses to which the Fourth Amendment might otherwise be put. The problem is not so much the answers provided by eighteenth-century common law—those are rare—but rather the limited range of the questions it asked.

To take perhaps the most obvious example, of late the Supreme Court has studiously avoided considerations of equality in assessing the reasonableness of searches and seizures. Constitutional challenges to discrimination, the Court has explained, should be raised under "the Equal Protection Clause, not the Fourth Amendment." Nevertheless even Professor Amar, who echoes Justice Scalia's call to return Fourth Amendment law to "first principles," suggests that constitutional reasonableness today may depend in part on considerations of race, class, and gender equity. These concerns, however, are difficult to read into the common law of 1791. Indeed, as I discuss later, eighteenth-century rules of search and seizure, far from reflecting a broad commitment to equality, systematically codified class privilege. So although the new Fourth Amendment originalism may not be to blame for the absence of race, class, and gender considerations from current search-and-seizure doctrine, the rhetoric of the new originalism makes correction of the absence less likely.

*   *   *

II. ASSESSING THE NEW ORIGINALISM

By its terms the Fourth Amendment does not prohibit searches and seizures "illegal at common law;" it prohibits searches and seizures that are "unreasonable." ...

...Justice Scalia, the chief proponent of the new Fourth Amendment originalism, is also the Court's most articulate defender of "textualism," the idea that the words in the Constitution, and in statutes, should be given their plain and natural meaning. Moreover, like some other self-professed "textualists," Justice Scalia has pointed to the common law as a model for how judges engaged in statutory or constitutional interpretation should *not* approach their work. In his Tanner Lectures, perhaps the fullest statement of his judicial philosophy, Scalia painted common-law judging as not just antidemocratic but self-indulgent: "intellectual fun" that amounts to "playing king—devising, out of the brilliance of one's own mind, those laws that ought to govern mankind."

* * *

... [T]he preeminent importance attached to eighteenth-century common law by the new Fourth Amendment originalism sits oddly with Scalia's repudiation of the common-law "mind-set," and even more oddly with his insistence that "[t]he text is the law, and it is the text that must be observed."

* * *

... [Moreover], the structural case for the new Fourth Amendment originalism has at least two serious weaknesses.

The first... is that it shares some of the evil it seeks to remedy: the untethered exercise of judicial power. By its terms the Fourth Amendment does not codify eighteenth-century common law, and the available evidence suggests that was not its purpose. For courts to read common law into the provision, in order to let it better accomplish what they take to be its basic function, is to engage in precisely what Scalia condemns: de facto amendment of the Constitution by unelected judges....

The second weakness... is that common law is a far less secure tether for Fourth Amendment rights than Scalia has suggested. In part this is due to the discretion judges must inevitably exercise in deciding whether or not common law provides an "answer" to modern search and seizure questions, notwithstanding changed circumstances. But there is a more basic problem. More often than not, eighteenth-century "common law" itself is wildly indeterminate—so much so that the new Fourth Amendment originalism may make search-and-seizure law more rather than less responsive to the vicissitudes of judicial predisposition.

* * *

Part II

THE FOURTH AMENDMENT TODAY

Chapter 2

WHAT CONSTITUTES A "SEARCH"?

INTRODUCTION

The Fourth Amendment is not implicated unless and until the government has engaged in a "search" or a "seizure." For many years, for a "search" within the meaning of the Fourth Amendment to have taken place, the Supreme Court required a physical trespass by the government into a constitutionally protected area. In 1967, the Court abandoned its physical trespass theory and established the modern test for a search. *Katz v. United States*, 389 U.S. 347 (1967). Under the *Katz* test, a search within the meaning of the Fourth Amendment takes place when the defendant manifests an actual expectation of privacy that society is willing to recognize as legitimate, justifiable, or reasonable. In the first excerpt, Peter Winn tells the behind-the-scenes story of how the "reasonable expectation of privacy" test—a test expressed in Justice Harlan's concurring opinion in *Katz*, not the majority opinion—came into being.

The reasonable expectation of privacy test appears to reflect a variety of different and sometimes conflicting concerns, rather than a single coherent theory. Whether a particular government action constitutes a search under the *Katz* test turns on a variety of factors, including whether the defendant knowingly exposed his illegal activity to public view, whether the defendant voluntarily conveyed information to a third party, whether the officer was in a lawful position to view the illegal activity, and whether the government intrusion involved a home, curtilage, or an "open field." In the second excerpt, "Four Models of Fourth Amendment Protection," Orin S. Kerr argues that the reasonable expectation of privacy test represents not one, but four distinct models of Fourth Amendment protection.

The remaining excerpts in this chapter critique the Supreme Court's current search jurisprudence. In "The Distribution of Fourth Amendment Privacy," William J. Stuntz demonstrates how the Court's privacy-centric search jurisprudence results in class- and race-based inequities in the distribution of Fourth Amendment protections. In "What Is a Search? Two Conceptual Flaws in Fourth Amendment Doctrine and Some Hints of a Remedy," Sherry F. Colb takes issue with the Court's heavy reliance on whether the defendant knowingly exposed his illegal activity to the public, arguing that the Court has repeatedly made two improper analytic moves: (1) equating the risk of exposure with inviting exposure, and (2) equating exposure to a limited audience with exposure to the world. In "Digital Dossiers and the Dissipation of Fourth Amendment Privacy," Daniel J. Solove critiques the Court's third-party doctrine—the rule that one who voluntarily conveys information to a third party forfeits any reasonable expectation of privacy in that information—in light of advances in modern technology. In "The Supreme Court, Criminal Procedure, and Judicial Integrity," Stephen A. Saltzburg critiques the Court's open fields doctrine, under which police trespass onto private property not immediately adjacent to the home is not considered a "search" within the meaning of the Fourth Amendment, even if the owner has taken steps to keep that property private by surrounding the property with a fence and "no trespassing" signs. In "Open Fields in the Inner City: Application of the Curtilage Doctrine to Urban and Suburban Areas," Carrie Leonetti critiques one application of the open fields doctrine. Leonetti argues that the common areas of an apartment, such as the hallway outside one's apartment door, should be viewed as curtilage, not open fields.

KATZ AND THE ORIGINS OF THE "REASONABLE EXPECTATION OF PRIVACY" TEST

Peter Winn

Why should we care about the history of *Katz v. United States?* The 1967 Supreme Court case, of course, formulated the "reasonable expectation of privacy" test that is used to decide when a governmental intrusion constitutes a "search" under the Fourth Amendment. But the test extends beyond the confines of the Constitution; it has found its way into common law and statutes, and even the laws of other countries. In short, *Katz v. United States* represents a great touchstone in the law of privacy, and Judge [Harvey] Schneider's memoir of his experience as the lawyer for Charles Katz gives us a glimpse into the origins of an important legal doctrine and a rare peek into the human side of the development of law.

*   *   *

Although the majority opinion is a masterful example of judicial politics, and presents a reasoned defense of the result, it is not without its flaws. It begins with a highly unusual attack on counsel—both the petitioner's attorneys as well as the government's—criticizing them for framing the issue as "whether a public telephone booth is a constitutionally protected area so that evidence obtained by attaching an electronic listening recording device to the top of such a booth is obtained in violation of the right to privacy of the user of the booth." However, this judicial "frame" was not invented by the lawyers, but had been used explicitly by the Court itself in numerous earlier Fourth Amendment cases.... Furthermore, when the Court granted *certiorari*, it framed the issues in precisely this manner.... Once the Court accepted this formulation, the parties would be expected to address only those issues in their briefs and argument.

*   *   *

As explained above, the Court's criticism is unfair because counsel addressed the precise issues on which the Court accepted *certiorari*. Moreover, the Court's criticism is surprisingly inaccurate. Katz's attorneys specifically argued in their opening brief that the old trespass test had been discredited and needed to be replaced with a test based not on property but on a right of privacy. Furthermore, [a] passage from the opinion...appears to have borrowed the specific language it used to make this point from the petitioner's brief. And one can find other echoes of the petitioner's briefs in the text of the majority opinion. Of course, it is not unusual for a court to borrow, without attribution, arguments, ideas, and even explicit passages from a brief filed by counsel. The practice exemplifies the fundamental collaborative nature of the legal process. Lawyers usually consider it a high compliment when a court borrows directly from their briefs, for it shows the court's respect for the quality of their work product. What is unusual is to see such borrowings accompanied by criticism of counsel for missing the point.

There is an even more surprising mistake in the majority opinion: When one listens to the oral argument or reads the transcript, one recognizes that it was counsel for the petitioner who first took the position that the manner in which the issues had been framed (by reference to a "constitutionally protected area") needed to be altered, and who reformulated the issues into exactly the manner ultimately adopted by the Court. It appears that the oral argument persuaded the Court to reformulate the issues. However, instead of acknowledging flaws in the earlier cases and correcting the analysis, the Court's opinion blames *counsel* for getting it wrong.

The Justices, of course, did not intentionally make what we now can see was a highly embarrassing mistake. The erroneous criticism of counsel first appears in the draft opinion prepared by Stewart's law clerk, who likely never attended the oral argument. The criticism of counsel for missing the point, after adopting arguments from the brief, is more difficult to explain. But whatever the explanation, no one appears to have noticed the problem before the opinion was published.

In addition to its embarrassing attack on counsel, the majority opinion contains an important weakness in its legal analysis. The opinion creates the impression of a revolutionary upheaval of the previous regime, while using criticism of counsel to sidestep the otherwise difficult job of addressing prior inconsistent case law with candor. By dismissing precedent without adequate analysis, it loses the ballast of history. While announcing a new understanding of the Fourth Amendment based on a right of privacy, it says nothing about how this newfound right is to be determined. In eliminating the trespass standard of *Olmstead*, it offers nothing by way of a standard to replace it. How then, has a Supreme Court case, which contains so many mistakes and which promised a legal revolution that it ultimately could never deliver, come to occupy such an unchallenged position in the modern legal Pantheon? The short answer is that the majority opinion has been largely ignored. Instead, most courts cite to the... concurring opinion by Justice Harlan:

> ...My understanding of the rule that has emerged from prior decisions is that there is a twofold requirement, first that a person has exhibited an actual (subjective) expectation of privacy and, second, that the expectation be one that society is prepared to recognize as "reasonable."...

Within a year, the Supreme Court started to use Harlan's "reasonable expectation of privacy" test as the standard in its Fourth Amendment jurisprudence. Within a decade, Harlan's test became so familiar that the Court officially recognized it as the essence of the *Katz* decision—a rare instance where a concurrence effectively replaced a majority opinion.

Before we go on, we should take a moment to analyze Harlan's concurrence, because, at first blush, its greatness is not at all obvious. Harlan characterizes the reasonable expectation of privacy test as "the rule which has emerged from prior decisions," but at the same time he expressly joins the Court in overruling *Olmstead*'s prior "trespass" regime. Because the Court's prior decisions follow the trespass rule, Harlan's position appears to be self-contradictory. Furthermore, as many academic commentators have pointed out, if a constitutionally cognizable "search" takes place when there is an expectation of privacy that "society is prepared to recognize as reasonable," but judges ultimately determine which expectations of privacy are objectively "reasonable," then Harlan's famous test appears to be circular.... According to this criticism, the famous test appears to boil down to "whatever the judges say it is." How, in spite of this apparent contradiction and circularity, and the endless criticism of the academy, has Harlan's test come to occupy such a central place in the law? The answer is that there is more to the test than its critics seem to realize.

Consider Harlan's allegedly paradoxical claim that the reasonable expectation of privacy test is "the rule that has emerged from prior decisions." As Harlan takes pains to point out in his concurrence, except for *Olmstead* and *Goldman*, *Katz* does not overrule any other prior cases—even though all the former cases ... were based on the old trespass model. Harlan then points out something obvious—the reasonable expectation of privacy test *is entirely consistent with these former trespass decisions.*

In fact, in overruling *Olmstead*'s narrow trespass test, the Court made only an incremental change in the old trespass standard—it removed the requirement that one hold a possessory interest to assert a claim under the Fourth Amendment. Since there is no property interest in a voice communicated over electric wires, and thus nothing to possess, the Court had to abandon *Olmstead*'s possessory interest requirement....

Harlan recognized that although it was appropriate to reject *Olmstead*'s technical and artificial possessory interest test, much of the old trespass doctrine, as reflected in prior case law, was still intact. Fourth Amendment violations before and after *Katz* still involved challenges to government intrusion into an area where a person had a legally protected interest—the essence of the traditional trespass concept. Thus, because Harlan's reasonable expectation of privacy test represents an essential continuity with prior law, the accusation of circularity misses the point. Harlan addressed this issue explicitly when he wrote: "As the Court's opinion states, 'the Fourth Amendment protects people, not places.' The question, however, is what protection it affords to those people. Generally, as here, the answer to that question requires reference to a 'place.'"

In this passage, Harlan pointed out the obvious—that our intuitions of privacy are essentially context-specific. In the context of the Fourth Amendment, they generally involve reference to a place. Places have well-defined pre-existing legal rules—determined in large part by the law of trespass—which govern our socially recognized and accepted expectations of privacy.

Thus, an objectively reasonable expectation of privacy necessarily must reference *other* norms independent of the idea of privacy itself. The test is not *just* what the judge says it is; the test must also incorporate a long tradition of what other judges and lawmakers have declared the law to be in the past. This tradition includes as an important aspect those norms underlying society's objective expectations of privacy—among which a central place is held by the law of property.

*　　*　　*

Where, then, did the reasonable expectation of privacy test come from? The test is not mentioned in the record of the lower courts, or in the pleadings and briefs filed in the Supreme Court. Until recently, most observers treated the test as if Harlan made it up out of thin air. However, as the few who have taken the time to read the transcripts or listen to the oral arguments know, the idea came from the lawyers—specifically one lawyer—Harvey (now Judge) Schneider who, with Burton Marks, represented the petitioner, Charles Katz.

In his accompanying article, Judge Schneider explains how, after the Court issued its decision in *Berger v. New York*, he realized that the days of the *Olmstead* trespass standard were numbered. In the days leading up to the oral argument, the young lawyer began to rethink his strategy. He suddenly realized that expectations of privacy should be based on an objective standard, one that could be formulated using the reasonable man standard from tort law. In an act of great courage, he decided to focus all of his energy during oral argument on articulating the new standard for the Court. As we have seen, the test had not been articulated in the briefs, and presenting it at oral argument arguably constituted a breach of protocol. Only a young and inexperienced lawyer would ever have tried such a thing....

And, as evidenced by the initial vote in conference, Schneider nearly lost his case. Justice Stewart's change of heart appeared to occur not because of anything Schneider said in oral argument, but because of the Justice's own separate concerns and the efforts of Stewart's new law clerk, who had not even heard the oral argument. Needless to say, Stewart's majority opinion makes no reference to the reasonable expectation of privacy test. On the other hand, Harlan, who always recognized the importance of oral argument, appears to have listened carefully to what the young lawyer said and recognized his point.

*   *   *

The credit for the reasonable expectation of privacy test thus belongs to two men: one of them, a bright, young, and relatively inexperienced lawyer who nevertheless had great talent and nerve; the other, a wise old judge who knew how to listen. To their lasting credit, both men saw the significance of an important legal idea when few others did, and had the courage to follow through with that idea, resulting in what is now universally recognized as the great cornerstone of Fourth Amendment jurisprudence.

FOUR MODELS OF FOURTH AMENDMENT PROTECTION

ORIN S. KERR

*   *   *

The reasonable expectation of privacy test is the central mystery of Fourth Amendment law. According to the Supreme Court, the Fourth Amendment regulates government conduct that violates an individual's reasonable expectation of privacy. But no one seems to know what makes an expectation of privacy constitutionally "reasonable."...Although four decades have passed since Justice Harlan introduced the test in his concurrence in *Katz v. United States*, the meaning of the phrase "reasonable expectation of privacy" remains remarkably opaque.

Among scholars, this state of affairs is widely considered an embarrassment. The Court's handiwork has been condemned as "distressingly unmanageable," "unstable," and "a series of inconsistent and bizarre results that [the Court] has left entirely undefended."...

The chaos prompts an obvious question: why can't the Supreme Court settle on a single test for what makes an expectation of privacy "reasonable"?...

This Article explains why the Supreme Court has not and cannot adopt a

74

single test for what makes an expectation of privacy "reasonable."...The Supreme Court has not and cannot adopt a single test for when an expectation is "reasonable" because no one test effectively and consistently distinguishes the more troublesome police practices that require Fourth Amendment scrutiny from the less troublesome practices that do not.

* * *

...Although the courts speak of a single "reasonable expectation of privacy" test, the one label masks several distinct but coexisting approaches. Four approaches predominate, together reflecting four different models of Fourth Amendment protection....

I. THE FOUR MODELS

* * *

A. THE PROBABILISTIC MODEL

The first model of the Fourth Amendment is what I term *the probabilistic model.* According to this approach, a reasonable expectation of privacy depends on the chance that a sensible person would predict that he would maintain his privacy. The inquiry is descriptive rather than normative: it tries to assess the likelihood that a person will be observed or a place investigated based on prevailing social practices. Under the probabilistic approach, a person has a reasonable expectation of privacy when the odds are very high that others will not successfully pry into his affairs. As those odds drop, the individual's expectation of privacy becomes less and less reasonable....

   Bond v. United States offers an example of the probabilistic approach. A border patrol agent boarded a bus at the Texas-Mexico border and conducted a brief search for narcotics by walking the length of the bus and squeezing soft luggage placed in the overhead compartment. A squeeze of the defendant's canvas bag revealed what appeared to be a "brick-like" object stored inside, and the agent then opened the bag and found drugs. In an opinion by Chief Justice Rehnquist, the Court held that the officer's "probing tactile examination" of the defendant's luggage violated his reasonable expectation of privacy. The key was that the agent's probing had exceeded the usual handling common among bus passengers:

> When a bus passenger places a bag in an overhead bin, he expects that other passengers or bus employees may move it for one reason or another. Thus, a bus passenger clearly expects that his bag may be handled. He does not expect that other passengers or bus employees will, as a matter of course, feel the bag in an exploratory manner.

The officer's conduct was a search because it was contrary to the reasonable expectations of bus passengers.

*   *   *

So far, so good. But there's a wrinkle: for every case in which the Court endorses the probabilistic model, you can find several others flatly rejecting it. In many cases, the Supreme Court has dismissed the probabilistic model as simply incorrect as a matter of basic Fourth Amendment law. Consider the Supreme Court's recent decision in *Illinois v. Caballes*. Caballes was stopped for speeding, and the officer brought a drug-sniffing dog to the scene. When the dog alerted the officer to the presence of drugs in the trunk, the officer searched the trunk and found marijuana. The Supreme Court held that the use of the dog to alert for the presence of drugs was not a search. According to Justice Stevens' majority opinion, the chance that the police would find out about the drugs in the trunk was completely irrelevant to the Fourth Amendment inquiry: "[T]he expectation 'that certain facts will not come to the attention of the authorities' is not the same as an interest in 'privacy that society is prepared to consider reasonable.'" As the Court emphasized twenty years earlier in *United States v. Jacobsen*, "The concept of an interest in privacy that society is prepared to recognize as reasonable is, by its very nature, critically different from the mere expectation, however well justified, that certain facts will not come to the attention of the authorities."

*   *   *

B. THE PRIVATE FACTS MODEL

The second model of Fourth Amendment protection is what I call *the private facts model*. The private facts model focuses on the information the government collects, and considers whether that information is private and worthy of constitutional protection. If the government obtains information that is particularly private, then the acquisition of that information is a search; if the information collected is not private or does not otherwise merit protection, then no search has occurred. The key question becomes what information the government collected rather than how it was obtained or whether the government's conduct was unexpected.

United States v. Jacobsen offers a helpful example. In *Jacobsen*, a cardboard box sent via Federal Express broke open during delivery. A white powder seeped out, and an FBI agent performed a chemical field test of the powder to determine if the powder was cocaine. The field test returned a positive result, leading to criminal charges against the package recipient. In an opinion by Justice Stevens, the Supreme Court held that a field test for narcotics could not violate a reasonable expectation of privacy.... Because the field test could only reveal evidence of a crime, "and no other arguably 'private' fact," it could not violate any expectation of privacy that was constitutionally "legitimate."

Dow Chemical Co. v. United States reflects a similar approach. The Environmental Protection Agency (EPA) hired a commercial photographer to take aerial photographs of a chemical plant to identify violations of environmental protection laws. The owner of the chemical plant, Dow Chemical, brought a civil suit claiming that the photography violated the Fourth Amendment. In an opinion by Chief Justice Burger, the Court rejected the Fourth Amendment challenge based in part on the limited information the photography revealed: "[T]he photographs here are not so revealing of intimate details as to raise constitutional concerns."

*   *   *

Once again, however, these cases tell only half of the story. The Supreme Court's search cases often ignore the private facts model, finding a search when no private information is obtained and concluding that no search occurs when even very invasive information is collected. For example, in *Arizona v. Hicks*, the police entered an apartment looking for a gunman who had fired shots from the apartment moments earlier. An officer came across expensive audio equipment in what was otherwise a ramshackle apartment, and picked up a turntable to check its serial number for a match with stolen equipment. In an opinion by Justice Scalia, the Court held that moving the stereo equipment to reveal the serial number violated the defendant's reasonable expectation of privacy. The fact that moving the turntable revealed only a serial number was irrelevant:

> It matters not that the search uncovered nothing of any great personal value to respondent—serial numbers rather than (what might conceivably have been hidden behind or under the equipment) letters or photographs. A search is a search, even if it happens to disclose nothing but the bottom of a turntable.

*   *   *

C. The Positive Law Model

The *positive law model* offers a third model of Fourth Amendment protection. When courts apply the positive law model, they look at whether there is some law that prohibits or restricts the government's action (other than the Fourth Amendment itself). If the government broke the law in order to obtain the information it did, the government conduct violated a reasonable expectation of privacy. This approach often focuses on whether the information collected was legally available to the public. If a member of the public could have accessed the information legally, then it does not violate a reasonable expectation of privacy for the government to do the same. The positive law approach is descriptive, not normative: it asks whether the government's access to the suspect's information was achieved legally based on preexisting legal doctrine.

*   *   *

...Consider Justice White's plurality opinion in *Florida v. Riley*. The facts of *Riley* are similar to those of *Ciraolo*: investigators flew a helicopter over the defendant's property at an altitude of 400 feet, and from that vantage point observed marijuana growing in his greenhouse. The government's brief invoked the positive law model, pointing out that Federal Aviation Administration (FAA) regulations banning fixed-wing aircraft from traveling below an altitude of 500 feet do not apply to helicopters. Because FAA regulations permitted helicopters to fly above Riley's property at that altitude, doing so did not violate his reasonable expectation of privacy. Justice White's plurality opinion agreed:

> We would have a different case if flying at that altitude had been contrary to law or regulation. But helicopters are not bound by the lower limits of the navigable airspace allowed to other aircraft. Any member of the public could legally have been flying over Riley's property in a helicopter at the altitude of 400 feet and could have observed Riley's greenhouse. The police officer did no more.... [I]t is of obvious importance that the helicopter in this case was *not* violating the law....

*   *   *

Much like the probabilistic model and the private facts model, the positive law model is only an occasional guide to Fourth Amendment protection. Some opinions embrace it and others reject it.

D. THE POLICY MODEL

The fourth and final model of Fourth Amendment protection is the *policy model*. Under the policy model, the reasonable expectation of privacy inquiry poses a policy question: should a particular set of police practices be regulated by the warrant requirement or should those practices remain unregulated by the Fourth Amendment? If the consequences of leaving conduct unregulated are particularly troublesome to civil liberties, then that conduct violates a reasonable expectation of privacy. On the other hand, if the practical consequences of regulating such conduct unnecessarily restrict government investigations given the gain to civil liberties protection, then any expectation of privacy is constitutionally unreasonable. Whether an expectation of privacy is reasonable hinges on a normative value judgment. Judges must consider the consequences of regulating a particular type of government activity, weigh privacy and security interests, and opt for the better rule.

*   *   *

Kyllo v. United States offers an illustration of the policy approach to the reasonable expectation of privacy test. Acting on the suspicion that Kyllo was growing marijuana in his home, federal agents pointed a thermal imaging device towards the exterior of his home to check for high temperatures that might indicate the use of heat lamps. The imaging device measured infrared radiation emanating from the walls and roof of the home.... Sitting in a parked car across the street, the agents used the device and found that one wall and the roof of Kyllo's garage were unusually hot. In his opinion for the Court, Justice Scalia reasoned that use of the device to monitor a home was a search because in "the long view" the use of sense-enhancing devices presented a major threat to privacy in the home.

*   *   *

THE DISTRIBUTION OF FOURTH AMENDMENT PRIVACY

William J. Stuntz

* * *

...Most of Fourth Amendment law is devoted to the regulation of searches, and searches are defined as anything agents of the government do that infringes a reasonable expectation of privacy. As every criminal procedure class learns, if the key to that definition is the word "expectation," the definition is circular. People expect what they think will happen, and what they think will happen is a function of what has happened in the past. By altering its behavior, the government can change how people expect it to behave. Thus, if the government is bound only to respect people's expectations, it is not bound at all, for it can easily condition the citizenry to expect little or no privacy.

So if it is to have any bite, Fourth Amendment privacy protection must be tied to something other than what people expect from the police. The law's solution is to tie its protection to what people expect from one another. People define, in their ordinary interactions with each other, the kinds of things they do and don't want to keep secret; once that private space has been so defined, the police should be required to respect it. This sounds like a brilliant idea, a way to permit the law to develop and adapt to changing circumstances without having judges pull their own intuitions about privacy out of thin air.

Two Supreme Court decisions from the early 1980s capture this idea. In *United States v. Knotts*, the police used an electronic tracking device to follow the movements of a suspect along the public streets.... [T]he Court held that the police could observe movements in public without any Fourth Amendment justification, because any member of the public might have observed the same thing. Because Knotts's travels were public to the world, they were public to the police.

In *United States v. Karo*, decided the next year, the police used a similar tracking device to follow several drums of chemicals into a private house; they continued to use the device to "observe" the movements of the chemicals within the house. As in *Knotts*, tracking the drums' movements in public was not a search. Tracking them once inside the house, though, was a different story. Because ordinary citizens could not have observed those movements, neither could the police, unless they complied with the rules governing house searches.

The principle that underlies *Knotts* and *Karo*—absent some special justification, the police can see and hear only those things that the rest of us can see and hear—has wide application; it is not too much to call it the defining principle of Fourth Amendment doctrine. Eavesdropping on telephone conversations is a "search." Overhearing a conversation on the street isn't. Jumping over a backyard fence to look around is a "search." Viewing the same yard from an airplane window isn't. Hiding in the bushes just outside the house and looking in the living room window is a "search." Standing in the street and peering through the open curtains into the living room isn't. The pattern is clear enough: the police can infringe privacy in ways that anyone else might infringe it, but not (meaning, again, not without special justification) in ways that differ from the sorts of things ordinary people might do. All these results seem designed to take the privacy people have, and use it to define the privacy that the police cannot invade without some good cause.

*   *   *

There are plenty of complications and counter-examples.... But for all its contradictions, the law retains a substantial degree of coherence. The things and places people keep secret from one another are surely more private, and hence their discovery more harmful to privacy, than the things and places people expose to the world. And among the places where people maintain their privacy, a hierarchy exists. Homes really *are* more private than other places; cars and containers we carry around are private, but less so than homes; clothing less so still. These propositions are not perfectly true, but the law must deal in generalizations, and they are good generalizations.

Perhaps *because* they are good generalizations, they have a substantial class bias. Consider how Fourth Amendment protection works in four major spheres: home, job, car, and street. Save for a small homeless population, rich and poor alike have homes. But the homes of the rich are larger and more comfortable, making it possible to live a larger portion of life in them. Privacy follows space, and people with money have more space than people without. People with more money are more likely to live in detached houses with yards; people with less money are more likely to live in apartment buildings with common hallways. Because others can hear (sometimes smell) from the hallway what goes on inside apartments, the police can too. My neighbors cannot freely surround my house to hear what is happening inside; consequently, neither can the police....

One finds a similar distributive tilt in the workplace. A police search of an enclosed office requires probable cause and a warrant. Consent of the employer is not enough. People who work on assembly lines or shop floors or hotel kitchens do not have offices; they share their work space with many others. When that space is open to the public, the police can see what it holds without justification. When that space is open only to employees, the police may need the consent of the employer, but not the consent of the suspected employee. In practice, probable cause and warrants are never needed.

With cars, the tilt is less substantial: one can enjoy as much, or as little, privacy in an old Chevrolet as in a new Lexus. Still, a substantial slice of the urban poor (in some cities, the urban middle class as well) use public transportation in place of cars. Fourth Amendment law treats passengers on subways and buses no differently than pedestrians on the street. And pedestrians receive less Fourth Amendment protection than drivers.

Which leads to the fourth sphere, the street. As with transport, there are two divides here: between cities and everyplace else, and between richer and poorer. Street life is mostly an urban phenomenon. It is also mostly a phenomenon of the lower and lower-middle classes. Again, poorer people have less comfortable homes; it is natural to want to spend less time, and do less, in them. Other forms of entertainment are more costly than sitting on a front stoop or wandering the streets and talking to friends. So among urban residential neighborhoods, one finds more pedestrian traffic in poorer neighborhoods than in wealthier ones.

And Fourth Amendment law makes it easy for police to stop and search pedestrians. Police can approach anyone and ask questions with no justification at all; as long as the encounter is no more coercive than any police-citizen encounter must be, it is deemed consensual, notwithstanding the fact that such conversations rarely seem optional to the suspect. That power is terribly important, for it gives the police the authority to initiate street encounters at will. ...

The general picture is clear enough. Fourth Amendment privacy is unequally distributed; it more closely resembles the right to buy political advertisements, which is useful only to those with money, than the right to vote, which almost all adult citizens share. Privacy, as Fourth Amendment law defines it, is something people tend to have a lot of only when they also have a lot of other things.

The temptation is to blame this feature of Fourth Amendment law on privacy's definition. By tying the definition of "searches" to the kind of privacy people actually have, the doctrine naturally tends to favor some classes of people over others, for people who have more privacy also have more, period. The solution, one might think, is a less positive, more normative definition of privacy. Ask not what privacy we actually have with each other; rather, ask what privacy we ought to have with the police. If rich and poor deserve the same level of privacy protection from the police, perhaps the law can simply give it to them.

That task is harder than it sounds. If by "privacy" one means the interest in not being observed (seen or heard), it is impossible. The problem is that, in general, the harm from being observed declines steeply with the addition of each new observer. If my wife and I have conversations that we wish to share only with each other, it is a real injury to each of us for a third party to listen in. If we live in an apartment building where our neighbors hear all our conversations because the walls are so thin, the addition of one more pair of ears is not particularly harmful. The point is not that poor people don't care about privacy; they surely do. Rather, the point is that, much of the time, the police don't take privacy (in the Fourth Amendment sense of the word) away from poor people, because those people have already lost it, and one cannot lose it twice. However the law of police searches is defined, if its goal is to protect against the harm of being observed, it will give most of its protection to people who can afford lives that allow limited observation. That excludes the urban poor.

Note: the urban poor, not simply the poor. People who live outside cities tend to have cars whatever their income level. People in trailer parks live in places that afford almost as much privacy as detached houses. It is poor people in cities who tend to live in large apartment buildings, to travel by bus or subway, and because of a combination of income and concentrated population, to spend more time on the street than do people in other places. This urban-nonurban divide creates another divide. Poverty in America is not exclusively an urban phenomenon. Poverty among certain population groups in certain parts of the country *is* almost exclusively an urban phenomenon. Poor whites are dispersed; they do not live in close proximity to large numbers of other poor whites. Poor blacks are more likely to live in cities, surrounded by other poor blacks. If the law is tilted against the urban poor, it is bound to have a racial tilt as well.

*   *   *

WHAT IS A SEARCH? TWO CONCEPTUAL FLAWS IN FOURTH AMENDMENT DOCTRINE AND SOME HINTS OF A REMEDY

SHERRY F. COLB

*   *   *

When determining what privacy the Fourth Amendment does and does not protect—what circumstances, in other words, give rise to a "reasonable expectation of privacy"—the Court asks: "What is a search?" To rule out activities that *do not* qualify, the Court denies privacy in whatever people "knowingly expose" to the public. If a person knowingly exposes some object or activity to the public, there has accordingly been no search. Absent a search, police may observe the thing that is "exposed" without having to obtain a warrant or otherwise justify their observations. . . .

In developing the category of things that are "knowingly exposed," and therefore not a search, the Court has repeatedly made two analytic moves that effectively rob the category of any firm boundaries: (1) It treats the risk of exposure through third-party wrongdoing as tantamount to an invitation for that exposure ("Move One"); and (2) it treats exposure to a limited audience as morally equivalent to exposure to the whole world ("Move Two").

Treating risk-taking as inviting exposure effectively excuses (and even justifies) what would otherwise be wrongful conduct by third parties, including the police. If a man lies down and falls into a deep sleep on a subway train, for example, he risks having his pocket picked. A pickpocket can easily swipe the sleeping man's wallet without encountering any resistance. We might even say colloquially that the sleeping man has "asked to have his pocket picked." This colloquialism does not, however, describe a legal justification for the pickpocket. We would not say, in other words, that the man on the train has willingly agreed to the taking of his wallet (as we would, for example, if he had abandoned the wallet in the street). Like taking candy from a baby, taking a wallet from a sleeping man remains a crime, no matter how easy it is to accomplish.

The second of the two moves, treating exposure to a limited audience as identical to exposure to the world, means failing to recognize degrees of privacy in the Fourth Amendment context. A person going on vacation, for example, might give a neighbor the key to her house and ask him to water her plants while she is gone. The neighbor now has explicit permission to observe what would otherwise be hidden from view, namely, the inside of the vacationer's home (at least those parts visible from areas through which he must travel to reach the plants). By granting this permission, the vacationer has forfeited a measure of privacy and has thus knowingly exposed part of her home to her neighbor. Still, if the neighbor were to invite his friends or family into the apartment to see the vacationer's personal items,... that act would go beyond the scope of the vacationer's permission and therefore represent an invasion of her privacy. There are degrees of privacy and, accordingly, degrees of exposure, and one might choose to forfeit some of her freedom from exposure without thereby forfeiting all of it.

* * *

II. MOVE ONE: EQUATING RISK AND INVITATION

*   *   *

A. TRASH

Perhaps the leading decision equating risk and invitation is *California v. Greenwood*. Suspecting narcotics trafficking, a police officer asked a garbage collector to segregate Greenwood's trash upon collection. After separating the target's garbage, the collector then gave it to the officer to permit her to rummage through it. The Supreme Court considered the following question: "[W]hether the Fourth Amendment prohibits the warrantless search and seizure of garbage left for collection outside the curtilage of a home." Did the officer, in other words, invade any "reasonable expectation of privacy" by obtaining and rummaging through Greenwood's trash, such that a Fourth Amendment search took place, triggering the warrant requirement?

The Court answered no to these questions and concluded that when a person leaves his trash at the curb, he knowingly exposes it to the public. When Greenwood placed his garbage on the street, the Court said, he took a significant risk that the bag would be torn open and its contents revealed. "It is common knowledge," the majority explained, "that plastic garbage bags left on or at the side of a public street are readily accessible to animals, children, scavengers, snoops, and other members of the public." In other words, children, raccoons, and snoops would have had access to the garbage, sitting out in public as it was, and they could have raided it, just as the police officer did.

*   *   *

By invoking the risk of snoops rummaging through Greenwood's garbage, the Court made Move One, described above. It treated a person who takes the risk that something might occur as having invited the materialization of that risk. Without explicitly articulating this equivalence, the Court permitted the officer to act as though the garbage, which was in fact safely enclosed within an opaque bag, had actually been strewn about by all manner of errant creatures in the neighborhood. By constructively inviting such exposure, Greenwood could not be heard to complain of the government's acceptance of the invitation.

The Supreme Court's approach to the facts of *Greenwood* was highly artificial. It is unpersuasive to argue that by putting out his garbage, Greenwood had knowingly relinquished the secrecy of its contents. When the garbage was at the curb, Greenwood's hypothetical snoopy neighbor might have had to violate the law to rummage through it in the way that the police officer did. To say that he invited the world to rummage through it was thus to confuse the risk of exposure, one that he can perhaps be said to have knowingly taken, and exposure itself, something that the police officer brought about in a manner that would have been wrongful conduct if attempted by a private "snoop."

To see further why the Court's equation of risk and invitation in *Greenwood* is destructive of privacy, consider what else a "snoop," raccoon, or child might have done.... A snoop, raccoon, or child might have climbed beyond the curb, onto the curtilage, and into Greenwood's house through an open window, perhaps proceeding to remove items from the shelves.... The Court presumably would not suggest, however, that these possibilities might justify the police in doing the same. The suggestion is nonetheless implicit in the "risk as invitation" argument that the Court adopts in *Greenwood.*

*   *   *

D. TRACKING DEVICES

Because bagged garbage and enclosed fields are better concealed than cars on the public roads, it should come as no surprise that the Court has ruled that police may—without a warrant or probable cause—track the whereabouts of cars as they travel.... In *United States v. Knotts*, police placed a beeper into a "five-gallon drum containing chloroform purchased by one of respondent's co-defendants" and thereby "monitor[ed] the progress of a car carrying the chloroform." The beeper enabled the police to track the car's whereabouts, even when they could no longer see the vehicle. The police had not obtained a warrant authorizing the tracking nor did the government argue that police had probable cause to justify a search. It claimed instead that neither a warrant nor probable cause (nor any alternative "reasonableness" measure) was required, because no reasonable expectation of privacy was implicated.

The Supreme Court agreed with the government and held that because the car in question was outside of the house and visible to the public, the use of a tracking device did not trigger Fourth Amendment requirements.

Tracking the movements of the person's car did not qualify, in other words, as a Fourth Amendment search. Tracking would only become a search at the point at which the item being monitored entered a nonvisible part of a private residence, where analogous visual surveillance would be impermissible.

The reasoning is now familiar. People who drive their cars on the road knowingly and continuously expose their whereabouts to the public. Since anyone and everyone can watch them and observe the places they go, there is no additional intrusion involved in police surveillance of them. This ceases to be true, however, once the car begins moving around inside a private residence.

Far from reflecting common values about privacy and the way people actually behave, however, the Court's analysis here is counterintuitive. Imagine that police officers presented you with the option of having them follow you everywhere you travel, keeping track of when you leave your house each day, where you go for recreation and how often you visit various people and places. Now imagine that as an alternative, the police propose tracking exactly where inside your garage your car is parked at any given time. Which of the two would you choose? Which of the two represents the greater invasion of privacy?

*　　*　　*

The *Knotts* reasoning is flawed because people do not expect to be followed when they move about in public areas. When you notice a person following you on the road, you are likely to feel unnerved. It is not that you suppose you are literally "invisible" in public. Occasionally, you will see or be seen by someone you know. Other times, you may go to two different places and run into the same acquaintance or stranger at both. Nonetheless, for the most part, you rightly anticipate a measure of public privacy. Unless you are a celebrity, you rely on a level of anonymity and mutual distance that comes with most public outings. If you know someone is following, you will therefore feel a sense of violation or intrusion.

*　　*　　*

The criminal law's recognition of stalking as an offense reflects the importance of being left alone, even out in public. "'Stalking' is generally defined as the 'willful, malicious, and repeated following and harassing of another person.'" If we think about what is wrong with stalking, it goes to a very elemental component of the individual's sense of security in her person, her ability to be left alone and to choose not to associate with others.

*   *   *

E. Electronic Eyes and Privacy in Public

To illustrate the importance of public privacy, let us take an arguably less controversial example than *Knotts* of police monitoring of what is broadly available to the public. There now exist technologies that can scan the eyes and faces of large crowds to identify a specific individual. A machine scans faces in the way that a computer might scan fingerprints. Police have used such technologies at football games, for example, to determine whether a particular target is in the audience. Following the Court's "public visibility" approach to the Fourth Amendment that we saw in *Knotts*, no one could plausibly object on privacy grounds to scanning. Yet we shall see that scanning does raise some difficult questions.

Sitting in the bleachers of a sporting event is arguably the essence of a public appearance. Anyone sitting nearby, and perhaps even a television audience, has visual access to the spectator's presence at the game. If the scanned individual did not want to be seen or identified there, then it seems he should have stayed home and watched the event on television.

This perspective, however, may not give us the whole story. An insightful letter to the editor of the *New York Times* convincingly challenged the idea that such scanning technology does no more than anyone sitting near the observed person could do. As the writer noted, under normal circumstances, we are in a position to "observe the observers." If someone stares at us (or points a television camera at us) in a public place, we tend to notice. Having noticed, we can take measures to put a stop to the staring or the filming. We can stare back and hope the other person will look away or blink. Because there is a social norm against staring, simply catching the offender will often do the trick. We can also behave differently for the few seconds that a camera is trained on us (as spectators often do by waving momentarily at television viewers). Such actions allow us to control the extent of our own exposure. Alternatively, we can change seats or leave the area altogether. Our ability to observe our observers thus gives us the power to rebuff, confront, and escape invasions of our privacy. Knowledge is power.

Not so with scanning technology (or hidden video cameras in the streets). With such devices, we can be watched wherever we go and have no idea at the time. The scanners, moreover, do not feel constrained by social norms of personal space. If we do not know that we are being observed, though, do we really "suffer" from the intrusion? The answer is that we do. Such technology is different from the unknown "watcher," because we know that the technology is available and may be in use. If the Supreme Court were to rule that the technology does not invade any reasonable expectation of privacy, as the logic in the precedents suggests it would do, the face scanner (or hidden camera) would always be a possibility whenever we left the house. Rather than living in blissful ignorance of constant surveillance, we might therefore find ourselves in a constant state of apprehension and self-consciousness whenever out in public. Our knowledge, however, unlike that of the observed who can see their own observers, does not give us any means of protecting ourselves.

*   *   *

DIGITAL DOSSIERS AND THE DISSIPATION OF FOURTH AMENDMENT PRIVACY

Daniel J. Solove

*   *   *

We live in the early stages of the Information Age, a time when technology has given us unprecedented abilities to communicate, transfer and share information, access data, and analyze a profound array of facts and ideas. The complete benefits of the Information Age do not simply come to us. We must "plug in" to join in. In other words, we must establish relationships with a panoply of companies. To connect to the Internet, we must subscribe to an ISP, such as America Online (AOL) or Earthlink. To be able to receive more than a few television channels, we need to open an account with a cable company. Phone service, mobile phone service, and other utilities require us to open accounts with a number of entities.

Further, life in modern society demands that we enter into numerous relationships with professionals (doctors, lawyers, accountants), businesses (restaurants, video rental stores), merchants (bookstores, mail catalog companies), publishing companies (magazines, newspapers), organizations (charities), financial institutions (banks, investment firms, credit card companies), landlords, employers, and other entities (insurance companies, security companies, travel agencies, car rental companies, hotels). Our relationships with all of these entities generate records containing personal information necessary to establish an account and record of our transactions, preferences, purchases, and activities. We are becoming a society of records, and these records are not held by us, but by third parties.

*　*　*

These record systems are becoming increasingly useful to law enforcement officials. Personal information can help the government detect fraud, espionage, fugitives, smuggling cartels, drug distribution rings, and terrorist cells. Information about a person's financial transactions, purchases, and religious and political beliefs can assist law enforcement in investigating suspected criminals, individuals providing money and assistance to terrorists, or profiling people for more thorough searches at airports.

... [F]rom pen registers and trap and trace devices, the government can obtain a list of all the phone numbers dialed to or from a particular location, potentially revealing the people with whom a person associates. From bank records, which contain one's account activity and check writing, the government can discover the various companies and professionals that a person does business with (ISP, telephone company, credit card company, magazine companies, doctors, attorneys, and so on). Credit card company records can reveal where one eats and shops and which cultural events one attends. The government can obtain one's travel destinations and activities from travel agent records. From hotel records, it can discover the numbers a person dialed and the pay-per-view movies a person watched. ... From video stores, the government can access an inventory of the videos that a person has rented.

*　*　*

Beyond the records described above, the Internet has the potential to become one of the government's greatest information-gathering tools. There are two significant aspects of the Internet that make it such a revolutionary data-collection device. First, it gives many individuals a false sense of privacy. The secrecy and anonymity of the Internet is often a mirage. People are rarely truly anonymous because ISPs keep records of a subscriber's screen name and pseudonyms. ISP account information can also include the subscriber's name, address, phone numbers, passwords, information about web surfing sessions and durations, credit card and bank account information. By learning a person's screen name, the government can identify the person behind the pseudonym postings to newsgroups or chat rooms. For example, in *McVeigh v. Cohen*, AOL provided a Navy official with the identity of an individual using a pseudonym who indicated he was gay and worked in the military. Based on this information, the Navy proceeded to initiate discharge proceedings under the "Don't Ask, Don't Tell" policy.

*   *   *

Websites often accumulate a great deal of information about their users. Through the use of a "cookie," which identifies a user by deploying a text file into the user's computer, websites can detect the previous website and parts of the site a user accessed. This data is called "clickstream data" because it records nearly every click of the mouse. Another information collection device, known as a "web bug," involves hidden pixel tags secretly planted on a user's hard drive that surreptitiously gather data about the user. Websites also collect data when people fill out online questionnaires pertaining to their hobbies, health, and interests. Further, a person's Internet postings are archived and do not readily disappear. As we invest more time on the Internet, strangers and unfamiliar organizations are keeping permanent records about our lives.

Thus, the government can glean a substantial amount of information about visitors to a particular website. For example, certain heath websites ask individuals to fill out questionnaires about their symptoms to determine whether they have a disease. Other websites have questionnaires relating to psychology and personality. From Internet retailers, the government can learn about the books, videos, music, and electronics that one purchases. Some Internet retailers, such as "Amazon.com," record all the purchases a person makes throughout the many years that the person has been shopping on the website. Also, retailers use surveys to identify how a person rates books and videos. Based on this information, the government can discover a consumer's interests, sexuality, political views, religious beliefs, and lifestyle. Further, if a person buys a gift from an Internet retailer and has it mailed to a friend, the government may learn the friend's name and address and develop a list of an individual's friends and acquaintances.

*   *   *

While life in the Information Age has brought us a dizzying amount of information, it has also placed a profound amount of information about our lives in the hands of numerous entities. These digital dossiers are increasingly becoming digital biographies, a horde of aggregated bits of information combined to reveal a portrait of who we are based upon what we buy, the organizations we belong to, how we navigate the Internet, and which shows and videos we watch. This information is not held by trusted friends or family members, but by large bureaucracies that we do not know very well or sometimes do not even know at all.

*   *   *

... [T]he Court held that there is no reasonable expectation in privacy for information known or exposed to third parties. In *United States v. Miller*, federal agents presented subpoenas to two banks to produce all of the financial records of the defendant.... The defendant challenged the subpoenas as a violation of the Fourth Amendment. The Court held that there was no reasonable expectation of privacy in financial records maintained by a bank. "[T]he Fourth Amendment does not prohibit the obtaining of information revealed to a third party and conveyed by him to Government authorities." The Court reasoned: "... All of the documents obtained, including financial statements and deposit slips, contain only information voluntarily conveyed to the banks and exposed to their employees in the ordinary course of business."

In *Smith v. Maryland*, police officers were attempting to track down a robber who had begun making obscene and harassing phone calls. At one point, the robber asked someone he had been calling to step out on her front porch, where she observed him drive by in his car. The police traced the license plate number and found that the car was registered to the defendant. Without a warrant, the police asked the telephone company to install a pen register to record the numbers dialed from the defendant's home. The Court concluded that there was no reasonable expectation of privacy in pen registers. Since people "know that they must convey numerical information to the phone company" and that the phone company records this information for billing purposes, people cannot "harbor any general expectation that the numbers they dial will remain secret."

Miller and *Smith* establish a general rule that if information is in the hands of third parties, then an individual can have no reasonable expectation of privacy in that information, which means that the Fourth Amendment does not apply. Individuals thus probably do not have a reasonable expectation of privacy in communications and records maintained by ISPs or computer network system administrators.

*   *   *

Smith and *Miller* have been extensively criticized throughout the past several decades. However, it is only recently that we are truly beginning to see the profound implications of the Court's third party doctrine.... Gathering information from third party records is an emerging law enforcement practice with as many potential dangers as the wiretapping in *Olmstead.* "The progress of science in furnishing the government with means of espionage is not likely to stop with wiretapping," Justice Brandeis observed in his *Olmstead* dissent. "Ways may some day be developed by which the government, without removing papers from secret drawers, can reproduce them in court, and by which it will be enabled to expose to a jury the most intimate occurrences of the home."

That day is here. Government information gathering from the extensive dossiers being assembled with modern computer technology poses one of the most significant threats to privacy of our times.

*   *   *

THE SUPREME COURT, CRIMINAL PROCEDURE, AND JUDICIAL INTEGRITY

Stephen A. Saltzburg

* * *

[T]he open fields doctrine...exemplifies the world in which the Supreme Court claims we live in versus the one most people actually live in. In *Oliver v. United States*, the Supreme Court turned the reasonable expectation of privacy analysis adopted in *Katz v. United States* on its head. *Katz* departed from the Court's prior decisions in *Olmstead v. United States* and *Goldman v. United States* and reasoned that the Fourth Amendment protects privacy irrespective of whether there is a technical trespass by the government.

So, what did the Court do in *Oliver*? It held that a person has an expectation of privacy only in the curtilage around a home, not elsewhere. As a result, trespasses that would almost surely have been searches prior to *Katz* are not searches. What sense does this make? One of the things many Americans aspire to is to own their own land as well as their homes. If they have two, three, seven, or twenty acres, they ought to be able to believe (as most non-lawyers still believe

98

because they do not read the United States Reports) that they have a right to exclude others, including the government, and to claim privacy in their land. But, under *Oliver*, if a landowner has three acres of land, two of which are outside the curtilage, the landowner fences his land with barbed-wire and electrified fencing, posts no-trespassing signs, plants trees around the fence to enhance privacy, buys large dogs to patrol the property, and with all of this in place then decides to run naked around his or her property, the government can knock down the fence, uproot the trees, shoot the dogs, and spy on the homeowner without violating the Fourth Amendment. This is so because the Supreme Court says that the private property is an open field. Of course, the field is as closed as any owner could make it, but the Court believes that the Fourth Amendment still is not implicated because an open field need not be either a field or open. So we have a doctrine which has no rationale and no identifying characteristics.

By the way, compare the phone booth in which Katz transmitted wagering information with the three-acre property I have described. The phone booth was located on a street, which is an open field in which there is no general expectation of privacy; the booth was owned by the telephone company; and Katz was fully in sight at all times. Notwithstanding these facts, the Supreme Court said that Katz's privacy was invaded. Surely, that invasion was a lesser intrusion than a trespass into private property against the posted wishes of and despite the fences employed by a homeowner.

What about shopping malls? The owners and tenants of such malls still believe that they are protected by the Fourth Amendment. But those malls are simply fields over which a cover is placed. If open fields need not be either genuine fields or open, why should malls or even office buildings be protected by the Fourth Amendment? There is not even curtilage there.

The answer is that they should be protected because private property is where people claim their privacy. That is most true of homeowners, and ironically, *Oliver* gives them the least amount of protection. Why? The answer is because police want to search for marijuana. Will the country suffer much if the Court were to admit that homeowners have a right to expect privacy in the property they have closed to the public? Surely the answer is no. There are so many other opportunities for law enforcement to gather information about large-scale drug trafficking that the loss of information that would occur if the Supreme Court protected the privacy of home owners against government trespass is not likely to be great.

*   *   *

OPEN FIELDS IN THE INNER CITY: APPLICATION OF THE CURTILAGE DOCTRINE TO URBAN AND SUBURBAN AREAS

CARRIE LEONETTI

* * *

The first standard for determining whether a search has occurred for Fourth Amendment purposes is whether the individual affected has a reasonable expectation of privacy in the area searched. In the case of multi-occupant dwellings, such as apartment complexes, hotels, and motels, this determination is complicated by the fact that residents do not occupy the entire dwelling and its surrounding areas alone. Instead, certain areas of the dwelling are shared among multiple residents.

...The Supreme Court has afforded apartments and hotel rooms status as "homes" under the Fourth Amendment.... Unfortunately, however, courts have also generally ended this protection at the inside of the door of an individual apartment or motel room, largely on the basis of the *Dunn* factors [(1) the proximity of the area to the home; (2) whether the area was within an enclosure surrounding the home; (3) the nature of the uses to which the area was put; and (4) the steps taken to protect the area from observation by passers-by].

*   *   *

This analytical loophole has encouraged the proliferation of two increasingly popular police investigatory techniques in urban areas and among multi-occupant dwellings: canine sniffs and knock-and-talks. Both canine sniffs and knock-and-talks involve an approach only to the outer door of an individual tenant's apartment or motel room, with the entry into the unit being justified later, either by consent or by probable cause developed during the initial approach of the unit. These techniques were designed by police to gain entry for a search without obtaining a warrant and, ultimately, to avoid the encumbrances caused by the protections provided by the Fourth Amendment.

The "knock-and-talk" is an investigatory method in which the police approach a dwelling, without probable cause or a warrant, knock on the door, identify themselves as police officers, and attempt to "talk" their way inside to conduct a search of the dwelling by gaining the occupant's verbal "consent." The knock-and-talk has become extremely popular with law enforcement agencies around the country, particularly in areas of high drug activity. Despite its popularity, however, few courts have addressed its constitutionality. Nonetheless, several federal circuit courts of appeal have found that the procedure does not offend the Fourth Amendment, regardless of the time of day or night at which the search takes place.

*   *   *

Applying a similar rationale, that a resident's privacy interest begins only inside the apartment or motel-room door, courts have held that dog sniffs of the exterior of urban dwellings, for the purpose of generating probable cause for entry therein, do not constitute searches for Fourth Amendment purposes.

*   *   *

One analytical device that courts have employed in declining to suppress the fruits of these investigatory techniques, and thereby avoiding the recognition and protection of privacy rights in the curtilage of more densely populated areas, is to rely upon a quasi-trespass theory within common areas of urban dwellings that are accessible to more than one occupant or tenant. In the context of multi-occupant dwellings, in particular, courts have generally permitted knock-and-talks and dog-sniff searches in common areas based on the theory that individual tenants lack the ability to exclude other occupants from them.

The problem with the common-area theory of curtilage is that *Katz's* reasonable-expectation-of-privacy test is not coextensive with the property concept of an exclusive right to exclude. The example of a single apartment with two roommates living in two separate bedrooms provides a useful analogy. While each roommate has a right to exclude the other from his or her bedroom, neither has a right to exclude the other from the common areas of that apartment. Nonetheless, the two tenants together have a collective right to exclude all but each other and their guests from the entire apartment. Therefore, while one roommate could consent to a search of the living room or kitchen on behalf of the other, it does not follow that the police could conduct a warrantless search of those areas of the dwelling simply because they are common to the two roommates.

This example demonstrates the fundamental fallacy with determining the boundaries of urban curtilage by applying only nineteenth-century trespass concepts and the twentieth-century *Dunn* factors to the twenty-first century reality of urban life. Like the two roommates in a shared apartment, each resident of an apartment building or motel is offended by the invasion of the common premises in the same manner that each member of a single-family household is affronted by the invasion of the curtilage.

The central principle of the Fourth Amendment is that a person may "retreat into his own home and there be free from unreasonable governmental intrusion." If privacy is confined only to areas that are exclusively occupied by a single tenant, then most Americans would be left with only a few hundred square feet in which to confine themselves from the increasing governmental intrusions of modern life. This mistakenly ignores the collective right that the residents of an apartment building, condominium complex, or hotel have to exclude all individuals that do not have a legitimate purpose there.

*   *   *

Ultimately, it is important to remember that the *Dunn* factors were not meant to be an exhaustive list, but rather were merely meant to illustrate the primary inquiry of the curtilage doctrine—namely, whether the area sought to be protected is one that is truly tied to the intimate activities of the home. Occupants of urban, multi-unit dwellings do participate in intimate activities associated with the privacy of a home that extend beyond the doors of their apartments into the common property of the building, such as barbequing on a back patio or sunbathing on a roof deck. These activities would clearly be factors, under *Dunn*, in determining the boundaries of curtilage on a large ranch-style home. There is no principled reason why the same activities should not generate a privacy interest in an urban setting, where privacy is all the more rare and sacred.

As the Court of Appeals of Indiana explained:

> Individuals who live in apartments often hang decorations on outside doors and place doormats on the ground outside the door. Further, individuals who have apartments that exit immediately outside often place and keep personal items on their steps or porches. Simply because one lives in an apartment does not mean that he or she does not at times occupy the space immediately outside of the apartment home. Thus, one who lives in an apartment also treats the area immediately outside his or her apartment home as his or her curtilage.

In the context of multi-occupant urban dwellings, only a broader look at the time, place, and manner of police intrusions into common areas, including the area immediately beyond the door to an individual unit, can inform the inquiry of whether the police presence there infringes upon a tenant's reasonable expectation of privacy and, therefore, constitutes a search for Fourth Amendment purposes. Employing this multi-textual definition of curtilage would recognize that residents in apartment buildings and hotels have a reasonable expectation of privacy, and therefore a *curtilage* interest exists, in all common areas of the dwelling in which the residents have a right to expect that none but their cohabitants and invited guests will enter. This definition of curtilage would include hallways and enclosed yards, each of which form the curtilage of an individual unit as to all but those invited there by the resident of any other unit. The police could constitutionally conduct a knock-and-talk or dog-sniff investigation in the common areas of such a dwelling, therefore, only with a warrant issued upon probable cause or consistent with one of the well-established exceptions to the warrant requirement, such as the consent of a resident or manager.

*   *   *

Chapter 3

WHAT CONSTITUTES
A "SEIZURE"?

INTRODUCTION

This chapter features several articles critiquing the Court's test for a "seizure" of the person. Under the traditional test for a seizure announced in *United States v. Mendenhall*, 446 U.S. 544 (1980), a person has been "seized" within the meaning of the Fourth Amendment if the reasonable person in his shoes would have felt he was not free to leave. In "The Supreme Court's Search for a Definition of a Seizure: What Is a 'Seizure' of a Person within the Meaning of the Fourth Amendment?," Thomas Clancy examines this test as applied in *INS v. Delgado*, 446 U.S. 210 (1984), where the Supreme Court held that factory workers subjected to an immigration raid were not seized even though INS agents blocked the exits while questioning the factory workers. Clancy notes that rather than ask whether the reasonable person in the factory workers' shoes would have felt free to leave as it should have, the Court examined whether the police action was reasonable.

In *Florida v. Bostick*, 501 U.S. 429 (1991), the Court modified the traditional test for a seizure, holding that in cases where a reasonable person would not feel free to leave due to factors outside the control of the police, the test for a seizure is whether the reasonable person in the defendant's shoes would have felt free to terminate the encounter with the police or decline the police officer's requests. In "(E)Racing the Fourth Amendment," Devon W. Carbado applies insights from Critical Race Theory to critique Justice O'Connor's color-blind analysis in *Florida v. Bostick*. In "'Black and Blue Encounters'—Some Preliminary Thoughts about Fourth Amendment Seizures: Should Race Matter?," Tracey Maclin argues that when determining whether a person has been seized, courts should consider the race of the person confronted by the police.

Florida v. Bostick's modified test for a seizure was subsequently applied in *United States v. Drayton*, 536 U.S. 194 (2002). In "No Need to Shout: Bus Sweeps and the Psychology of Coercion," Janice Nadler applies insights from social psychology to critique the Court's conclusion in *Drayton* that two black males were not seized when confronted by white officers during a bus sweep for drugs.

THE SUPREME COURT'S SEARCH FOR A DEFINITION OF A SEIZURE: WHAT IS A "SEIZURE" OF A PERSON WITHIN THE MEANING OF THE FOURTH AMENDMENT?

Thomas K. Clancy

* * *

...In *United States v. Mendenhall,* Justice Stewart made the first attempt to formulate a test to measure when a seizure short of a physical restraint occurs, proposing the "reasonable person" test.... In his opinion, joined in relevant part only by Justice Rehnquist, he wrote: "a person has been 'seized' within the meaning of the Fourth Amendment only if, in view of all of the circumstances surrounding the incident, a reasonable person would have believed that he was not free to leave."

* * *

INS v. Delgado... produced the first majority opinion utilizing the reasonable person standard. The case involved the individual questioning of workers concerning their citizenship status by Immigration and Naturalization Service agents during factory surveys. Several named plaintiffs, who were workers in the affected factories, sued the INS. At the beginning of each survey, several agents positioned themselves near the building's exits. Other agents dispersed throughout the factory to question employees at their work stations. The agents displayed badges, carried walkie-talkies, and were armed. The agents approached the employees and, after identifying themselves, asked questions relating to the employee's citizenship. If the employee gave a credible response, the agents moved on; if not, the employee was asked to produce immigration papers. During each survey, employees continued to work and were free to walk around within the factory.

*   *   *

The majority, in an opinion written by Justice Rehnquist, rejected the claim that the entire factory work force was seized for the duration of the survey when the INS agents were placed near the exits. The majority reasoned that people at work "[o]rdinarily" have their freedom to move about "meaningfully restricted" by their "voluntary obligations to their employers." The majority noted that, when the surveys were initiated, people went about their ordinary business;... the workers were not prevented from moving about the factories.... The majority concluded that, since most workers could have no reasonable fear that they would be detained upon leaving, no seizure of the work force as a whole occurred.

*   *   *

Only Justices Brennan and Marshall dissented. Although agreeing that the reasonable person standard applied, Brennan stated in the dissent that the most "striking" aspect of the majority's opinion was its "studied air of unreality." Brennan said that the Court's avoidance of the conclusion that a seizure resulted was "rooted more in fantasy than in the record of this case." He believed that a seizure occurred when the factory workers were "accosted by the INS agents and questioned concerning their right to remain in the United States." He reasoned that the manner in which the surveys were conducted demonstrated a "'show of authority' of sufficient size and force to overbear the will of any reasonable person." The majority's reasoning was flawed,

Brennan believed, based on its failure to consider the circumstances surrounding the questioning: a large number of agents systematically moved through the workers; suspected illegal aliens were handcuffed and taken away; all exits were guarded by agents; and, as the agents moved through the factory, they showed their badges and directed "pointed questions" at the workers. Brennan also considered the plaintiffs' testimony, which demonstrated their belief that they had to answer the agents' questions. Given the surrounding circumstances, Brennan concluded that those feelings of constraint were reasonable and, therefore, further concluded that seizures had taken place.

*   *   *

The reasonable person analysis, as employed by the increasingly conservative majority of the Court, has become strained and divorced from the plain meaning of the words of the test itself. In *INS v. Delgado*, there was no real attempt by the majority to determine if a reasonable person would believe that he or she was not free to leave. Such an analysis would entail determining what a reasonable person in the suspect's position would believe based on the police behavior. Instead, the majority looked to the objective factors of the encounter and focused on the reasonableness of the police's conduct, without regard to the conduct's impact on the mind of a reasonable person in the suspect's position.

*   *   *

In summary, two currents have been at work in the cases. First, there has not been a consensus of what the reasonable person test means, and *Delgado* suggests a trend toward a general reasonableness test, divorced from what a reasonable suspect would believe. Second, unusually expansive dicta has obscured the actual results in the cases. These two tendencies have suggested a broader test than is actually employed. Many lower courts, utilizing the dicta emanating from above, have applied the reasonable person test broadly, while others have not. Rather than produce stability and predictability, the reasonable person test has produced the opposite. It thus has failed as an effective test.

*   *   *

(E)RACING THE FOURTH AMENDMENT

DEVON W. CARBADO

* * *

It's been almost two years since I pledged allegiance to the United States of America—that is to say, became an American citizen. Before that, I was a permanent resident of America and a citizen of the United Kingdom.

Yet, I became a black American long before I acquired American citizenship. Unlike citizenship, black racial naturalization was always available to me, even as I tried to make myself unavailable for that particular Americanization process. Given the negative images of black Americans on 1970s British television and the intra-racial tensions between blacks in the U.K. and blacks in America, I was not eager, upon my arrival to the United States, to assert a black American identity....

But I became a black American anyway. Before I freely embraced that identity it was ascribed to me.

* * *

...I was closely followed or completely ignored when I visited department stores. Women clutched their purses upon encountering me in elevators. People crossed the street to avoid me. The seat beside me on the bus was almost always racially available for another black person. Already I wanted to be a black American no more.

*   *   *

Like many black Americans, I developed the ability to cope with, manage, and sometimes even normalize certain micro-aggressive racial encounters....

I have not, however, been able to normalize my experiences with the police. They continue to jar me. The very sight of the police in my rear view mirror is unnerving. Far from comforting, this sight of justice (the paradigmatic site for injustice) engenders feelings of vulnerability: How will I be over-policed this time? Do I have my driver's license, insurance, etc.? How am I dressed? Is my UCLA parking sticker visible? Will any of this even matter? Should it?

And what precisely will be my racial exit strategy this time? How will I make the officers comfortable? Should I? Will I have time—the racial opportunity—to demonstrate my respectability? Should I have to? Will they perceive me to be a good or a bad black?

These questions are part of black people's collective consciousness. They are symptomatic of a particular colorline anxiety: a police state of mind. This racial dis-ease is inflicted on black people ostensibly to cure the problem of crime. Its social effect, however, is to make white people feel good about, and comfortable with, their own racial identity and to make black people feel bad about, and uncomfortable with, being black.

My first racial episode with over-policing occurred only two weeks after I purchased my first car: a $1,500 yellow, convertible Triumph Spit Fire. I had been living in America for a year; my brother had been in the States for under a month. It was about nine p.m., and we were on our way to a friend's house.

Our trip was interrupted by the blare of a siren. We were in Inglewood, a predominantly black neighborhood south of Los Angeles; a police car had signaled us to pull over. One officer approached my window; the other stationed himself beside the passenger door. He directed his flashlight into the interior of the car, locating its beam, alternatively, on our faces. The characters: two black boys. The racial stage was set.

"Anything wrong, officers?" I asked, attempting to discern the face behind the flashlight. Neither officer responded. Against my racial script, I inquired again as to whether we had done anything wrong. Again, no response. Instead, one of the officers instructed, "Step outside the car with your hands on your heads." Effectively rehearsing our blackness, we did as he asked. He then told us to sit on the side of the curb. Grudgingly, we complied. Though we were both learning our parts, the racial theater was well underway.

As we sat on the pavement, "racially exposed," our backs to the officers, our feet in the road, I asked a third time whether we had done anything wrong. One officer responded, rather curtly, that I should "shut up and not make any trouble." Perhaps foolishly, I insisted on knowing why we were being stopped. "We have a right to know, don't we? We're not criminals, after all."

Today I might have acted differently, less defiantly. But my strange career with race, at least in America, had only just begun. In other words, I had not yet lived in America long enough to learn the ways of the police, the racial conventions of black and white police encounters, the so-called rules of the game: "Don't move. Don't turn around. Don't give some rookie an excuse to shoot you." No one had explained to me that "if you get pulled over by the police "[n]ever get into a verbal confrontation.... Never! Comply with the officer. If it means getting down on the ground, then get down on the ground. Comply with *whatever* the officer is asking you to do." It had not occurred to me that my encounter with these officers was potentially life threatening. This was one of my many racial blind spots. Eventually, I would develop my second sight.

The officer discerned that I was not American. Presumably, my accent provided the clue, although my lack of racial etiquette—mouthing off to white police officers in a "high-crime" area in the middle of the night—might have suggested that I was an outsider to the racial dynamics of police encounters. My assertion of my rights, my attempts to maintain my dignity, my confronting authority (each a function of my pre-invisibility blackness) might have signaled that I was not from here and, more importantly, that I had not been racially socialized into, or internalized the racial survival strategy of, performing obedience for the police. From the officer's perspective, we were, in that moment, defiant ones.

The officer looked at my brother and me, seemingly puzzled. He needed more information racially to process us, to make sense of what he might have experienced as a moment of racial incongruity. While there was no disjuncture between how we looked and the phenotypic cues for black identity, our performance of blackness could have created a racial indeterminacy problem that had to be fixed. That is, to the extent that the officers harbored an a priori investment in our blackness (that we were criminals or thugs), our English accents might have challenged it. At best, this challenge was partial, however; racial inscription was inevitable. The officer could see—with his "inner eyes"—that we had the souls of black folk. He simply needed to confirm our racial stock so that he could freely trade on our blackness.

"Where are you guys from?"

"The U.K.," my brother responded.

"The what?"

"England."

"England?"

"Yes, England."

"You were born in England?"

"Yes."

"What part?"

"Birmingham."

"Uhmm...." We were strange fruit. Our racial identity had to be grounded.

"Where are your parents from?"

"The West Indies."

We were at last racially intelligible. Our English identity had been dislocated, falsified—or at least buried among our diasporic roots.

"How long has he been in America?" the officer wanted to know, pointing at me.

"About a year," my brother responded.

"Well, tell him that if he doesn't want to find himself in jail, he should shut the fuck up."

The history of racial violence in his words existentially moved us. We were now squarely within a sub-region of the borders of American Blackness. Our rite of passage was almost complete.

My brother nudged me several times with his elbows. "Cool it," he muttered under his breath. The intense look in his eyes inflected his words. "Don't provoke them."

By this time, my brother needn't have said anything. I was beginning to see the white over black racial picture. We had the right to do whatever they wanted us to do, a reasonable expectation of uncertainty. With that awareness,

I simply sat there. Quietly. My brother did the same. We were in a racial state of rightlessness, effectively outside the reach of the Fourth Amendment. The experience, in other words, was disciplinary. Although I didn't know it at the time, we were one step closer to becoming black Americans. Unwillingly, we were participating in a naturalization ceremony within which our submission to authority reflected and reproduced black racial subjectivity. We were being "pushed" and "pulled" through the racial body of America to be born again. A new motherland awaited us. Eventually we would belong to her. Her racial burden was to make us Naturalized Sons.

Without our consent, one of the officers rummaged through the entire car—no doubt in search of ex post probable cause; the other watched over us. The search yielded nothing. (No drugs.) (No stolen property.) (No weapons.) Ostensibly, we were free to leave.

But what if the search had resulted in the production of incriminating evidence? That is, what if the officers' racial suspicions were confirmed? Would that have rendered their conduct legitimate? Would they thereby become "good" cops? Would that have made us "bad" blacks—blacks who confirm negative stereotypes, blacks who are undeserving of public sympathy, blacks who discredit the race?

One of the officers asked for my driver's license, which I provided. My brother was then asked for his. He explained that he didn't have one because he had been in the country only a few weeks.

"Do you have any identification?"

"No. My passport is at home." We both knew that this was the wrong response.

The officers requested that we stand up, which we did. Pursuant to black letter law, or the law on the street for black people, they forced us against the side of the patrol car. Spread-eagled, they frisked and searched us. (Still no guns.) (Still no drugs.) (Still no stolen property.)

The entire incident lasted approximately twenty minutes. Neither officer provided us with an explanation as to why we were stopped. Nor did either officer apologize. By this time, I understood that we were not in a position to demand the latter, even as I did not understand that, in some sense, the entire event was racially predetermined. The encounter ended when one of the officers muttered through the back of his head, "You're free to go."

"Pardon?"

"I said you can go now."

And that was that. The racial bonding was over (for now). I wanted to say something like, "Are you absolutely certain, Officer? We really don't mind the intrusion, Officer. Do carry on with the search. Honest." But the burden of blackness in that moment rendered those thoughts unspeakable. Thus, I simply watched in silence as they left.

The encounter left us more racially aware and less racially intact. In other words, we were growing into our American profile. Still, the officers did not physically abuse us, we did not "kiss concrete," and we managed to escape jail. Relative to some black and Blue encounters, and considering my initial racial faux pas—questioning authority/asserting rights—we got off easy.

Subsequent to that experience, I have had several other incidents with the police. In this respect, and like many black people, I am a repeat player. While each racial game bears mention (as part of a broader informal naturalization process that structured the racial terms upon which I became American), I shall recount only one more here. This encounter, too, occurred on my way to American citizenship. And, like the first, it facilitated my (intra)racial integration into black American life.

Two of my brothers and my brother-in-law had just arrived from England. On our way from the airport, we stopped at my sister's apartment, which was in a predominantly white neighborhood. After letting us in, my sister left to perform errands. It was about two o'clock in the afternoon; my brothers wanted some tea. I showed one of them to the kitchen. After about five minutes, we heard the kettle whistling. "Get the kettle, will you." There was no answer. My other brother went to see what was going on. Finally the kettle stopped whistling, but he never returned. My brother-in-law and I were convinced that my brothers were engaged in some sort of prank. "What are they doing in there?" Together, we went into the kitchen. At the door were two police officers. Guns drawn, they instructed us to exit the apartment. With our hands in the air, we did so.

Outside, both of my brothers were pinned against the wall at gunpoint. There were eight officers. Each was visibly edgy, nervous and apprehensive. Passersby comfortably engaged in conspicuous racial consumption. Their eyes were all over our bodies. The racial product was a familiar public spectacle: white law enforcement officers disciplining black men....

The officers wanted to know whether there was anyone else inside. We answered in the negative. "What's going on?" my brother-in-law inquired. The officer responded that they had received a call from a neighbor reporting that several black men had entered an apartment with guns. "Rubbish, we're just coming in from the airport."

"Do you have any drugs?"

"Of course not. Look, this is a mistake." The officers did not believe us.... The body of evidence—that is to say, our race—was uncontestable....

"May we look inside the apartment?"

"Sure," my brother in-law "consented." "Whatever it takes to get this over."

Two officers entered the apartment. After about two minutes, they came out shaking their heads, presumably signaling that they were not at a crime scene. In fact, we were not criminals. Based on "bad" information—but information that was presumed to be good—they had made an "error." "Sometimes these things happen." At least, they were willing to apologize.

"Look, we're really sorry about this, but when we get a call that there are [black] men with guns, we take it quite seriously. Again, we really are sorry for the inconvenience." With that apology, the officers departed. Our privacy had been invaded, we experienced a loss of dignity, and our blackness had been established—once more—as a crime of identity. But that was our law-enforcement cross to bear. In other words, the police were simply doing their job: acting on racial intelligence. And we were simply shouldering our racial burden: disconfirming the assumption that we were criminals. No one was really injured. Presumably, the neighbors felt a little safer.

My eyes followed each officer into his car. As they drove off, one of them turned his head to witness the after-spectacle: the four of us (racially) traumatized in the gunned-down position they had left us. Our eyes met for a couple of seconds, and then he looked away. It was over. The racial transaction—routinized social power freely expended upon black bodies—was complete. Another day in the life, for the police and for us.

Simple injustice.

We went inside, drank our tea, and didn't much talk about what had transpired. Perhaps we didn't know how to talk about it. Perhaps we were too shocked. Perhaps we wanted to put the incident behind us—to move on, to start forgetting. Perhaps we needed time to recover our dignity, to repossess our bodies....

We relayed the incident to my sister. She was furious. "Bloody bastards!" She lodged a complaint with the Beverly Hills Police Department. She called the local paper. She contacted the NAACP. "No, nobody was shot." "No, they were not physically abused." "Yes, I suppose everyone is alright."

Of course, nothing became of her complaints. After all, the police were "protecting and serving." We, like other blacks in America, were the unfortunate but necessary casualties of the war against crime. We were impossible witnesses to police abuse. Eventually, we would learn that within America's racial environment, policed black identity is a natural and national resource. It is the raw material for a nation-building project to make America feel safer—ostensibly for all of us.

*   *   *

II. RACE AND THE "FREE TO LEAVE" TEST

*   *   *

The "free to leave" test—the test the Supreme Court applies to determine whether a particular police activity is a seizure of the person that implicates the Fourth Amendment—constitutes a specific doctrinal site within which the construction of race exploits and exacerbates existing racial inequalities. Two cases in particular bear this out: *Florida v. Bostick* and *INS v. Delgado*.... [T]o the extent that scholars engage either of these cases, they pay almost no attention to the race-constructing ideologies that underlie them. The dominant way of understanding *Bostick*, for example, is that it constitutes an instance in which the Supreme Court ignores race. While not entirely inaccurate, this understanding obscures the racial productivity of *Bostick*—that is, the Court's construction and reification of race in that case. Re-reading *Bostick* and *Delgado* as cases that are actively engaged in constructing race helps to make the point that colorblindness is not in fact race neutral, but instead reflects a particular racial preference that systematically burdens nonwhites.

*   *   *

In *Bostick*, two armed Broward County Sheriff officers wearing bright green "raid" jackets boarded a Greyhound bus at Fort Lauderdale. The bus had made a temporary stop on its way from Miami to Atlanta. When the officers entered the bus, the bus driver exited, closing the door behind him. Without suspecting any individual passenger of wrongdoing, the officers approached

Terrance Bostick, who was asleep in the back of the bus. One of the officers asked to see Bostick's ticket and a piece of identification. Bostick obliged, providing the officer with a Florida driver's license and a ticket stub, both of which the officer returned to Bostick. The officers then explained that they were narcotics agents and asked for Bostick's permission to search his luggage. Upon searching Bostick's luggage the officers found approximately one pound of cocaine, and they arrested him. Subsequently, Bostick was charged with trafficking in narcotics, and he pleaded no contest.

Writing for the Court, Justice O'Connor "refrain[ed] from deciding whether or not a seizure occurred in this case." She maintained, however, that the facts left "some doubt" that Bostick was seized. In other words, she implicitly suggested that the encounter was consensual; that at all times, Bostick was free to leave. Central to her analysis is the notion that an individual's interaction with the police does not become a seizure simply because the officer asks that individual a few questions, requests that the individual produce identification, or seeks permission to search the individual's personal effects. "[A]s long as the police do not convey a message that compliance with their request is required," a seizure has not occurred. Justice O'Connor's opinion invites the conclusion that neither the officers' communication nor their conduct toward Bostick conveyed a message of compulsory compliance.

*   *   *

...Nowhere in Justice O'Connor's opinion does she entertain the possibility that Bostick may have been targeted because he is black. In fact, Justice O'Connor does not even mention Bostick's race. Nor does she mention the race of the officers. In this sense, an argument can be made that Justice O'Connor's analysis ignores race. This argument, however, is only partially correct. That is, while it is fair to say that Justice O'Connor's analysis ignores the fact that Bostick is black and the officers are white, it is more accurate to say that her analysis constructs Bostick and the officers with the racial ideology of colorblindness. In other words, the problem is not that Justice O'Connor does not see race, but rather that she sees race in a particular way. Her decision to see Bostick as a man and not as a black man does not ignore race; it constructs race.

*   *   *

That Justice O'Connor is of the view that, by and large, race does not and should not matter is clear from her race jurisprudence in the Fourteenth Amendment context. According to Justice O'Connor, "[r]acial classifications of any sort pose the risk of lasting harm to our society. They reinforce the belief, held by too many for too much of our history, that individuals should be judged by the color of their skin." For Justice O'Connor, "'the individual is important, not his race, his creed, or his color.'" This normative commitment about race, although articulated in a different doctrinal context, helps to explain Justice O'Connor's construction of Bostick and the police officers. From Justice O'Connor's perspective, textually referencing their respective racial identities would entrench existing negative racial impressions of—that is, stigmatize—both. The thinking might be that, because of stereotypes, the starting point for conceptualizing an interaction between a black man and a white police officer might be that the former is a criminal and the latter a racist. To disrupt these social meanings, and to prevent the attribution of them to Bostick and the police officers, Justice O'Connor constructs these parties as "individuals."

*   *   *

Justice O'Connor's commitment to individualism (not race) obscures the fact that individualism as an ideological concept is itself racializing and thus race-constructing. To appreciate how, assume that Justice O'Connor's construction of Bostick and the police officers as individuals without races disrupts both the social meaning of Bostick as a criminal and the social meaning of the police as racist cops. This disruption does not eliminate race; Bostick remains black and the police officers remain white. The disruption merely re-defines what blackness vis-à-vis Bostick and whiteness vis-à-vis the police officers signify. Under this redefinition, Bostick becomes a black man without the presumption of criminality and the police become white officers without the presumption of a racist identity. In the abstract, both disruptions might make sense. But in the context of *Bostick*, they obscure that Bostick may have held and acted on a racial presumption that the police officers were racists and the police may have held and acted on a racial presumption that Bostick was a criminal.

*   *   *

The more fundamental problem with Justice O'Connor's analysis is that it does not explicitly engage race. Throughout her opinion, race remains unspeakable. A more careful analysis would, at the very least, have racialized Bostick's interaction with the officers.... Part of the circumstances of the encounter was race—more particularly, Bostick's race and the race of the police officers. The interaction of black male identity with white male police authority creates a physically confining social situation every bit as real as (and operating independently from) being on a bus. Most, if not all, black people—especially black men—are apprehensive about police encounters. They grow up with racial stories of police abuse—witnessing them as public spectacles in the media, observing them firsthand in their communities, and experiencing them as daily realities. Put another way, race-based policing is part of black people's collective consciousness. Thus, when black people encounter the police, "[t]hey don't know whether justice will be meted out or whether judge, jury and executioner is pulling up behind them." Yet, Justice O'Connor situates her seizure analysis outside of this racial reality. She removes Bostick and the police officers from a social context in which race is material to a discursive, socially constructed world in which it is not. At no time does Justice O'Connor consider how Bostick, or a man in his racial position, might have experienced two white police officers crowded around him on a bus. She race neutralizes the encounter. Bostick's race, the race of the officers, and the relationship between the two receive no textual engagement in her analysis. Thus, her opinion fails to consider that Bostick may have been the target of a particular racial preference.

Perhaps Justice O'Connor does not discuss the racial dimensions of the encounter for the same reason that she discounts the coercive aspects of police encounters on buses. With respect to the latter, she argued that, to the extent that "Bostick's movements were 'confined'...this was the natural result of his decision to take the bus; it says nothing about whether or not the police conduct at issue was coercive." In other words, "Bostick's freedom of movement was restricted by a factor independent of police conduct—*i.e.*, by his being a passenger on a bus." Given this fact, Justice O'Connor's test for whether Bostick was seized is not whether a person in his position would have felt free to leave, but rather whether that person would have felt free to terminate the encounter. The Court's analysis reflects the idea that because Bostick chose to board the Greyhound bus, and because the police had nothing to do with that decision, it is constitutionally permissible for the officers to exploit Bostick's vulnerability as a bus passenger.

A similar argument about police culpability—or the lack thereof—can be made more broadly with respect to race and racial vulnerability. The argument would be that to the extent that Bostick's encounter with the officers reflects a degree of coercion that derived from the black/white racial interaction between Bostick's race and the race of the officers, that coercion existed apart from the conduct of the officers. "[I]t says nothing about whether or not [their] conduct...was coercive." The police officers did not make Bostick black. They found him that way. Nor did they make themselves white. Finally, neither officer is to be blamed for black people's general distrust of and apprehensions about the police. They have a right simply to do their jobs without being burdened by contemporary racial realities. Finally, to the extent that police officers, like the officers in *Bostick*, merely exploit or take advantage of (racial) circumstances they did not themselves create, no Fourth Amendment problem exists.

*   *   *

"BLACK AND BLUE ENCOUNTERS"—SOME PRELIMINARY THOUGHTS ABOUT FOURTH AMENDMENT SEIZURES: SHOULD RACE MATTER?

TRACEY MACLIN

I. INTRODUCTION

*   *   *

Currently, the Court supposes that there is an *average, hypothetical,* reasonable person out there to serve as the model for deciding Fourth Amendment cases. For example, the Court has said that a reasonable person will not feel coerced when federal drug agents accost her in an airport and ask to see her identification and airline ticket. The Court takes this position even when the person approached has not been expressly informed of her right to decline to cooperate with agents' inquiries. Similarly, no seizure occurs, according to the Court, when federal agents enter a factory to systematically question workers about their citizenship while other agents are positioned at the exits of the factory.

* * *

I have argued elsewhere that the Court's definition of seizure is wholly unrealistic. The average, reasonable individual—whether he or she be found on the street, in an airport lobby, inside a factory, or seated on a bus or train—will not feel free to walk away from a typical police confrontation. Common sense teaches that most of us do not have the chutzpah or stupidity to tell a police officer to "get lost" after he has stopped us and asked for identification or questioned us about possible criminal conduct. Indeed, practically every constitutional scholar who has considered the issue has agreed that the average, reasonable person will not feel free to leave a law enforcement official who has approached and addressed questions to them.

But even if I am mistaken in saying that the current state of the law is out of touch with the perspective of the *average, hypothetical, reasonable* person that the Court has in mind when it formulates the Fourth Amendment standards, I submit that the dynamics surrounding an encounter between a police officer and a black male are quite different from those that surround an encounter between an officer and the so-called average, reasonable person. My tentative proposal is that the Court should disregard the notion that there is an average, hypothetical, reasonable person out there by which to judge the constitutionality of police encounters. When assessing the coercive nature of an encounter, the Court should consider the race of the person confronted by the police, and how that person's race might have influenced his attitude toward the encounter.

* * *

IV. IS A RACE-NEUTRAL APPROACH PREFERABLE?

...As I stated earlier, my thesis is that the Court should, when assessing whether a police encounter constitutes a seizure under the Fourth Amendment, consider the race of the person confronted. Currently, the Court assesses the coercive nature of a police encounter by considering the *totality of the circumstances* surrounding the confrontation. All I want the Court to do is to consider the role race might play, along with the other factors it considers, when judging the constitutionality of the encounter.

Some will no doubt object to the explicit use of race in deciding constitutional questions. Understandably, some will ask: If we really wish to live in a future non-racial society, shouldn't we be moving away from procedures and decisions in which people are classified by their race?

I too would like to see a future in which decision-makers will not have to consider the race of individuals in deciding important legal and constitutional questions. But in *today's* world, where the anger and distrust between black males and the police is rising, not decreasing, we must recall Justice Blackmun's familiar stance in the affirmative action debate. "In order to get beyond racism, we must first take account of race. There is no other way."

A harmonious future will not be achieved by ignoring the realities of today. Many black males, especially black teenagers, still view police officers as oppressors and part of a system designed to keep them in their place.

*   *   *

A second objection I have heard against my thesis is that my solution is a form of "affirmative action" for black males. This criticism apparently stems from the notion that black men are somehow receiving special advantage or benefit under a theory that considers their race in assessing the coerciveness of a police encounter. Some see my proposal as creating a separate Fourth Amendment standard for black men. Nothing could be further from the truth.

Under my approach, black males would only receive what the Fourth Amendment already guarantees them. That is, their constitutional right not to be stopped and detained by police officers who lack objective reasons for the seizure. The Court currently measures that right by assessing the coercive character of the police confrontation.

My position simply recognizes that, for most black men, the typical police confrontation is not a consensual encounter. Black men simply do not trust police officers to respect their rights. Although many black men *know* of their right to walk away from a police encounter, I submit that most do not trust the police to respect their decision to do so. I only propose that the Court consider race when assessing the coercive nature of a police confrontation. Indeed, why would the Court *want* to ignore this reality? If the Court were to acknowledge and take account of the coercive dynamics that surround police confrontations involving black males, it would only be enforcing what the Constitution already establishes. Black men would get no special treatment under this approach[;] they would only receive what the Fourth Amendment guarantees them.

This leads to a third objection to my thesis. This objection claims that if the Court were to acknowledge the role race plays in police confrontations with black males, it might be forced to do the same in the case of Hispanics, Asian-Americans, women, and other ethnic and social groups who have had run-ins with the police.

You will pardon me if I label this objection a "fear of too much justice." At bottom, this rejection does not refute my main point—which is that police confrontations involving black males ordinarily are coercive—but instead, seeks to dismiss it by arguing that recognition of this reality may cause the Court to address the claims of other groups.

If my thesis compels the Court at some future date to face the fact that, for example, Mexican-Americans, Native Americans, or some other ethnic group experience tensions with the law enforcement officials, then so much the better. In the meantime, it strikes me as curious why society and the Court would want to deny the fact that one group, black males, currently experiences real tensions between themselves and the police. Just because similar claims may be presented by other groups today or at some future date is no reason not to consider the case of black males who have sufficient cause for complaint now.

A more substantive objection to my thesis is that it relies too heavily on the *subjective perceptions* of black males. Professor Wayne LaFave, the nation's foremost search and seizure scholar, has eschewed a Fourth Amendment standard that measures the seizure question by the subjective perceptions of the person confronted. In his view, "any test intended to determine what street encounters are not seizures must be expressed in terms that can be understood and applied by the officer." Asking a police officer to decide or guess whether a person feels free to leave would require predictive skills that neither the police nor anyone else possesses.

I must admit that this objection does cause me trouble. It troubles me not because it casts doubt on my original premise that police confrontations are inherently coercive. It is troubling because of the deep roots in our justice system that require lawyers to address legal questions in the framework of the average, hypothetical, reasonable person. But the Court claims to be committed to considering the *totality of the circumstances* in deciding whether a police confrontation constitutes a seizure. If this is true, the Court should include the consideration of race in order to gain a full view of the circumstances and dynamics surrounding the encounter.

Moreover, just as logic suggests that in evaluating the severity and pervasiveness of a sexual harassment complaint a "reasonable woman" standard makes more sense than a "reasonable person" standard, so too in assessing the coerciveness surrounding a police encounter, the Court should focus on the perspective of the person who is on the other side of the police confrontation. Continued use of a reasonable person test runs the risk that majoritarian values and perceptions of police practices will go unchallenged. Scholars of police-community relations tell us that perceptions of the police vary among different economic and ethnic communities. Thus, it makes no sense to devise Fourth Amendment rules as if we lived in a nation where there are no differences among us.

Furthermore, guidance and understanding may be promoted, and not undermined, if police officers are provided information regarding how their investigative tactics are perceived by different segments of the community. Under my model, police officers will not be asked to "guess" whether a particular person feels free to leave depending on his or her skin color. Rather, under my proposal, police departments would be encouraged to keep abreast of minority groups' perceptions of police behavior and investigative tactics, and to make sure that the officers on-the-beat are kept updated about these perceptions.

*   *   *

Finally, even if it were to cause some initial hesitancy and confusion among police officers, I would still favor taking account of the subjective perceptions of black males in assessing police confrontations. The Fourth Amendment, after all, guarantees the rights of persons, not the police. While it is important for the Court to provide guidance to the officer on the beat, it is equally, if not more important, to consider the perspective of the individual who is the subject of a police intrusion. Recently, however, it seems the Rehnquist Court is more concerned about the needs and interests of police officers, than the rights of individuals. This is regrettable. As Professor Yale Kamisar asked me once, "Whose Amendment Is It, Anyway?"

This leads to my final explanation why the court should move in the direction that I am proposing. In his acclaimed book, *Justice Without Trial*, Jerome Skolnick observed that those who write about criminal procedural rules too often "fail to give sufficient consideration to the simple notion that legal practices must have a differential impact in a stratified and racially constructed society." ... It is evident, however, from the reasoning in [*California v.*] *Hodari* [*D.*] and [*Florida v.*] *Bostick* that a majority of the Supreme Court has neither paid sufficient attention to Skolnick's caution, nor come to grips with the perspective of black males who are targeted by the police.

Consider, for example, Justice Scalia's gratuitous suggestion in *Hodari* that the prosecution was mistaken in conceding that there was no reasonable suspicion to seize Hodari, who ran when he saw a patrol car. Justice Scalia intimated that it is reasonable to detain young men who "scatter in panic upon the mere sighting of the police." For Scalia, the prosecution's concession contradicted proverbial common sense, whereupon he noted that "The wicked flee when no man persueth."

From a police perspective, Justice Scalia's remarks may make sense. "Flight from an approaching patrol car implies guilt; an innocent person, patrolmen reason, would have nothing to fear from the police and would not [run] away," as did Hodari. Of course, this viewpoint never considers that Hodari, a black youth, may have had alternative reasons for wanting to avoid the cops. Many persons who have never committed a crime have ambivalent or negative attitudes about the police. Perhaps, a youth like Hodari flees at the sight of police because he does not wish to drop his pants, as many black youths in Boston have been forced to do, just because cops suspect he belongs to a gang or is selling drugs.

Or maybe Hodari has had an older sibling or friend roughed up by the police, and does not wish to undergo a similar experience with the approaching officers. Perhaps Hodari has seen the video-tape of the Los Angeles police beating and kicking Rodney King, or he has seen the NBC video of Don Jackson, a former police officer himself, being pushed through a store window by Long Beach, California, police officers for no reason. Maybe Hodari believed that the officer who wants to ask him "What's going on here?" may engage in similar brutality in his case. As California Assemblyman Curtis Tucker was quoted as saying: "When black people in Los Angeles see a police car approaching, 'They don't know whether justice will be meted out or whether judge, jury and executioner is pulling up behind them.'"

*   *   *

Thus, it comes as no surprise that some black men go out of their way to be calm and extremely congenial when approached by a police officer. A black man's silence in the face of police demands should not be interpreted as co-operation, however. His silent exterior masks a complex reaction of fear, anger and distrust that must be kept under wraps in order to avoid a more intense and violent confrontation that history has too often shown places the black man in an overmatched and vulnerable position. When faced with this reality, the *Bostick* Court's confidence in the ability of bus passengers like Bostick to "just say no" to armed drug agents seems a bit strained.

* * *

CONCLUSION

I think it accurate, but sad, to say that many black persons were not surprised when they saw or read about the police brutality suffered by Rodney King at the hands of twenty-one police officers earlier this year. For many blacks, it is a joke to speak about Fourth Amendment protection, and more accurate to describe their status in relation to the police as "sub-citizens." That such a state of affairs exists during the time when we celebrate the bicentennial of the Bill of Rights is particularly unfortunate, but not surprising.

Justice Thurgood Marshall recently reminded us that society still has a long journey to travel in order to achieve the ideals and principles enshrined in our Constitution. In the context of its Fourth Amendment jurisprudence, the Court can take a step in the direction Justice Marshall had in mind by dis-carding the notion that there is an average, reasonable person out there by which to judge the constitutionality of police encounters.

When assessing a challenged police confrontation, the Court should con-sider the race of the citizen and how the citizen's race might have influenced his attitude toward the encounter. If the Court is sincerely interested in ana-lyzing the dynamics of police-citizen encounters, it should abandon a naive theory of the Fourth Amendment, and consider the real world that exists on the street.

NO NEED TO SHOUT:
BUS SWEEPS AND THE PSYCHOLOGY OF COERCION

JANICE NADLER

*   *   *

Christopher Drayton and Clifton Brown, two young African-American men, boarded a Greyhound bus in Fort Lauderdale, Florida, intending to go to Indianapolis. About 10 hours into the trip, the bus made a scheduled stop in Tallahassee, Florida, where the passengers disembarked from the bus during the 45-minute stopover. About five minutes prior to the scheduled departure, after the passengers had reboarded, the driver took the passengers' tickets and went inside the bus terminal building to complete paperwork. At that point, three plainclothes police officers from the Tallahassee Police Department Drug Interdiction Team boarded the bus. One officer knelt backward in the driver's seat, where he could observe everyone on the bus. Another officer stood at the back of the bus. A third officer, Officer Lang, began questioning passengers individually. Officer Lang approached individual passengers from the rear, leaned over their shoulder, placed his face 12–18 inches from theirs, and held up his badge. He introduced himself as Investigator Lang from the Tallahassee Police Department and informed them that he was conducting bus interdiction to make sure there were no drugs or weapons on the bus. He told them that he would like their cooperation and asked them to identify their carry-on baggage. Sometimes he asked permission to search a passenger's baggage.

After speaking with three passengers, and searching the bag of one of those passengers, Officer Lang approached Drayton and Brown. In response to Officer Lang's request to identify their baggage, Drayton and Brown pointed to a bag in the overhead compartment. Officer Lang asked for permission to search it, and Brown agreed. The bag was searched and no contraband was found. The officer then asked Brown for permission to check his person for weapons, which Brown gave. Officer Lang noticed hard objects in Brown's upper thigh area that were "inconsistent with the human anatomy." Those objects turned out to be two packages of cocaine taped to Brown's thighs. After handcuffing Brown and escorting him off the bus, police then asked Drayton's permission to search his person, and similar cocaine packages were found on Drayton's person. The two men were convicted in federal court of narcotics offenses.

Prior to trial, Drayton and Brown moved to suppress the cocaine on two grounds. First they claimed that they had been unlawfully seized by police and the search was a fruit of the unlawful seizure. Second, they claimed that even if they had not been seized, they had not consented voluntarily to the search. The trial judge denied the defendants' motion to suppress, ruling that they had not been seized, and that their consent was voluntarily given. The Eleventh Circuit reversed the convictions. It held that when Drayton and Brown consented to the search of their persons, that consent was coerced and not voluntary, and as a result the cocaine should have been suppressed.

*   *   *

The Supreme Court granted certiorari and reversed....Justice Kennedy, writing for the majority, held that Drayton and Brown had not been seized because a reasonable person in the situation would have felt free to terminate the encounter with the police. Further, the Court concluded that Drayton and Brown's permission to search their persons had been voluntarily given under the totality of the circumstances. The Court noted that the police officers did not command passengers to answer their questions; instead they spoke in polite, quiet voices, and asked permission first before searching bags or persons. The Court concluded that the passengers cooperated not because they were coerced but because they knew that doing so would enhance their own safety.

*   *   *

The "free to terminate the encounter" test evolved from the basic proposition that the Fourth Amendment does not prohibit law enforcement officers from approaching citizens on the street and asking questions, even in the absence of individualized suspicion. So long as the encounter remains consensual, then no Fourth Amendment interests are implicated.

*   *   *

This standard demands both consideration of the totality of the circumstances and a determination of the citizen's voluntary consent: either consent to engage in the encounter or consent to have the police search. The standard thus requires an examination of the following question: How would a reasonable person in these circumstances feel? Would a reasonable person, seeing what the bus passengers saw, hearing what the bus passengers heard, and knowing what the bus passengers knew, feel free to terminate the encounter, or to say no to the request to search? Note that the question of whether a reasonable person would feel free to terminate the encounter, or refuse the request to search, must necessarily be answered from the perspective of the citizen. By necessity, to answer the "free to refuse" question, the focus cannot be on the police perspective, and what the police did or could have done differently, and whether what the police did seems reasonable. The police could honestly view their actions as restrained and discreet in a situation where, at the same time, a reasonable person would feel coerced.

This distinction between citizen perspective and police perspective is a crucial one. As I shall demonstrate later, the Court's analysis...in *Drayton* is at bottom based on a judgment about the reasonableness of police conduct under the circumstances.... [T]the Court's real (but unstated) concern was whether the police conduct was acceptable (in a general policy sense) under the circumstances (no guns drawn, no explicit threats uttered). Having been satisfied implicitly that the police did not engage in abusive conduct, the

Court then directly concluded that there must have been no seizure and no unconsented search.

Although the police conduct in...*Drayton* may have been reasonable under the circumstances, it does not follow that there was no seizure and no unconsented search for Fourth Amendment purposes. The standard for determining whether a citizen has been seized or subjected to an involuntary search focuses on whether a reasonable person in the situation would feel free to refuse the police requests. As I argue later, empirical evidence suggests that reasonable citizens in the same situation in which Drayton and Brown found themselves would not, in fact, feel free to refuse the police requests.

*　　*　　*

II. FEELING FREE TO REFUSE
AND THE REASONABLE PERSON:
THE EVIDENCE FROM SOCIAL SCIENCE

*　　*　　*

The social psychology of compliance is the study of the conditions under which people accede to requests made by others. Thus, empirical evidence on the social psychology of compliance can assist in determining when a citizen's response to a police officer's request to search is voluntary and when it is "no more than acquiescence to a claim of lawful authority."...

1. *Compliance with authority.* Whether a request results in acquiescence depends a great deal on whether the requester is a legitimately constituted authority. As a general matter, persons with such authority exert an enormous amount of influence over our decisions. In many ways, it is logical that this is the case: the reason for their inordinate influence is that their position of authority signals that they possess information and power that is greater than our own. Throughout the course of our lives we learn that taking the advice of people like parents, teachers, supervisors, oncologists, and plumbers is beneficial for us, both because of their ability to enlighten us and because we depend on their good graces. For example, patients are in the habit of following the advice of their doctors because that advice usually turns out well. ...For most people, most of the time, conforming to the wishes of persons

with authority makes a great deal of sense. "It makes so much sense, in fact, that people often do so when it makes no sense at all."

*   *   *

Perhaps the most well-known scientific study of compliance with authority is the set of obedience studies conducted by Stanley Milgram, who investigated the extent to which people would comply with a request to perform an apparently harmful action. Milgram's subjects, who were adults from all walks of life, were informed that they would be participating in an experiment on the effects of punishment on learning. Upon arrival in the laboratory, the subject was assigned (through an apparently random procedure) to assume the role of "teacher," while the other "subject" (actually a confederate of the experimenter) was assigned to be the "learner." The subject was informed that it is his or her job to teach a series of word pairs to the learner. In full view of the subject, the learner was then strapped into a chair, and an electrode was taped to his wrist. As teacher, the subject's job was to administer shocks to the learner, by pressing switches on a shock generator, each time the learner made an error in recalling a word. Before beginning the learning task, the experimenter asked the subject to press the electrode to his or her own arm to experience a mild (but real) shock such as the one the learner would receive.

The subject was then led to an adjacent room where he or she could hear, but not see, the learner. The subject was seated in front of the shock generator, which was a box with 30 lever switches, labeled in 15-volt increments from 15 to 450 volts. The levers were also labeled with accompanying descriptions of the shock intensities, ranging from "slight shock" to "danger: severe shock." The last two switches were labeled "XXX." The experimenter informed the subject that he or she was to increase the shock level by 15 volts with each incorrect answer given by the learner.

After administering the first few shocks, the subject hears the learner protest about the painfulness of the shocks. When the shock level reaches 300 volts, the learner pounds on the wall in protest and stops participating in the word-recall task. The learner protests that his heart is bothering him, and his verbal protests become agonizing screams. Eventually, there is complete silence after each shock. Throughout the experiment, if the subject questions the procedure because of the learner's reaction, the experimenter responds by saying, "Please continue." If the subject expresses reluctance to continue, the experimenter says,

"The experiment requires that you continue." If the subject becomes very insistent, the experimenter says, "You have no choice; you must go on."

Unbeknownst to the subjects, the shocks delivered to the learner are not real. Even though they believed they were delivering real shocks, most people participating in this experiment (over 65%) continued on until the very end, beyond the "danger: severe shock" level and all the way to "XXX." One hundred percent of all participants continued shocking the learner even after he protested that he was in pain.

There are obvious differences between the situation in which Milgram's subjects found themselves and the situation of the passengers on Drayton and Brown's bus. Most prominently, unlike in the Milgram experiments, no one was telling the bus passengers "you must continue." But there are similarities also. Instead of an experimenter in a white lab coat expecting cooperation, the bus passengers faced a police officer with a badge (and a gun) expecting cooperation. Like the role of the white lab coat in the Milgram experiments, the role of the police officer's displayed badge in *Drayton* should not be underestimated. In *Drayton*, Officer Lang leaned in at close range and held up his badge. Despite Milgram's empirical demonstration of the power of authorities to command compliance, the Court flatly rejected the notion that a police badge exerts pressure on passengers, holding that factors such as the presence of badges, uniforms, or guns "should have little weight in the analysis." At the same time that one officer leaned in close to passengers and displayed his badge, another officer had taken the driver's seat. With one officer in the back, one in the driver's seat, and another displaying his badge, the officers had essentially commandeered the bus. From the passengers' perspective, the message was clear that the bus was going nowhere until the officers were satisfied that they had received cooperation. Aside from the obvious message that the continuation of the trip was dependent on the officers achieving their goal of receiving passenger cooperation, the more subtle message was conveyed through symbols of authority such as the officers' positioning on the bus and the display of the badge 12–18 inches from each passenger's face. Even though the police were not in uniform, the symbols of authority were quite strong. The main point here is that in both situations, people are coerced to comply when they would prefer to refuse.

*   *   *

2. *Social validation.* In new or ambiguous situations, people often decide upon the correct course of action for themselves by following other people's actions. The rule of thumb of "consensus equals correctness" has been shown to influence behavior across a wide array of contexts. For example, amusement park visitors use this rule of thumb when deciding whether to litter; pedestrians use it when deciding whether to stop and look up at an empty spot in the sky; college students use it when deciding whether to donate blood; and, sadly, troubled individuals use it when deciding whether to end their own lives....

Obviously, the "consensus equals correctness" rule of thumb does not determine all of our behavior at all times. The extent to which we follow the decisions of other people depends, among other things, on the ambiguity of the situation, the number of other people present, and whether those other people are similar to oneself. People are especially likely to comply with a request when it appears that other people like themselves have already done so. It is for this reason that bartenders often "salt" their tip jars at the beginning of their shift, and that political activists often display a long list of other people who have already signed onto the cause.

The socially validating effects of the decisions of similar others also explain why an onlooker in an emergency is unlikely to give aid when other bystanders are present.... Genuine emergencies are often not recognized as such when there are several bystanders; each person present decides that because nobody else looks worried, there must be nothing wrong. Ironically, often nobody else looks worried because everyone is looking surreptitiously at the reactions of others to decide the seriousness of the situation.

*   *   *

The influence of the behavior of others can be so great that people end up responding in a way that every bone in their body is telling them is wrong, but they do it anyway. The classic demonstration of the immense pressure exerted by social validation is Solomon Asch's 1950s studies on conformity. The task in the experiment was simple. A board at the front of the room depicted several straight lines. On the left side of the board was a single "target" line. On the right side were three "comparison" lines. The subject was asked to choose the one comparison line that was the same length as the target line. The task was quite easy—participants working on their own chose the correct comparison line 98% of the time. This high accuracy rate decreased dramatically, however, when the subject publicly stated his or her judgment in the presence of several other "subjects," each of whom stated that the matching line was line B (rather than the correct answer, line A). In this situation, accuracy dropped precipitously, with over 75% of subjects giving wrong answers. In interviews after the experiment, subjects mentioned that they went along with the majority because they believed that the majority must have been right: either their own eyesight was failing them, or they misunderstood the instructions (maybe they were to judge line width, not length). In this way, "the judgments of others are taken to be a more or less trustworthy source of information about the objective reality." The appropriate response is powerfully dictated by the responses of others who went before.

*   *   *

At the point when the officers had approached Drayton and Brown, they had already addressed three other passengers, none of whom attempted to terminate the encounter. In addition, the officers had already requested consent to search from one of the other passengers, which was granted. Using the rule of thumb that consensus equals correctness, a reasonable innocent person in Drayton's and Brown's shoes would have concluded that consenting was the correct thing to do. There were 25–30 passengers on the bus. No one asked the officers why they were doing what they were doing or questioned them. All passengers they addressed did what was asked unquestioningly. No one tried to get up and leave. No one tried to interfere or even politely intervene. All signals pointed to polite cooperation as the rule of the day. In a totality of the circumstances analysis of whether a reasonable person would have felt free to refuse the officer's requests or terminate the encounter, the influence of the "consensus equals correctness" heuristic on decisions to comply is a factor that must be considered, and one that law enforcement conducting bus sweeps use to their advantage.

C. SOCIAL CONTEXT, POLITENESS, AND THE LOGIC OF CONVERSATION

In its analysis of the totality of the circumstances, the *Drayton* opinion focused heavily on the tone of the conversation between the police officer and the citizens. The Court pointed to the officer's quiet and polite tone of voice, the fact that he did not state or suggest that citizens he spoke with were required to answer, that he talked to passengers one by one, and that he did not say or suggest that passengers could not leave the bus or could not terminate the encounter. The Court noted that the encounter contained "no threat, no command, not even an authoritative tone of voice." Focusing on the officer who kneeled backward in the driver's seat to observe the passengers, the Court noted that he "did nothing to intimidate passengers, and he said nothing to suggest that people could not exit and indeed he left the aisle clear."

* * *

Focusing narrowly on the tone and language used by the police makes plausible the notion that voluntary cooperation and consent were the only thoughts on the minds of passengers on the bus that day. But the Court's intense focus on precisely what Officer Lang did and did not say is problematic, because in doing so it neglected what the passengers actually experienced when they listened to the officers' polite tone and requests for permission.

* * *

From the passengers' perspective, the officers appeared to board the bus with a specific goal in mind. The fact that a police officer was occupying the driver's seat in the absence of the driver gives rise to the natural inference that the officers intend to achieve their goal before the bus would continue on its regular route. Officer Lang testified that he approached each individual passenger, introduced himself while holding his badge, and told the passenger that he was looking for illegal drugs and weapons. Officer Lang announced his goal at the outset, and the meaning of the speaker's intentions was therefore clear to the passenger: he is a police officer (an authority) and intends to look for illegal contraband.

Having understood the speaker's meaning and intentions, the next thing that the passengers heard was an indirect request: "Would you mind if I searched your bag?" Phrased directly, the request would be something like: "Let me search your bag." The question "Would you mind if..." is interpreted as the same thing as the direct request, but phrased more politely. The indirect request is more polite because it threatens the listener's status less than the direct request. So in all likelihood, this statement was interpreted by passengers as the officers informing the passenger what he would do, albeit in a polite fashion.

The context of discourse is crucial in the understanding of it; this is especially true when the speaker is making a request. Perceived coercion is determined by the speaker's authority and the speaker's language working together. Because authorities such as police officers direct the actions of others, the listener is likely to conclude that an utterance is in fact a directive, or an order to be followed. For example, citizens generally do not interpret "Can I please see your license and registration?" as spoken by a police officer as a genuine request; it is a command, and everyone understands this.

*　　*　　*

The influence of the speaker's authority on perceived meaning has been demonstrated empirically. In one study, participants assumed the role of an employee who was late for work. The employee was advised, either by her boss or by her co-worker, not to be late anymore. The results revealed that when a peer is speaking, the listener perceives imperatives ("don't be late again") as more coercive than suggestions ("try not to be late again"). But when an authority (such as the boss) is speaking, there is no such difference in perceived coercion—forcefulness of language does not matter. The authors conclude, "those who have authority apparently need not activate coercive potential through their discourse. Their roles are sufficient to do so." So, when authorities use softened discourse—suggestions rather than imperatives— they can exert control without being face-threatening.

*　　*　　*

Chapter 4

TERRY STOPS AND FRISKS

INTRODUCTION

Until the 1960s, it was widely assumed that police officers needed probable cause to engage in any kind of search or seizure. In *Terry v. Ohio*, 392 U.S. 1 (1968), the Court for the first time held that an officer may briefly seize an individual and search him for weapons upon less than probable cause. The *Terry* Court did not use the specific words "reasonable suspicion," but in later cases, the Court made clear that its decision in *Terry* meant that an officer could engage in a brief seizure of the person (a *Terry* stop) upon reasonable suspicion of criminal activity and conduct a limited patdown search of the outer clothing for weapons (a *Terry* frisk) upon reasonable suspicion that the individual stopped was armed and dangerous.

The excerpts in this chapter examine the *Terry* decision and offer both critique and explanation for this historic decision. In "*Terry v. Ohio* at Thirty-Five: A Revisionist View," Lewis R. Katz takes a close look at the testimony of Officer McFadden, the police officer who stopped Terry and his companions, and reveals that the officer was not consistent in his telling of the facts, an inconsistency replicated by the *Terry* decision itself. Katz also critiques the reasonable suspicion standard, arguing that it allows police to stop almost anyone in a high-crime neighborhood.

In "Stopping the Usual Suspects: Race and the Fourth Amendment," Anthony C. Thompson provides a racial rereading of *Terry v. Ohio*, an opinion that is almost entirely devoid of any reference to race. Thompson suggests that the Court was hard-pressed to make sense of Officer McFadden's otherwise perplexing decision to stop and frisk the men. Without racial context, Officer McFadden's decision to stop and frisk Terry and his companions appears to have been based on nothing more than an impermissible hunch. According to Thompson, the Court used a "police officer-as-expert" narrative to explain Officer McFadden's decision so it would not appear that the Court was approving a police officer's bare hunch.

In "*Terry v. Ohio*, the Warren Court, and the Fourth Amendment: A Law Clerk's Perspective," Earl C. Dudley Jr., the law clerk who worked for Chief Justice Earl Warren on *Terry v. Ohio*, discusses the historical and political factors that may have contributed to the decision in *Terry v. Ohio*. Interestingly, Dudley notes that in the discussions preceding the decision, Justice Brennan, usually remembered as a strong proponent of the Warrant Preference view, suggested reading the Fourth Amendment as two separate clauses. This suggestion enabled the Court to conclude that since all the Fourth Amendment requires is reasonableness, not probable cause, police do not violate the Fourth Amendment when they briefly detain individuals on less than probable cause.

Finally, in "Let's Not Bury *Terry*: A Call for Rejuvenation of the Proportionality Principle," Christopher Slobogin argues that in allowing police to briefly detain individuals on less than probable cause while retaining the probable cause standard for arrests, the Court in *Terry* established the correct framework for determining the validity of a seizure of the person. Both in this article and in his 2007 book on the Fourth Amendment, Slobogin argues that the Court should embrace the proportionality principle reflected in *Terry* and apply it across the board to all searches and seizures.

TERRY V. OHIO AT THIRTY-FIVE: A REVISIONIST VIEW

Lewis R. Katz

* * *

On Halloween mid-afternoon in 1963, Martin McFadden, a plain clothes Cleveland Police detective, was patrolling his regular beat in downtown Cleveland. He was looking for shoplifters and pickpockets, as he had done for over 35 years. McFadden testified "that he had developed routine habits of observation over the years and that he would 'stand and watch people or walk and watch people at many intervals of the day.'"

Officer McFadden observed two black men, John Terry and Richard Chilton. He testified that when he looked at Terry and Chilton standing on the street, "*they didn't look right to me at the time,*" although he was not acquainted with either man by name or sight, and he had received "[a]bsolutely no information regarding [the] men at all." Officer McFadden did not explain what about the two men "didn't look right" to him. The two men were dressed in topcoats, the standard dress of the day. They were engaged in no unusual behavior when they initially attracted McFadden's attention. When pressed on what about the two men attracted his interest and whether he would pursue them as he did if he saw them that day across from the court house, Officer McFadden replied, "I really don't know."

What happened as McFadden studied Terry and Chilton depends upon which version of Officer McFadden's statement of the facts one reads and in which court opinion the facts appear. McFadden watched the men over a period [of] ten minutes. He watched as one of the two men left the other and walked down the street and looked inside a shop window and continued walking, and then walked back to the other man, again looking in the shop window. The second man then repeated the same behavior. That behavior is the critical conduct which gives rise to the stop in this case. If they did it once or twice each, their behavior was pretty unremarkable. So, how many times they looked in the store window is crucial. In the police report filed the same day as the incident, Officer McFadden wrote that the men did this "about three times each." Between the day of the event when he wrote the police report and his memory was freshest, and the suppression hearing, which was almost one year to the day after the event, Officer McFadden's memory changed. At the suppression hearing three times each became "at least four or five times apiece," which later turned into four to six trips each. Moreover, at trial, when asked how many trips he observed, Officer McFadden replied, "about four trips, three to four trips, maybe four to five trips, maybe a little more, it might be a little less. *I don't know, I didn't count the trips.*" The Ohio Court of Appeals decision in the case picked up on the uncertainty and asserted that the men separated and looked in the window "at least two to five times" each. However, by the time the fact worked its way into Chief Justice Warren's majority opinion in the Supreme Court, the number expands exponentially. He wrote that the men did this "between five or six times apiece— in all roughly a dozen trips." Later in the majority opinion, Chief Justice Warren came up with still another number when he described Terry and Chilton's behavior: "where these men pace alternately along an identical route, pausing to stare in the same store window roughly twenty-four times." The body of law which stems from *Terry* is dependent upon this single fact.

Officer McFadden was never sure which store was the subject of the suspects' attention. At the suppression hearing he admitted he had no experience in observing the activities of individuals who were "casing" a store for a robbery. In the police report, Officer McFadden indicated that they were looking in an airline ticket office; at the suppression hearing, the Detective mentioned an airline office or a jewelry store. Chief Justice Warren (wisely) chose not to focus on this issue. If the men were "casing a ... stickup," as Officer McFadden believed, a downtown airline office would be unlikely to produce significant cash. Even in 1963, airline tickets were rarely purchased with cash. A jewelry store would be a more lucrative target. Terry and Chilton's street behavior and the supposed target of their interest are extremely important issues because they are all that set apart these suspects from any other two people on the street, unless it was their race.

The third man, Carl Katz, a white man, approached Terry and Chilton in conversation. McFadden did not know the white man either. McFadden suspected that the two black men were "casing a job, a stick-up," and he feared they may have a gun. Cleveland was a segregated city, and police lore had it that the only time whites and blacks congregated was to plan or commit a crime. When Terry and Chilton walked on, turning a corner and walking down the street, they stopped in front of Zucker's, a men's clothing store, where they met up again with Katz. At that point, McFadden decided to act.

Officer McFadden walked over to the three men, identified himself as a police officer, and asked for their names. McFadden testified that he received a mumbled response to his inquiry. McFadden then immediately grabbed Terry, spun him around, and "patted down the outside of his clothing. When Officer McFadden felt a pistol in the inside breast pocket of Terry's overcoat, the Supreme Court reported that McFadden, then, reached inside the overcoat to retrieve the pistol but was unable to do so. He ordered all three men into the clothing store where he removed Terry's overcoat and removed a .38-caliber automatic pistol. He then ordered all three men to face the wall, and proceeded to pat-down "the outer clothing of Chilton and the third man, Katz," finding a .38-caliber revolver in Chilton's pocket, but no weapon on Carl Katz.

*　　*　　*

PART V: REASONABLE SUSPICION

Not only has the Court excluded a significant portion of citizen-police encounters from Fourth Amendment scrutiny, it has categorically broadened police power to make legal investigatory stops. ... Chief Justice Warren's majority opinion [in *Terry v. Ohio*] never used the term "reasonable suspicion," instead writing of "unusual conduct" which leads a police officer "reasonably to conclude in light of his experience that criminal activity may be afoot." It was only in Justice Harlan's concurring opinion in *Sibron* that the "reasonable suspicion" standard was articulated. In applying this diluted-cause standard, the Warren Court claimed the need to distinguish facts and circumstances from inarticulate hunches, but failed to do so when they validated the stop of Terry and Chilton based on Officer McFadden's statements that the two "didn't look right" and that McFadden "just didn't like 'em." Thus, the current standard for a stop was forever grounded upon the very type of inarticulate hunch that the Court said was an insufficient basis for a *Terry* stop. From the outset, the *Terry* "reasonable suspicion" test exhibited the form of a standard devoid of any real substance. Consequently, later courts relying on this standard mired in vagary have further weakened "reasonable suspicion" to uphold stops based on nothing or very little more than race or socioeconomic status.

*   *   *

In the years since *Terry*, the standard of reasonable suspicion has become more problematic by the emphasis upon two factors. The first is the officer's experience. In *Terry*, the Court said that Officer McFadden's conclusion that criminal activity was afoot was reasonable "in light of his experience." However, Chief Justice Warren failed to elaborate on the relevant experience. Officer McFadden, an expert at identifying shoplifters and pickpockets, testified that he had never apprehended a robber.

*   *   *

The second problematic factor is the weight given to the locale where the stop takes place. The Supreme Court has made it clear that the neighborhood where a suspect is found is not enough, alone, to justify an investigatory stop. In *Brown v. Texas*, the Court said that "[appellant's being] in a neighborhood frequented by drug users, standing alone, is not a basis for concluding that appellant himself was engaged in criminal conduct."

Nonetheless, the Supreme Court has used locale as an appropriate element in the *Terry* equation, and in one of the earliest stop and frisk cases, *Adams v. Williams*, it appeared to be the critical component. In *Illinois v.*

Wardlow, Chief Justice Rehnquist wrote that "[a]n individual's presence" in a high crime area "standing alone, is not enough to support a reasonable, particularized suspicion that the person is committing a crime" but immediately undermined that statement:

> But officers are not required to ignore the relevant characteristics of a location in determining whether the circumstances are sufficiently suspicious to warrant further investigation. Accordingly, we have previously noted the fact that the stop occurred in a "high crime area" among the relevant contextual considerations in a *Terry* analysis.

... The clear message is that in "high crime" or "high drug activity" areas, i.e., the inner city, the possibility of criminal activity is so substantial as to make everyone in the area subject to police inquiry.

Consequently, lower courts give enormous weight to this collateral factor, often requiring little more than some other innocuous bits of information to fulfill the reasonable suspicion requirement justifying a stop. Thus, "high crime area" becomes a centerpiece of the *Terry* analysis, serving almost as a talismanic signal justifying investigative stops. Location in America, in this context, is a proxy for race or ethnicity. By sanctioning investigative stops on little more than the area in which the stop takes place, the phrase "high crime area" has the effect of criminalizing race. It is as though a black man standing on a street corner or sitting in a legally parked car has become the equivalent to "driving while black" for motorists.

One of the best illustrations of both points, substituting a police officer's expertise for an objective evaluation and substituting locale for facts, is an Ohio case, *State v. Bobo,* where three officers from the Cleveland Police Department Narcotics Unit, "in an unmarked police car, were investigating an area of the city known for heavy drug activity." The officers "noticed a car with two occupants legally parked on the street near an open field." The officers circled the block and returned to the parked vehicle where, now, only one occupant of the car was visible. One of the officers testified that Marvin Bobo popped up on the passenger's side of the front seat, looked at the police officers, and then disappeared once again "as if to hide something under the front seat." The officers approached Bobo's vehicle on foot, asked him to step out, and conducted a search. The officers found a weapon under the front seat. Bobo was arrested and charged with two weapons offenses. No drugs were found on Bobo, on his companion, or in the car. Bobo's motion to suppress the gun and the police officers' testimony about the gun was denied by the trial court, which then found the defendant guilty. The court of appeals reversed the conviction on the ground that the investigative stop was illegal because "there were not articulable facts to justify the officers' reasonable suspicion that... [Bobo] was engaged in criminal activity."

The Ohio Supreme Court disagreed and reversed the appellate court, finding that the stop was reasonable. The court's conclusion in *Bobo* rested on four factors: (1) "the area in which Bobo was parked was an area noted for the number of drug transactions which occurred there"; (2) "the stop was made at approximately 11:20 p.m."; (3) "the circumstances surrounding the stop must 'be viewed through the eyes of a reasonable and cautious police officer on the scene, guided by his experience and training'"; and (4) "the officers' observation of Bobo popping up and then ducking down or leaning forward." It is instructive to note that the state argued that the arresting officer's twenty years of experience "and numerous years in the surveillance of drug and weapon activity" should weigh heavily in the assessment of the facts. After all, we are told that the officer knew how drug transactions went down and knew how to assess a suspect's "gesture...in ducking under his seat." Notice was not taken that the usual drug transaction is quick; the buyer and seller do not linger. The officers did not see any other persons walking up to the car. Moreover, the officers were not in a [marked] police car. Persons parked in a high drug area who see a vehicle with three men observing their parked car coming around the block again and stopping behind the parked car might well be frightened and prompted to move around perhaps in preparation for pulling away from the curb if they feel further threatened.

Bobo is indicative of how stops in the inner city are viewed by reviewing courts. The critical factors cited by the court were the area where Bobo was parked, the time of day, and the experience of the officers; everything else was terribly ambiguous. Arguably, area and time of day are not meant to be the foundation upon which a stop is made. Yet *Bobo* stands for the proposition that every person coming and going at night on an urban street in a "high crime" or "high drug activity" locale is subject to being stopped, questioned, and possibly searched. Although *Terry* held that an officer's experience requires her to draw inferences from facts, not to draw conclusions from nothing, in *Bobo* it was merely a ubiquitous claim of furtive gestures that sealed the case. Such outcomes could not have been the intent of the Court in *Terry*, but have become reality. There was no drug deal in Bobo's car that night. The person parked in the car with Bobo was a woman, and "[t]he facts in this case indicate that, if anything, a romantic tryst, not a drug deal or any other illegal activity, was occurring in the car." While these facts resulted in imprisonment of a guilty man in *Bobo*, similarly weak facts are responsible for the constant seizures of countless innocent citizens whose only "crime" is being poor, a minority, or in a high crime neighborhood. This deplorable repercussion stems from the striking failures of *Terry* and its progeny.

*   *   *

STOPPING THE USUAL SUSPECTS: RACE AND THE FOURTH AMENDMENT

ANTHONY C. THOMPSON

*   *   *

The Supreme Court's decision in *Terry v. Ohio* is well known for the Fourth Amendment rule it announced: The police can conduct limited seizures of the person (now commonly known as "*Terry* stops") and limited patdowns of a person ("*Terry* frisks") based on a quantum of suspicion that is less substantial than the "probable cause" standard that the police must satisfy when conducting full-blown arrests and equivalent seizures of the person. In reading the decision, one would see no reason to view the case as relevant to the issue of racially motivated searches and seizures. Yet, closer review of the case—especially when supplemented with an examination of the briefs and the trial court record in the case—reveals an important racial dimension.

In the majority opinion's statement of facts, Chief Justice Warren described Detective Martin McFadden's observations of two men, John Terry and Richard Chilton, standing on a street corner in "downtown Cleveland."

There is no mention of the race of any of these individuals. The decision states that McFadden "had never seen the two men before, and he was unable to say precisely what first drew his eye to them." McFadden (who was in plain clothes) watched first one individual, then the other, walk back and forth in front of a store window and look in the window as they passed. At one point in this sequence of events, as the two individuals were standing together on the corner, "a third man approached them and engaged them briefly in conversation" then "left the two others and walked west on Euclid Avenue"; after again "pacing, peering, and conferring," Chilton and Terry headed "west on Euclid Avenue, following the path taken earlier by the third man." The Court's decision also does not mention the race of "the third man."

Having concluded that Chilton and Terry were in the process of "'casing a job, a stick-up,'" McFadden followed them down the street. He observed them "stop . . . to talk to the same man who had conferred with them earlier on the street corner." "Deciding that the situation was ripe for direct action," McFadden approached the group, identified himself as a police officer, and asked for their names. The men "'mumbled something' in response to [the officer's] inquiries," which caused the officer to "grab[ ] petitioner Terry, sp[i]n him around so they were facing the other two, . . . and pat[ ] down the outside of his clothing." Finding a gun on Terry, the officer patted down the other two and also found a gun in Chilton's overcoat.

The Court presented the foregoing facts, which represent the key portions of the *Terry* opinion's factual presentation, in entirely race-neutral terms. When treatises recite the facts of *Terry*, they generally follow the Court's lead. But an examination of the trial court record reveals that John Terry and Richard Chilton were African American; "the third man," Katz, was white; Detective McFadden also was white.

The Court's legal analysis was almost entirely devoid of references to race. . . . The Court's discussion focused almost exclusively on doctrinal aspects of Fourth Amendment law and practical considerations in adapting Fourth Amendment rules to "the need for law enforcement officers to protect themselves and other prospective victims of violence."

*   *   *

When one adds the missing racial element to the Court's statement of facts, certain otherwise inexplicable events suddenly become much more comprehensible. Detective McFadden's assertion that "he was unable to say precisely what first drew his eye to [Terry and Chilton]," an assertion accepted by the trial court and uncritically recited by the Supreme Court, assumes a new meaning when one views *Terry* as a case in which a white detective noticed—and then focused his attention on—two black men who were doing nothing more than standing on a street corner in downtown Cleveland in the middle of the afternoon. The Court quoted Detective McFadden's statement that "they didn't look right to me at the time," but gave no explanation for what "'didn't look right'" meant to McFadden because he himself had offered no such explanation in his testimony.

With the element of race restored to the case, it is more readily apparent why these two men "didn't look right" to him. This inference becomes even clearer when one considers the officer's elaboration on this point in his testimony at the trial:

Q. Well, at what point did you consider their actions unusual?

A. Well, to be truthful with you, I didn't like them. I was just attracted to them, and I surmised that there was something going on when one of them left the other one and did the walking up, walk up past the store and stopped and looked in and come back again.

*   *   *

The Court stripped away the racial dimension of the case by removing all references to the participants' race. Although one cannot, of course, reconstruct the reasons for this rhetorical choice, it seems evident at least that this was a conscious choice. In his suppression hearing testimony, Detective McFadden repeatedly referred to the "third man" (Katz) as a "white man"; the lawyers who questioned McFadden did so as well. Yet, the Court's opinion refers to him only as "the third man" or by name.

The removal of race from the case presented the Court with a dilemma, however. To determine whether to uphold McFadden's actions under the new "stop and frisk" doctrine, the Court had to ascertain precisely why McFadden stopped and frisked Terry. After all, an essential element of pre-*Terry* "probable cause" doctrine—and one the Court carried forward to the new "stop and frisk" rule—was that a search and seizure had to be supported by specific facts that could be weighed by an objective magistrate. But, with race eliminated from the case, the most obvious explanation for McFadden's suspicions and his subsequent actions was unavailable. The Court was left with McFadden's testimony that "he was unable to say precisely what first drew his eye to them."

*   *   *

What the Court did to "make sense" of McFadden's actions is best understood in the terms of narrative theory. As others have explained, a sound judicial opinion requires coherent factual and legal narratives. Such narratives permit the judges to clarify the events in their own minds and to present the facts and law in a manner that the legal community will generally accept. In *Terry*, the narrative upon which the Court settled was one of the "police officer as expert." To explain Detective McFadden's immediate distrust of the two men on the street corner, the Court stated:

> He had never seen the two men before, and he was unable to say precisely what first drew his eye to them. However, he testified that he had been a policeman for 39 years and a detective for 35 and that he had been assigned to patrol this vicinity of downtown Cleveland for shoplifters and pickpockets for 30 years. He explained ... that he would "stand and watch people or walk and watch people at many intervals of the day." He added: "Now, in this case when I looked over they didn't look right to me at the time."

The Court took McFadden's statement that could easily be construed in racial terms ("they didn't look right to me") and transformed it into a highly skilled officer's instinctive assessment that something in the situation seemed awry and worthy of investigation. And the court accomplished this transformation in a manner quite familiar to those who study narrative: not explicitly (which would have been impossible since McFadden's testimony lacked such a direct link) but by juxtaposing two apparently unconnected subjects.

After acknowledging that each of the acts observed by McFadden was "perhaps innocent in itself" and consistent with the actions of individuals who are not engaged in criminal activity, the Court invoked the expertise of the detective to declare that "[i]t would have been poor police work indeed for an officer of 30 years' experience in the detection of thievery from stores in this same neighborhood to have failed to investigate this behavior further."

*   *   *

An independent examination of McFadden's suppression hearing testimony provides cause to be skeptical of the Court's characterizations of his expertise. Of course, the Court in the *Terry* opinion does not claim for McFadden any experience in recognizing "casing," for the Court could not have done so. Instead, it implies such expertise by saying that McFadden "testified that he had been a policeman for 39 years and a detective for 35 and that he had been assigned to patrol this vicinity of downtown Cleveland for shoplifters and pickpockets for 30 years." ... The "police officer as expert" narrative allowed the Court in *Terry* to present a coherent, raceless narrative about why McFadden acted as he did. Moreover, and more important for the broader canvas of Fourth Amendment jurisprudence on which the Court was painting, this device permitted the Court to denounce judicial reliance on police "hunches" in a case in which the Court was doing the very thing it was nominally condemning....

In stripping away race from the case and substituting the officer-as-expert narrative, the Court in *Terry* essentially created a conceptual construct: an officer who was unaffected by considerations of race and who could be trusted even in a race-laden case like *Terry* to be acting on the basis of legitimate indicia of criminal activity. Such an officer could be trusted with the expanded powers conferred by the *Terry* opinion, notwithstanding the dire warnings of the Legal Defense Fund.

Of course, even if the "Detective McFaddens" of the world could be trusted to perform in a race-neutral manner, that still left the other kind of officer described in the Legal Defense Fund brief: the officer who would abuse expanded search and seizure powers unjustly to stop and frisk African Americans and other members of "'unpopular racial and religious minorities.'" To deal with this concern, the Court once again constructed a narrative. This time, the Court's narrative focused on the Court itself describing the limits of judicial power, and specifically the limitations of lawmakers in construing the Fourth Amendment. The Court stated:

> The wholesale harassment by certain elements of the police community, of which minority groups, particularly Negroes, frequently complain, will not be stopped by the exclusion of any evidence from any criminal trial. Yet a rigid and unthinking application of the exclusionary rule in futile protest against practices which it can never be used effectively to control, may exact a high toll in human injury and frustration of efforts to prevent crime.

Although the Court in this passage appears to accept the validity of the complaints of "wholesale harassment" of "minority groups," the Court attributes these abuses to "certain elements of the police community." In essence, the Court divides the world of police officers into "good cops" (the "Detective McFaddens" of the world, who can be trusted) and "rogue cops" (the ones who might be expected to abuse whatever powers have been delegated to them).

*   *   *

Although the Court appeared to assume in *Terry*... that police officers can make assessments of criminality independent of whatever attitudes the officers may have about race, the social scientific research shows that the stereotypic judgments and biases that an individual brings to an event fundamentally shape perception. Research suggests that negative attitudes toward African Americans create a perceptual norm of viewing African Americans as more prone to criminal conduct.

*   *   *

The effects of these phenomena are not limited to police officers whom one can easily characterize as "biased." Of course, some law enforcement officers consciously act on the basis of racial bias in denominating behavior as "suspicious." Such officers embrace stereotypes and allow personal biases to dictate their behavior. But "dominative racists" are not the only class of discriminators. Especially as it has become less socially acceptable to acknowledge racial prejudices and because people increasingly tend to view themselves as egalitarian, discriminatory treatment is often the product of unconscious racism.

*   *   *

TERRY V. OHIO, THE WARREN COURT, AND THE FOURTH AMENDMENT: A LAW CLERK'S PERSPECTIVE

EARL C. DUDLEY JR.

I feel very much like one who, to use a current term, has been "outed" from a closet in which I have resided for thirty years. When John Barrett first invited me last fall to participate in this conference, he told me that he had learned from my co-clerk Ty Brown that I was the law clerk who worked for Chief Justice Warren on *Terry v. Ohio* and its companion cases. I responded that I had no difficulty acknowledging in a private conversation with a fellow academic that I had been the Chief's law clerk on *Terry*, but that I had never spoken in public—or even in any detail in private—about my work for the Chief Justice on any case. This was because of the stress he placed on confidentiality. I still recall vividly our first meeting with Chief Justice Warren in the fall of 1967. He told us that he considered us his lawyers and that our work for him was covered by the attorney-client privilege. He acknowledged that we would discuss the work of the Court with clerks from other chambers, but said that he expected what was said and done in his chambers to remain there.

John said that he would honor my views but that he hoped I would in any

153

event attend the conference. We did not speak again until February, and this time John said there was something I should know. He had recently been doing research at the Library of Congress and had been given access to the Warren papers. He had read—and indeed made copies of—many of the preliminary drafts and memoranda I had prepared for the Chief in *Terry, Sibron,* and *Peters.* So much for the attorney-client privilege!

John was kind enough to send me copies of the memos that he had copied from the *Terry* file, and so I had the eerie experience of rereading words I had written thirty years ago on a topic that has continued to interest me, one which in recent years I have come to teach in law school regularly.

Despite my trip down memory lane, what I want to say about *Terry,* its companions, and its progeny derives, not so much from those once-confidential drafts and memos, but largely from the opinions as published and the historical setting in which the Court first ventured into the world of "stop and frisk."

First the historical setting. Two powerful political and legal vectors intersected in the *Terry* cases in 1968.

In 1960, the Civil Rights movement, which had largely received support and encouragement from the Supreme Court, but had relatively little to show for it, took its case from the courthouses to the streets. While bus boycotts and rallies and demonstrations in support of lunch-counter sit-ins and of voting rights for black citizens effectively dramatized the continuing scourge of racism, they also created a backlash even among those sympathetic to the underlying cause. At the same time, despite legislative victories such as the Civil Rights Act of 1964 and the Voting Rights Act of 1965, frustration at the slow rate of progress boiled over into riots in urban ghettoes from Newark to Detroit to Los Angeles. It was the decade of the long, hot summers. When opponents of the Vietnam War also took to the streets beginning in about 1967, political tension and violence escalated even further. Only two months before *Terry* was handed down, there was a major outbreak of rioting in many cities, including Washington, D.C., in the wake of the assassination of Dr. Martin Luther King, Jr.

At the same time, the Supreme Court had come under heavy fire for its decisions enforcing the constitutional claims of those accused of crimes. In 1964 the Court's criminal procedure decisions were for the first time a major target of the Republican presidential campaign, and similar attacks were to be expected in the upcoming 1968 election.

In this context the police made a politically powerful and commonsensical argument that they needed greater authority to deal with street encounters that always had the potential to escalate into violence. Several states passed statutes authorizing "stop and frisk" tactics, and the courts of other states recognized such authority under common law and state constitutional rubrics.

Individually, the Justices of the Supreme Court may have felt differing degrees of sympathy with the arguments of the police, but collectively they were unwilling to be—or to be perceived as—the agents who tied the hands of the police in dealing with intensely dangerous and recurring situations on city streets.

On the other hand, many of the Justices were skeptical about the scope of the authority claimed by the police. The President's Commission on Law Enforcement and the Administration of Justice, chaired by Attorney General Katzenbach, had just issued its massive report, which was critical of many police practices, including some aspects of so-called "aggressive patrol" tactics in urban ghettoes.

Moreover, there was some reluctance to recognize authority on the part of the police to detain a person for investigative purposes on less than the traditional standard of probable cause. Such detention could quickly expand for all purposes into an arrest. Nor was there universal trust in the neutrality of the authorities. While the red-baiting fever of the 1950s had eased somewhat, J. Edgar Hoover was still the Director of the FBI, the House Committee on Un-American Activities and its counterpart, the Senate Permanent Subcommittee on Investigations, were still very powerful, ... and political tensions ran high on a number of fronts....

I recall not being surprised by the vote to affirm in *Terry*, though I was taken a bit aback by its initial unanimity. (Justice Douglas voted at first with the majority but later changed his vote.) This unanimity, I soon learned, masked an almost complete lack of consensus about just *how* simultaneously to recognize and to cabin this new police authority. The Court's fumbling effort to find a satisfactory solution to this problem, and the evident difficulty of that effort, are for the most part plain on the face of the published opinions.

One thing, I suppose, that is not apparent from the published opinions is the evolution of *Terry*'s solution to the doctrinal conundrum that confronted the Court.

Without ever facing an explicit challenge on the point, the Court had historically read the Fourth Amendment's two clauses *in pari materia*. The Warrant Clause's standard of "probable cause" had been taken to define the "reasonableness" of a search and seizure, even where obtaining a warrant was excused as impracticable. This made a good deal of sense, for while the Court had occasionally wavered, it had generally encouraged law enforcement officers to go before a magistrate whenever possible before conducting a search, and it seemed anomalous to recognize a broader authority in the police acting alone than that which a magistrate could grant them under the Warrant Clause.

*   *   *

It was Justice Brennan who suggested, after the initial Warren draft had sat for several weeks without collecting any votes, what emerged eventually as the doctrinal solution—the analytical separation of the amendment's two clauses. In a context—swiftly developing street encounters—where obtaining a warrant was inherently impracticable, Justice Brennan argued, the strictures of the Warrant Clause were simply inapplicable, and the definition of a "reasonable" search could and should be cut free from the standard of "probable cause." Convinced that this offered a more sensible way to analyze the new authority that the Court was prepared to recognize, the Chief Justice incorporated this approach into a new draft. This doctrinal move led to the defection of Justice Douglas.

*   *   *

LET'S NOT BURY *TERRY*:
A CALL FOR REJUVENATION
OF THE PROPORTIONALITY PRINCIPLE

CHRISTOPHER SLOBOGIN

*   *   *

... Thirty years ago *Terry v. Ohio* established a conceptual framework for the Fourth Amendment that makes more sense than any alternative the courts or commentators have come up with since. That framework, which I call the proportionality principle, is very simple: A search or seizure is reasonable if the strength of its justification is roughly proportionate to the level of intrusion associated with the police action. As the Court put it, "there is 'no ready test for determining reasonableness other than by balancing the need to search or seize against the invasion which the search or seizure entails.'"

*   *   *

If only the Court had applied *Terry*'s proportionality framework in a consistent fashion and extended it to the entire Fourth Amendment universe, we'd be in much better shape than we are today. Contrary to the suggestions of many commentators, I think that if the promise of *Terry* had been realized by the Court, our law regulating search and seizure would be more, not less, coherent. We would have more protection of individual privacy, not less. And race would be less of an issue in the law enforcement context, not the all-pervasive problem it is now.

*   *   *

In this paper I try to make the case for rejuvenating and restructuring *Terry*'s proportionality principle.

*   *   *

I. WHY *TERRY* WAS RIGHT:
THE CASE FOR PROPORTIONALITY

Terry was right, not only in its specific holding, but with respect to its general approach to the Fourth Amendment. *Terry* only purported to deal directly with the constitutionality of a frisk. Basing its decision on the Reasonableness Clause of the Fourth Amendment, *Terry* held that police may conduct a pat down of the outer clothing if they have a reasonable suspicion that doing so will prevent harm to themselves or others. This relaxation of the probable cause standard can be, and in large part was, justified on proportionality grounds because a pat down is less invasive than a full search, it does not require probable cause.

This rationale makes perfect sense, if one accepts two propositions: (1) the principal interest the Fourth Amendment protects is individual security from government infringement on privacy, property, and autonomy (the latter in the sense of ability to control one's movements and maintain dignity), and (2) the greater the threat to that security, the greater justification the government should have to show. I think both propositions are correct.

*   *   *

Terry recognized that one justification standard was not enough, and it created reasonable suspicion to help fill the void. But the Supreme Court has never seriously followed up on Terry's insight that government justifications can and should come in all shapes and sizes....

The Court should develop a justification hierarchy that consists of at least four tiers, and that applies across the board to all searches and seizures. To probable cause and reasonable suspicion should be added a higher clear and convincing standard and a lower relevance standard....

1. THE FOUR (?) TIERS

The best place to start is probable cause, because it is the standard with which we are most familiar—except that we don't really know what it means. It is often defined as a more-likely-than-not finding, or perhaps a level of certainty just a little below that. But can we be serious about that definition? Are we really willing to allow police to arrest someone when there is a 50% chance they have the wrong person? Are we willing to let the police ransack a house when there is a one-in-two chance they've got the wrong place?

Then there's reasonable suspicion, defined by a group of federal judges as approximately a 30% level of certainty. Apparently a stop may constitutionally consist of a fifteen to twenty minute detention. Are we really willing to subject two innocent people to such inconvenience, embarrassment, and discomfort in order to nab one bad actor?

These questions may strike some as meaningless at best and disingenuous at worst, given the difficulty of translating percentages into anything police and magistrates can use on the street.... To get some idea of the type of justification we want to require for invasive police actions, we need to think about analogous normative queries.

If it were left up to me, I'd require arrests and searches of houses, car interiors and luggage to be based on clear and convincing justification (usually quantitatively defined at about a 75% level of certainty), a stance which might not be that far from the position of some courts and even some police officers on the matter. For more invasive actions (e.g., a body cavity search; electronic surveillance; perusal of private diaries; particularly prolonged, invasive undercover operations), I would additionally require clear and convincing proof that the evidence thereby sought is crucial to the state's case and that the search will be conducted in the least intrusive manner possible. For prolonged stops and similarly invasive seizures, I would require what we presently call probable cause (i.e., a 50% likelihood); the same standard should apply to undercover intrusions of the same approximate length. For short stops, pat downs, and many of the actions that the Court excludes from Fourth Amendment oversight—e.g., flyovers, searches of open fields and garbage, and more than casual encounters at roadblocks and on the street—I would require reasonable suspicion, which I would define to be something like a 20% to 30% chance of success.

That leaves the lowest standard—what I'm calling the relevance standard—to be defined. Evidence at trial is relevant if it has any tendency to make a fact in issue more probable than not. The relevance standard would require police to articulate a reason for believing their action has some tendency to lead to information that would help solve a crime or apprehend a suspect. Put statistically and arbitrarily, it might require a 5%–10% success rate. Using legal terminology, the relevance standard could be said to require demonstration of an "objective credible belief" that a "legitimate law enforcement objective" will be achieved through the police action. I would apply this standard to all but the most casual police-citizen questioning as well as to regulatory inspections of businesses and homes.

Under a proportionality approach, the animating inquiry in setting these levels of suspicion should be how much explanation for a given intrusion is necessary to convince an innocent person subjected to it that the police acted reasonably. The innocent person who is arrested will expect a "damn good reason" for the inconvenience. The innocent person who is stopped on the street for a brief interrogation is likely to be satisfied with a much less extensive explanation for the interruption. The official excuse for a mistaken action should be adequate, but need be no more than adequate, to dissipate the umbrage the action excites. This is the central insight of the proportionality principle: The justification for a search or seizure should nullify its intrusiveness, no more and no less.

*   *   *

Chapter 5

RACIAL PROFILING

INTRODUCTION

For years, black and brown motorists have been stopped and pulled over at rates greatly disproportionate to their presence in the community, a practice that has been called "Driving While Black (or Brown)." The propriety and effectiveness of racial profiling, the practice by law enforcement officials of detaining individuals based at least in part on their race, ethnicity, or national origin, is a subject that has divided reasonable minds for years.

In *Whren v. United States*, 517 U.S. 806 (1996), the Supreme Court stepped into this debate and gave police officers a green light to continue the practice of racial profiling. The *Whren* Court held that if a police officer observes a traffic violation, this gives the officer the authority to pull over the motorist. The Court further held that the officer's true motive for stopping the motorist is irrelevant. Even if the officer's real reason for stopping the motorist is a hunch (based in part on the motorist's race) that he or she is involved in some kind of criminal activity, the stop does not violate the Fourth Amendment.

In the first excerpt, David A. Harris, the nation's leading expert on racial profiling, provides a persuasive critique of the *Whren* decision. In "'Driving While Black' and All Other Traffic Offenses: The Supreme Court and Pretextual Traffic Stops," Harris argues that *Whren* approves two alarming police practices. First, contrary to the usual Fourth Amendment rule that police officers need some level of justification (probable cause to believe the person has committed a crime or reasonable suspicion of criminal activity) to detain an individual, *Whren* makes it possible for the police to stop any motorist, since no driver can drive three blocks without committing some traffic violation. Second, police officers will not use their discretionary power against all motorists, but instead will disproportionately stop African American and Latino drivers.

The second excerpt illustrates that the problem of racial profiling extends well beyond Driving While Black. In "'Walking While Black': Encounters with the Police on My Street," Paul Butler, an African American law professor, describes the experience of being stopped and followed by three black police officers while walking in his racially integrated, upper-middle-class neighborhood.

In "Cultural Context Matters: *Terry's* 'Seesaw Effect,'" Frank Rudy Cooper examines how Rudy Giuliani was able to win the 1994 mayoral election and impose an extreme form of racial profiling in New York City, even though Giuliani was a Republican running for mayor in a city where Democrats outnumbered Republicans five to one. Cooper theorizes that even though overall crime rates actually went down during the previous mayor's term, fear of crime and implicit racial bias led liberal whites to support Giuliani.

Just before the attacks on the World Trade Center and the Pentagon on September 11, 2001, civil liberties advocates had reached a high point in their fight against racial profiling. Polls indicated that just before September 11, 80 percent of Americans opposed racial profiling. After September 11, however, there was a marked reversal of public opinion with 70 percent of Americans believing that some form of racial profiling was necessary and acceptable to ensure public safety. Even African Americans and Latinos, who had been some of the strongest opponents of racial profiling prior to 9/11, supported the ethnic or religious profiling of Middle Easterners and Muslims. In "Profiling Terror," Sharon L. Davies critiques the arguments in support of the profiling of Arabs and Muslims in the wake of 9/11.

The debate surrounding the July 2009 arrest of Dr. Henry Louis Gates Jr., a Harvard professor and one of the nation's prominent African American scholars, suggests that the issue of racial profiling is as controversial today as it was when it first became a hot topic. Gates had just returned home from an overseas trip, and had trouble opening his front door with his key. Gates and his driver tried to push the door open. A neighbor in Gates's predominantly white, middle-class neighborhood called the police because she thought the two men were trying to break into Gates's home. A white police sergeant responding to the burglary call arrested Gates for disorderly conduct after it was clear that Gates was not a burglar and the home he was suspected of burglarizing was in fact his own. Gates had provided the officer with his identification, which showed that he lived in the home, but then argued with the officer, accusing the officer of harassing him because he was a black man. Controversy over the case erupted when President Barack Obama opined that the police sergeant had "acted stupidly" in arresting Gates. President Obama was careful to state that he did not know what role race played in the arrest of Gates, but also noted that this country has a long history of blacks and Latinos being stopped disproportionately by law enforcement. The Cambridge police department demanded an apology from President Obama. He responded by inviting both Gates and the police sergeant to the White House for a beer. While many blacks thought it obvious that Gates was arrested because he was black, many whites were offended at the suggestion that race may have influenced the officer's decision to arrest Gates. The excerpts that follow explore the history and current state of the law regarding racial profiling in this country.

"DRIVING WHILE BLACK" AND ALL OTHER TRAFFIC OFFENSES: THE SUPREME COURT AND PRETEXTUAL TRAFFIC STOPS

David A. Harris

I. INTRODUCTION

The Supreme Court's decision in *Whren v. United States* could not have surprised many observers of the Court's Fourth Amendment jurisprudence. In *Whren*, police officers used traffic violations as a pretext to stop a car and investigate possible drug offenses; the officers had neither probable cause nor reasonable suspicion to stop the driver for narcotics crimes. In the Supreme Court, the government advocated the "could have" standard: any time the police *could have* stopped the defendant for a traffic infraction, it does not matter that police *actually* stopped him to investigate a crime for which the police had little or no evidence. The defense asked the Court to adopt a "would have" rule: a seizure based on a traffic stop would only stand if a reasonable officer *would have* made this particular stop. The Court sided with the government. If police witness a traffic violation, the Court said, they have the simplest and clearest type of probable cause imaginable for a stop. Requiring more would force lower courts to make post hoc Fourth Amendment judgments based on either the mindset of a reasonable officer or the actual (perhaps ulterior) motives of the arresting officer, neither one of which the Court saw as necessary, useful, or relevant to the task of judging the constitutionality of a seizure. After *Whren*, courts will not ask whether police conducted a traffic stop because officers felt the occupants of the car were involved in some other crime about which they had only a hunch; rather, once a driver commits a traffic infraction, the officer's "real" purpose will make no difference at all.

... *Whren* ... approves two alarming law enforcement practices. . . . [B]oth represent profoundly dangerous developments for a free society, especially one dedicated to the equal treatment of all citizens.

First, the comprehensive scope of state traffic codes makes them extremely powerful tools under *Whren*. These codes regulate the details of driving in ways both big and small, obvious and arcane. In the most literal sense, no driver can avoid violating *some* traffic law during a short drive, even with the most careful attention. Fairly read, *Whren* says that any traffic violation can support a stop, no matter what the real reason for it is; this makes any citizen fair game for a stop, almost any time, anywhere, virtually at the whim of police. Given how important an activity driving has become in American society, *Whren* changes the Fourth Amendment's rule that police must have a reason to forcibly interfere in our business—some basis to suspect wrongdoing that is more than a hunch. Simply put, that rule no longer applies when a person drives a car.

This alone should worry us, but the second police practice *Whren* approves is in fact far worse. It is this: Police will *not* subject *all* drivers to traffic stops in the way *Whren* allows. Rather, if past practice is any indication, they will use the traffic code to stop a hugely disproportionate number of African-Americans and Hispanics. We know this because *it is exactly what has been happening already*, even before receiving the Supreme Court's imprimatur in *Whren*. In fact, the stopping of black drivers, just to see what officers can find, has become so common in some places that this practice has its own name: African-Americans sometimes say they have been stopped for the offense of "driving while black." With *Whren*, we should expect African-Americans and Hispanics to experience an even greater number of pretextual traffic stops.

And once police stop a car, they often search it, either by obtaining consent, using a drug sniffing dog, or by some other means. In fact, searching cars for narcotics is perhaps *the* major motivation for making these stops.

Under a Constitution that restrains the government vis-à-vis the individual and that puts some limits on what the authorities may do in the pursuit of the guilty, the power of the police to stop any particular driver, at almost any time, seems oddly out of place. And with the words "equal justice under law" carved into the stone of the Supreme Court itself, one might think that the use of police power in one of its rawest forms against members of particular racial or ethnic groups might prompt the Court to show some interest in curbing such abuses. The defendant-petitioners presented both of these arguments—the almost arbitrary power over any driver inherent in the "could have" approach, and the racially biased use of traffic stops—to the Court. Yet the Court paid little attention to these obvious implications of its decision. *Whren* is more than a missed opportunity for the Court to rein in some police practices that strike at the heart of the ideas of freedom and equal treatment; *Whren* represents a clear step in the other direction—toward authoritarianism, toward racist policing, and toward a view of minorities as criminals, rather than citizens.

*   *   *

IV. WHO WILL BE STOPPED?

Once we understand that *Whren* will permit police to stop anyone driving a car whenever they observe the ever-present violations of the traffic code, the question becomes *who* the police will stop. . . . [W]hile *Whren* certainly makes it *possible* for the police to stop anyone, the fact is that police *will not* stop *just anyone*. In fact, police will use the immense discretionary power *Whren* gives them mostly to stop African-Americans and Hispanics. I say this not to imply that individual officers will act out of racist motivations. Though some will, I believe most will not. Rather, my point is that whatever their motivation, viewed as a whole, pretextual stops will be used against African-Americans and Hispanics in percentages wildly out of proportion to their numbers in the driving population.

*   *   *

Here are four different stories of pretextual stops. They originate from different areas of the country: Florida in the South, Maryland in the Northeast, Illinois in the Midwest, and Colorado in the West. All involve independent police agencies. Other stories of this type of police activity exist, but those presented here are among the best documented. Each of them teaches the same lesson. And with *Whren* on the books, we should expect more of what these stories tell, not less.

A. VOLUSIA COUNTY, FLORIDA

Located in central Florida, Volusia County surrounds a busy stretch of Interstate 95. In the late 1980's, this portion of highway became the focus of Sheriff Bob Vogel and his deputies. Using a group of officers called the Selective Enforcement Team, Vogel operated a major drug interdiction effort against drivers moving narcotics by car through his jurisdiction. The deputies aimed not only to make arrests, but to make seizures of cash and vehicles, which their agency would keep.

As with most police agencies, the Volusia County Sheriff's Department did not keep records of stops and searches in which no arrests or seizures occurred in the three years that the Selective Enforcement Team operated. Thus no one might ever have learned about the Selective Enforcement Team's practices, except for one thing: Volusia County deputies' were cars fitted with video cameras. Deputies taped some of the I-95 stops; using Florida's public records law, the *Orlando Sentinel* obtained 148 hours of the videotapes.... [T]he tapes the newspaper obtained documented almost 1,100 stops, and they showed a number of undeniable patterns.

First, even though African-Americans and Hispanics make up only about five percent of the drivers on the county's stretch of I-95, more than *seventy percent* of all drivers stopped were either African-American or Hispanic. The tapes put this in stark terms. One African-American man said he was stopped seven times by police; another said that he was stopped twice *within minutes*. Looking at figures for all of Florida, seventy percent is vastly out of proportion to the percentage of Blacks among Floridians of driving age (11.7 percent), the percentage of Blacks among all Florida drivers convicted of traffic offenses in 1991 (15.1 percent), or to the percentage of Blacks in the nation's population as a whole (12 percent).... Second, the deputies not only stopped black and Hispanic drivers more often than whites; they also stopped them *for longer periods of time.* According to the videotapes, deputies detained Blacks and Hispanics for twice as long as they detained whites. Third, the tapes showed that police followed a stop with a search roughly half the time; *eighty percent* of the cars searched belonged to Black or Hispanic drivers.

It should not surprise anyone to know that deputies said they made these 1,100 stops based on "legitimate traffic violations." Violations ranged from "swerving" (243), to exceeding the speed limit by up to ten miles per hour (128), burned-out license tag lights (71), improper license tags (46), failure to signal before a lane change (45), to a smattering of others. Even so, only nine of the nearly eleven hundred drivers stopped—considerably less than one percent—received tickets, and deputies even released several drivers who admitted to crimes, including drunk driving, without any charges. The tapes also showed that the seizure of cash remained an important goal of the stops, with deputies seizing money almost three times as often as they arrested anyone for drugs. With regard to the seizures of cash, race also played a role: Ninety percent of the drivers from whom cash was taken, but who were not arrested, were Black or Hispanic.

*   *   *

B. Robert Wilkins and the Maryland State Police

In the early morning hours of May 8, 1992, a Maryland State Police officer stopped a new rental car carrying four African-Americans on Interstate 68. The four, all relatives, were returning to the Washington, D.C., area from a family member's funeral in Chicago. After obtaining the driver's license, the officer asked the driver to step out of the car and sign a form giving consent to a search. At that point, Robert Wilkins, one of the passengers in the car, identified himself as an attorney with a 9:30 a.m. court appearance in the District of Columbia Superior Court. Wilkins told the officer that he had no right to search the car without arresting the driver; the officer replied that such searches were "routine." After all, the officer said, if Wilkins and his relatives had "nothing to hide, then what [was] the problem?" Another officer joined the first, and they detained the group for an additional half hour while other officers brought a drug-sniffing dog to the scene. The driver asked whether he would receive a ticket; the officer said he would only give the driver a warning. The driver asked that the warning be written so that the group could leave, and Wilkins asserted that continued detention in order to bring the dog violated the Constitution; the officer ignored both of them. When the dog arrived, the officers ordered Wilkins and his relatives out of the car, despite their expressed fears of the dog and the fact that it was raining. They were forced to stand in the rain as the dog sniffed in and around the car. When the dog failed to react in any way, Wilkins and the others were then allowed back in the car—while the officer who had stopped them wrote the driver a $105 speeding ticket.

Civil rights lawyers sometimes say that despite the volume of complaints they receive about racially biased traffic stops, victims of this treatment feel reluctant to become plaintiffs in legal actions for redress. Perhaps they fear retaliation; others may want to avoid the hassle of becoming involved in a very public way in complex and often politically charged litigation. Still others may fear that opposing lawyers may discover dirt in their pasts and use it against them. Not so with Robert Wilkins. A Harvard Law School graduate, Wilkins worked as a public defender for the highly-regarded Public Defender Service in Washington, D.C. As an attorney with an active practice in criminal law, he was no doubt thoroughly familiar with the law that governed the situation in which he and his family members found themselves. The prospect of public litigation against a police agency obviously did not scare him. Individually and on behalf of a class of all others treated similarly, he and his family members sued the Maryland State Police, supervisory and command personnel at the agency, and the individual officers involved. They alleged civil rights violations and other wrongs, stating that the officers had illegally stopped and detained them on the basis of a "profile" that targeted people based on their race. State Police officials denied Wilkins' allegations; a spokesman said the practice of stopping a disproportionate number of blacks simply represented "an unfortunate byproduct of sound police policies." The implication was clear: African-Americans commit the most crime; to stop crime, we must stop African-Americans. Officials maintained this supposedly race-neutral explanation even in the face of an official document that surfaced during litigation. Dated just days before the State Police officers stopped Wilkins and his family members, it warned officers operating in Allegheny County—the very county in which police stopped the Wilkins group—to watch for "dealers and couriers (traffickers) [who] are predominantly black males and black females...utilizing Interstate 68..."

The case eventually produced a settlement, in which the Maryland State

Police agreed not to use any race-based drug courier profiles and to cease using "race as a factor for the development of policies for stopping, detaining, and searching motorists." The State Police also agreed to conduct training that would reflect the prohibition on the use of race as both departmental policy and state law, and to pay monetary damages and attorney's fees. Perhaps more significantly, the State Police agreed that for a period of three years, they would:

> maintain computer records of all stops in which a consent to search was given by a motorist stopped on any Maryland roadway by the Maryland State Police and all stops on any Maryland roadway by Maryland State Police in which a search by a drug-detecting dog is made....

The State Police have, in fact, maintained these records, and submitted them to the court. The latest figures ... bear a striking similarity to the information revealed by the Volusia County videotapes. Of the 732 citizens detained and searched by the Maryland State Police, 75% were African-Americans, and 5% were Hispanics.... Sad to say, the numbers show that very little has changed, despite the Wilkins suit and the Settlement Agreement.

C. Peso Chavez and the Illinois State Police

During recent years, African-Americans and Hispanics have made hundreds of complaints to the Illinois affiliate of the American Civil Liberties Union, alleging that the Illinois State Police targeted them for pretextual traffic stops. The ACLU eventually filed suit; a man named Peso Chavez became the lead plaintiff. However, Mr. Chavez's 1994 encounter with the Illinois State Police did not happen by chance.

Chavez was a private investigator with twenty years of experience and a former elected official in Santa Fe, New Mexico. In 1994, a lawyer for an Hispanic man who alleged that Illinois State Police had stopped him illegally hired Chavez to drive a late model sedan across areas of Illinois that had been the source of complaints of illegal stops and searches of minority motorists. The plan called for Chavez, a man with an Hispanic appearance, to drive cautiously, taking care not to break the traffic laws; a paralegal in another car would follow at a distance to observe his driving. The idea was a "reverse sting"—an attempt to catch police in the act of making illegal stops and searches.

On February 18, 1993, in Bureau County, Illinois, Officer Thomas of the Illinois State Police began to follow Chavez. He followed Chavez for twenty miles, through Bureau and LaSalle Counties. Eventually, Thomas activated his emergency lights and pulled Chavez over. Thomas was soon joined at the scene by another officer. Officer Thomas told Chavez that he had stopped him for a traffic violation, and asked Chavez for his license and rental agreement. Chavez supplied both. After questioning Chavez, Thomas gave Chavez a warning for failing to signal when changing lanes. This supposed infraction was an obvious and unfounded pretext for the stop; the paralegal following Chavez saw no such violation. The other officer then asked Chavez if he could search his car. Chavez asked whether he had to allow the search; the officer said that he wanted a drug-sniffing dog to walk around Chavez' car. Chavez unequivocally refused and asked to be allowed to leave, but the officers detained him. Another officer then led a dog around Chavez' car; the officers told Chavez that the dog had "alerted" to the presence of narcotics, and ordered him into the back seat of a patrol car. For the next hour, Chavez watched as the interior, trunk, and engine compartment of his car were thoroughly searched. The police opened his luggage and searched through his personal possessions. Meanwhile, an officer in the patrol car with Chavez questioned him about his personal life. The police found nothing, and eventually allowed Chavez to leave.

*   *   *

"WALKING WHILE BLACK":
ENCOUNTERS WITH THE POLICE ON MY STREET

PAUL BUTLER

Sometimes being a scholar of criminal procedure and a black man seems redundant.

I am walking in the most beautiful neighborhood in the District of Columbia. Though I'm coming home from work, I feel as though I'm on a nature walk: I spy deer and raccoons and hear ridiculously noisy birds. And even more unusual in Washington: black *and* white people. Living next door to each other. It's more like Disney World than the stereotypical image of Washington, D.C.

It is the neighborhood where I am fortunate enough to reside, and I am ashamed that the walk is unfamiliar; it is occasioned by my broken car. The time is about 9 p.m., and the streets are mostly deserted. When I'm about three blocks from home, a Metropolitan Police car, passing by, slows down. I keep walking, and the car makes a right turn, circles the block, and meets me. There are three officers inside. Their greeting is, "Do you live around here?"

I have been in this place before. I know that answering the question will be the beginning, not the end, of an unpleasant conversation—"Where do you live?" "It's kind of cold to be walking, isn't it?" "Can I see some I.D.?"—that I don't feel like having.

So I ask a question instead: "Why do you want to know?" The three officers exchange a glance—the "we got a smartass on our hands" glance. I get it a lot.

"Is it against the law to walk on the sidewalk if I don't live around here?" When no response is immediately forthcoming, I say, "Have a nice evening, officers," and head toward home.

The police now use an investigative technique that probably has a name other than cat-and-mouse, but that is the most accurate description. They park their car on the side of the road, turn off their lights, and watch me walk. When I pass out of their range of vision, they zip the car up to where they can see me.

In this fashion we arrive on the block where I live. I have a question, and so I stop and wait. For once, I have the power to summon the police immediately, quicker even than the president, who lives about seven miles away. Sure enough, as soon as I pause, the car does too. The police and I have a conversation, consisting mostly of questions.

"Why are you following me?"

"Why won't you tell us where you live?"

"What made you stop me?"

"We don't see a lot of people walking in this neighborhood."

"Are you following me because I'm black?"

"No, we're black too."

This answer is true, but it is not responsive. I ask the officers if they have ever been followed around a store by a security guard. They all say yes. The senior officer—a sergeant—says that it doesn't bother her because she knows she's not a thief.

I ask if that's how the kid in the Eddie Bauer case should have felt. A Prince George's County police officer, moonlighting as a security guard, made an African-American teen-ager take off the shirt he was wearing and go home to get a receipt in order to prove that he had not stolen the shirt from the store. Testifying about how that made him feel, the black man-child cried. The case had been in the news the previous week because a jury awarded the boy $850,000. Nonetheless, the sergeant says she isn't aware of it.

The officers tell me that they're suspicious because this is not a neighborhood where they usually see people walking. Furthermore, they know every-body who lives in the neighborhood and they don't know me. I ask if they know who lives there, pointing down the road to the house where I have lived for 14 months. Yes, they answer, yes, they do.

And so I walk. I walk up my stairs. I sit on my porch. I wait. I wait because I am a professor of criminal procedure. I wait because I remember the last time, with different officers, in a different place, when I "cooperated." Which meant that I let them search my car. Or rather, I let one search while the other watched me. With his hand resting near his gun. On 16th Street. Cars whizzed by. I pretended that I was invisible.

Now the officers park their car and position its spotlight on my face. All three of them join me on my porch.

"Do you live here?"

"Yes, I do."

"Can we see some identification?"

"No, you may not."

During the antebellum period of our nation's history, blacks were required to carry proof of their status, slave or free, at all times. Any black unsupervised by a white was suspect. In North Carolina, to make it easier for law enforcement, non-slave blacks had to wear shoulder patches with the word "free."

The District of Columbia, through its three agents standing on my porch, tells me: "If you live here, go inside. It's too cold to be out."

I am content where I am. So, the police announce, are they. They will not leave me until I produce some I.D. or enter the house.

I have arrived home late because I worked late, writing about a book for the *Harvard Law Review*. The book, which I'm carrying in my knapsack, is *Race, Crime and the Law*, by Randall Kennedy. Since apparently none of us has anything better to do, I take the book out of my sack and show the officers chapter 4, "Race, Law, and Suspicion: Using Color as a Proxy for Dangerousness." The chapter contains several stories just like this one. It quotes Harvard Professor Henry Louis Gates Jr.... "There's a moving violation that many African-Americans know as D.W.B.: Driving While Black."

But this, I announce, is the first time I've ever heard of "walking while black." I point to the big window of my beautiful house. I tell the police that I have seen people, mostly white, walking down the street at all times of the day and night, and I have never heard them questioned about their right to be there. That is why I will not show them my identification. This is not apartheid South Africa, and I don't need a pass card.

The officers are not interested. In fact, they announce, they're getting angry. There have been burglaries in this neighborhood and car vandalism. The police are just doing their job, and I—I am wasting the taxpayers' money. One officer theorizes that I'm homeless. Another believes that I'm on drugs. The one thing of which they are certain is that I don't live here in the house on whose porch I sit. And when they find out who I "really" am, I will be guilty of unlawful entry, a misdemeanor....

The sergeant tells me that since I'm being "evasive," she will interview my neighbors. The two officers who remain radio for backup. They give the dispatcher the wrong address, and I correct them. Soon a second patrol car, with two more officers, arrives. I am cold but stubborn.

Finally, my neighbor comes outside and identifies me. I'm free now—free to be left alone. Free to walk on a public street. Free to sit on my porch, even if it is cold.

But first, we—the five law enforcement officers and I—look to my neighbor for vindication, a moral to justify the last hour of our lives. My neighbor is black like us. He says that he is always happy to see police patrolling the neighborhood. But, he adds, many white people walk late at night, and they are not questioned about their right to be there. My neighbor tells the officers that they are always welcome to stop by his house for coffee. And he goes home. The sergeant invites me to a crime prevention meeting at the police station in a few weeks. Then the five officers get into their two cars and drive away.

As for me, I'm still searching for a moral. My neighborhood does not seem so beautiful anymore. I got my car repaired right away: I had enjoyed the walk, but I dreaded the next set of officers. Sometimes I prefer to leave criminal procedure at the office. Sometimes I like a walk to be simply a walk.

But sometimes I am willing for my walk to serve as a hypothetical, for the police, and for you, reader, about the Fourth Amendment and its protection against unreasonable government intrusion. If I had a television show, I would say, "Kids, don't try this at home." It is unfortunate, but other uppity Negroes have gotten themselves shot for less than what I did. The officers I encountered were professional, even if the male officers were not especially polite. They never led me to believe that they would physically harm me or even falsely arrest me. It is sad that I should feel grateful for that, but I do.

One reason that I felt safer with the officers was because they were

African-American. They might stop me because I'm black, but I didn't think they would be as quick on the draw as nonblack officers, who are more susceptible to the hype. The black officer's construct of me—a black man walking in a neighborhood where people don't often walk at night—was burglary suspect, or homeless person, or drug addict. The white officer's construct—even during a traffic stop—is violent black man. At least that is what is communicated by the approach with the hand on the gun, the order to exit the car, and the patdown search. Not every time, but often enough.

Because the officers were black, I was especially angry. They should've known better.

What is reasonable law enforcement? There are neighborhoods in this city that covet police officers as concerned about crime prevention as these officers seemed to be. Like my neighbor, I had been pleased to see police patrols—at least until the police patrolled me. Still, I could excuse the intrusion as the price of life in the big city if everybody had to pay the price. But everybody does not. Ultimately, my protest is less about privacy and more about discrimination.

Most courts say that police may consider race in assessing suspicion. It is probably true that there are more black than white burglars and car thieves in the District. In *United States v. Weaver*, 966 F. 2d 391 (1992), the U.S. Court of Appeals for the 8th Circuit said of racial profiles:

> [F]acts are not to be ignored simply because they may be unpleasant.... [R]ace, when coupled with other factors [is a lawful] factor in the decision to approach and ultimately detain [a suspect]. We wish it were otherwise, but we take the facts as they are presented to us, not as we would like them to be.

But the fact is also that most of the black people who walk in my neighborhood are, like me, law-abiding. And the fact is that some white people are not law-abiding. Race is so imprecise a proxy for criminality that it is, in the end, useless.

The police officers made me an offer before they left. If I wanted to know when they stopped white people who walked in my neighborhood, they would tell me. They would ring my doorbell any time, day or night, to let me know.

Ironically, considering the officers' lack of interest in Professor Kennedy's book, their offer is also his suggestion. Kennedy believes in colorblindness, including in assessments of suspicion. He writes:

[I]nstead of placing a racial tax on [minorities], government should, if necessary, increase taxes across the board.... [It] should be forced to inconvenience everyone... by subjecting all... to questioning. The reform I support, in other words, does not entail lessened policing. It only insists that the costs of policing be allocated on a nonracial basis.

I turned down the offer, thinking that the police might begin to question every walker in my neighborhood just to make a point. That would not make me feel any safer, and it would inconvenience the neighbors.

In retrospect, I made the wrong decision. I hadn't wanted to draw the enmity of my neighbors by causing them to be treated like criminal suspects. Or like black men. Sometimes the law gets me confused about the difference. Kennedy is correct: It is a confusion everyone should share.

CULTURAL CONTEXT MATTERS: *TERRY*'S "SEESAW EFFECT"

Frank Rudy Cooper

* * *

IV. FIRST STAGE OF TERRY'S SEESAW EFFECT IN NEW YORK CITY: THE RISE OF SUPPORT FOR EXTREME RACIAL PROFILING

* * *

[The] evidence [that New York City adopted an extreme form of racial profiling in the mid-1990s] is substantial. New York State Attorney General Eliot Spitzer compiled a report that found that NYPD officers disproportionately stopped and frisked blacks and Hispanics. The Attorney General found that in areas where blacks comprised 26% of the population, they accounted for 50% of the area's stops. Hispanics, comprising 24% of the population, accounted for 33% of the stops. Whites, however, comprising 43% of the population, accounted for only 13% of the stops. The figures for Giuliani's pet project, the Street Crimes Unit (SCU), were even more dramatic: 63% of people stopped by the unit were black. Following the Attorney General's report, investigators for New York City's Civilian Complaint Review Board determined that NYPD officers routinely failed to file paperwork, and thus the official police department statistics may have underestimated the extent of racial profiling. Furthermore, a federal investigation into the SCU also ensued after the highly-publicized shooting by police officers of Amadou Diallo, a black man. Prosecutors found that blacks and Hispanics were disproportionately stopped and frisked, and that the imbalance could not be explained by crime rates in the City's racial minority neighborhoods. This Part of the Article examines why New Yorkers initially supported the mayoral candidate who would eventually enact such an extreme form of racial profiling.

A. GIULIANI'S RACIALIZED CAMPAIGN

Consider the 1993 New York City mayoral campaign between black, incumbent Mayor David Dinkins and white, former United States Attorney Rudolph Giuliani. A fundamental fact of New York City politics is that Democrats outnumber Republicans by a ratio of five to one. So why did Giuliani, a member of the Republican party, win the mayoral election? He won because racial majorities outnumber racial minorities by more than three to one.

Giuliani waged political war on blacks and Hispanics by arguing that the NYPD should be granted greater power to control crime. Giuliani made it clear he wanted more aggressive policing, stating that those who make New Yorkers feel threatened "'have to be removed from the streets.'" According to Giuliani, New Yorkers had "'their eyes down'" because of a social malaise resulting from rampant crime. The candidate ran a series of commercials featuring "testimonials of crime-weary New Yorkers." As examples of the city's deterioration, the ads pointed to the menacing "'squeegee men'" and promised to crack down on street drug dealers, panhandlers, and homeless people. With about $1 million more in cash than Mayor Dinkins, Giuliani flooded the airwaves with images of homelessness and crime. Giuliani's message was rhetorically powerful. Indeed, it was effective although crime had decreased during Dinkins' term.

The media noted the race-based nature of Giuliani's anti-crime appeal. In an article titled *A Race About Race*, New York's *Newsday* declared that Giuliani was consciously cultivating a "silent majority." Giuliani wanted that majority to associate Dinkins with favoritism towards blacks. Dinkins countered by arguing that the city's racial tensions would have been worse had he not been mayor and claimed Giuliani failed to campaign in minority neighborhoods. Giuliani shrewdly argued that the Reverend Al Sharpton, an extremely unpopular figure among the city's whites at the time, had been asking black church leaders not to meet with Giuliani. Moreover, the candidate secured a Puerto Rican running mate, self-proclaiming their candidacies a "City of Fusion" ticket, thereby insulating him from charges of ultra-conservatism.

Having fought off Dinkins' challenges to his racial politics, Giuliani was free to link Dinkins to crime. "Crown Heights" became Giuliani's battle cry, ostensible evidence of Dinkins' "soft on crime" approach. The Crown Heights neighborhood had recently witnessed massive, violent riots by racial minorities in response to a white, Jewish man's hit-and-run killing of a black child. Giuliani contended that he would have quelled the four-day riot sooner had he been mayor. Giuliani's attacks seemed to suggest that had the Mayor not been black, the riots would have been quelled sooner.

Dinkins' popularity dropped dramatically when the governor of the State of New York, Mario Cuomo, ordered a report to determine whether Dinkins should have responded sooner in the Crown Heights incident. The order was probably a deciding factor in sealing Giuliani's election. Dinkins accepted the Crown Heights report's conclusions that he should have questioned and overruled the tactics of his police commanders before the third night of violence. Afterwards, Dinkins' supporters reasoned that the Governor's report might have moved the crucial white swing voters to the Giuliani camp.

B. How Liberal Whites Justified Supporting Giuliani's Race-Based Anti-Crime Theme

Giuliani's funding advantage does not adequately explain how he won in a city where Democrats outnumber Republicans five to one. Giuliani's victory is explained by examining why many liberal whites switched from supporting Dinkins during the previous election to supporting Giuliani. Why would this presumably non-prejudiced group of whites vote for Giuliani? The answer is that those white liberals were oblivious to the implicit prejudice in Giuliani's campaign.

We can consider the failure to predict Giuliani would racially profile in light of the theory of cultural norms discussed in Part II. Liberals could not see the prejudice of Giuliani's political tactics because of the operation of background social norms. Background social norms lead whites (1) not to think of themselves as belonging to a race, (2) to think of perspectives they share with other whites but not with racial minorities as being race-neutral, and (3) not to think of problems primarily faced by racial minorities as part of their own world. Here, even though overall crime dropped during Dinkins' term as mayor, many whites perceived crime as having recently risen. Either of two things could explain that disconnect: (1) the media tricked white liberals into believing overall crime had risen; or (2) crime had only recently moved from racial minority communities to white communities, causing an actual rise in the crime rate in white communities. While the media certainly overstated the comparative prevalence of crime during Dinkins' term, it is the increase in crime in white neighborhoods that explains why Giuliani's anti-crime theme had traction with white liberals.

New York City's liberal whites ignored late 1980s crime when it was concentrated in racial minority communities. Accordingly, liberal whites honestly believed crime increased overall during the Dinkins era, even though, at worst, crime rose in white neighborhoods while falling by a greater percentage in racial minority neighborhoods. Liberal whites adopted a "Not in My Back Yard" approach to crime without feeling prejudiced because background social norms allowed them to believe crime was a new problem. Again, scholars suggest socially empowered groups, such as American whites, often think of themselves as not belonging to any particular group. Because whiteness is the epistemological norm in this country, whites have the privilege of thinking of themselves as having no racial perspective. In early 1990s New York City, background social norms allowed whites to ignore crime while it was merely a racial minority problem without feeling that blindness was itself a racial perspective.

Because the crime problem was perceived as a new problem, the crime problem served as a race-neutral justification for supporting Giuliani. White liberals believed they were responding to Giuliani's anti-crime message rather than his implicitly race-based message. While the candidate's liberal, racial majority supporters were neither intentionally nor subconsciously prejudiced, they were normatively prejudiced. After all, "[t]he public knows, without having to be told," that anti-crime policies will be aimed at racial minorities.

Prevailing cultural identity norms allowed liberal, racial majority voters to engage in an act of denial whereby they could support Giuliani without thinking about the fact they were adopting a race-based policy.

*   *   *

PROFILING TERROR

SHARON L. DAVIES

*   *   *

Following the attack on the World Trade Center on September 11, 2001, the nation's debate over racial profiling turned an abrupt corner. In the wake of the horrendous events of that day and the sudden loss of thousands of innocent lives, the public's view of racial profiling lurched from dramatically against the practice to decidedly in its favor. As fear of additional terrorist attacks gripped the nation and public anger over the acts grew, worried citizens began to reconsider their prior opposition to racial profiling, and proposals that actively urged law enforcement agents to take an especially hard look at persons of Middle Eastern descent abounded. These included calls for the initiation of national identification cards, the enhanced surveillance of Arab-appearing persons in airports and flight schools, the reduction or discontinuation of student visas for nationals of Middle Eastern states, the expansion of governmental authority to arrest immigrants with "links" to terrorist organizations and to accelerate their deportation, the enhancement of governmental authority to intercept privileged attorney-client communications, and the establishment of military tribunals to prosecute suspected terrorists free of the process burdens and defense rights that apply in federal court.

A new label—"ethnic profiling"—quickly emerged and the practice it described was met with shrugs of resignation rather than shouts of protest, signaling a sea change in the nation's thinking about profiling practices from its new, post-9/11 perspective. Perhaps most tellingly, the sentiment favoring this ostensibly new breed of profiling seeped even across racial lines, appealing to those who had resented being the objects of the reviled practice only days before.

In the face of this sudden shift in popular thinking, racial profiling opponents feared that the government would use the public's new tolerance for race-conscious policing as a reason to renegotiate commitments it had only recently made to oppose racial profiling practices. In the days immediately following the attacks, however, government officials struck a more cautionary chord, at least in public. Even as legal commentators could find no constitutional obstacle to ethnic profiling practices, the United States Attorney General proclaimed the government's determination to abide by its commitment to oppose race or ethnic conscious policing practices. And the Department of Transportation issued a directive to all airlines warning that targeting Arab Americans, Muslims, or Sikhs would violate federal law.

Despite the government's assurances, however, fear for the rights of Arab-Americans grew as the soothing words of these public officials began to collide with information that federal agents had in fact begun to round up persons of Middle-Eastern descent and place them under arrest. In a little over a month, the number of people taken into federal custody mushroomed from dozens, to hundreds, to over one thousand. And despite round-the-clock news coverage of every conceivable aspect of the September 11 story, remarkably little was known publicly about the identity of those prisoners, the grounds for their detention, the nature of the legal charges against them, or what had led federal agents to arrest them.

If any doubts remained about the ethnic premises underlying the government's 9/11 investigation, those doubts were eliminated as information about the identity of those arrested after September 11 began to emerge, and the Attorney General announced the government's plan to interview more than five thousand persons of Middle Eastern ancestry in search of information about al Qaeda and other terrorist organizations. The Department of Justice expanded this group of interviewees four months later to include approximately 3,000 additional men who had entered the United States on non-immigrant visas from countries with an al Qaeda presence. The interview campaign made clear that the government, too, had concluded that shared heritage with the suicide bombers made individuals fair targets of suspicion after all.

And there was broad-based support for the view that it should. Even as it became apparent that ethnicity figured more heavily into the government's post-9/11 investigation than it at first cared to admit, one popular reaction was: so what? After all, all nineteen of the 9/11 suicide hijackers were nationals of Middle Eastern states. Didn't simple common sense mandate that government investigators of the events factor the shared ethnicity of additional suspects into their decisions of whom to question, detain, arrest, or search? Post-9/11 polls showed that many believed the answer was yes, and that continued loyalty to an anti-profiling position after the attacks would impose senseless costs on a nation suddenly at war with terrorism.

Before long, leading criminal justice scholars began to concur, if somewhat apologetically. The gravity of the danger posed by future terrorist threats justified some degree of ethnic profiling, these experts counseled, though for different reasons. The profiling of Arabs and Muslims is distinguishable from profiling of African Americans and Latinos, some argued. An across-the-board opposition to profiling practices may be inadvisable, others wrote, particularly in times of grave national peril. Attempts to prohibit profiling outright have always been futile, still another argued, thus the best we can hope to do is to trim the resentment caused by race-based practices by more closely monitoring how aggressively the police interact with those targeted. All of these scholars acknowledged that ethnic profiling would impose costs on innocent targets, but each believed that the nation's security demanded such costs, provided that safeguards were adopted to protect against police excesses.

This Article rejects the suggestion that Arab or Middle Eastern heritage provides an appropriate basis of suspicion of individuals in the aftermath of the September 11 attacks. In a nation that claims upwards of 3.5 million persons of Arab ancestry, the ethnic characteristic of Arab descent, standing alone, possesses no useful predictive power for separating the September 11 terrorists' accomplices and other terrorist wannabees from innocent Americans. It is a variable that is incapable of sufficiently narrowing what I call the "circle of suspicion" to warrant the kind of reliance pro-profiling arguments would place upon it.

* * *

II. IDENTIFYING THE LIMITS ON THE USE OF RACE IN CRIMINAL INVESTIGATIONS

Before we can evaluate the spate of calls for Middle Eastern profiling, it is important to understand how the legal system reacted to the actions of federal and state investigators who factored the race or ethnicity of a suspect into their interdiction or detention decisions prior to September 11....

A. DRAWING LINES—THE PRE-SEPTEMBER 11 POSITION ON POLICE CONSIDERATION OF RACE OR ETHNICITY.

A review of pre-9/11 authorities reveals that the police have always been permitted to factor a suspect's racial or ethnic characteristics into investigations in which the race or ethnicity of the perpetrator of a particular crime is known....

Situation #1—Victim Specifies Offender's Race.

Even before September 11, any statement that race or ethnicity could never be a factor in the reasonable suspicion calculus would clearly have been overblown. It has never been accepted as law, even by those most adamantly opposed to racial profiling practices, and for good reason....

To see this point, let us pause to consider how such a race-blind investigative approach would play out in the context of an assault on a victim who was able to provide specific identifying information about her assailant to the police. Suppose Victim is robbed at gun-point in broad daylight by a Caucasian male in his early 20s wearing blue jeans and a white tee shirt. Victim willingly hands over her bag and her assailant flees on foot. The police arrive on the scene within one minute. Victim quickly describes the event and provides important identifying features of Assailant, including his race, gender, approximate age, and clothing. What can the police do to apprehend the perpetrator of this robbery?

It should be evident that any rule that required the police to take a completely race-blind investigative approach in this context would lead to absurd results. Under that approach the answer would have to be that the police could consider as a possible suspect any young man in the area wearing jeans and a white tee shirt. They might even worry about focusing their suspicions on young males, for fear that considerations of age or gender might also violate the rights of those stopped. The inefficiency of this approach alone should be enough to convince any reasonable thinker of its unworkability. The police would have to question indiscriminately every jean-and-tee-shirt-clad person, male or female, black or white, young or old, who was found in the immediate area. Beyond efficiency concerns, such an approach would have little assurance of apprehending the person actually responsible for robbing Victim. No legal thinker could claim that the law requires such an approach. It does not.

*   *   *

Situation #2—Victim Specifies Offender's Race, Redux— Geographical and Temporal Considerations.

The courts faced more difficult line-drawing questions in the situation where a crime victim supplied racially-identifying information to the police, but surrounding demographics or the response time that it took to apprehend a suspect limited the value of that information as a basis for individualized suspicion. To see the complexities involved in such a case, we can simply add a few facts to our first situation, where Victim provided the police helpful identifying information about her assailant to the police, including racial information (*He* / was *young* / and *white* / and wore *jeans* / and a *white* / *tee-shirt*).

Suppose that after receiving Victim's description, the police realized the area in which Victim was attacked was filled with young, white males with a penchant for wearing jeans and white tee-shirts. Could the police stop every young, jean-clad white male in the general vicinity to investigate further? Suppose they did, but the sweep yielded no suspect. Could the police continue their sweep the next day, as hundreds of college students fitting the general description of the culprit made their way toward their classes?

1. *Brown v. City of Oneonta.*

Those familiar with the facts of *Brown v. City of Oneonta* know that the preceding hypothetical is no far-fetched scenario constructed merely to make a point. Complaints about such a sweep were filed by a class of African Americans residing in Oneonta, New York, following a police investigation that reached every black male on a university campus and all other non-whites discovered within the city limits over a five-day period. The police conducted the sweep after receiving a breaking-and-entering report from a seventy-seven-year-old woman in the early morning hours of September 1992. The woman told the police that a man had entered her home, attacked her, and then fled with a small wound on his hand. The woman was able to describe her assailant only as a young, black male, having seen only a part of his arm during their struggle. The police used a canine unit to track the perpetrator's scent toward a nearby university, but the dog lost the trail of the scent after only a few hundred yards. Undaunted, the police requested a comprehensive list of all black male students from university administrators. With this list, the police then attempted to locate, question, and examine the hands of every black male student. When those efforts failed to lead to an arrest, the police combed the city streets of Oneonta over the next several days, stopping and questioning and inspecting the hands of every person of color they saw.

The United States Court of Appeals for the Second Circuit split on the question of whether to review the case *en banc*, and disagreed vehemently about the equal protection claims advanced by the plaintiff class, but the court agreed on the validity of the Fourth Amendment claims of those among the class who could show that they were subject to seizures by the officers who confronted them. The court noted the defendants' failure to dispute the merits of the plaintiffs' Fourth Amendment claims, writing that defendants would have faced such "difficulty demonstrating reasonable suspicion" on the facts of the case [and] that they declined even to "attempt to do so."...

To the extent that *Oneonta* attracted scholarly attention before September 11, commentators embraced the decision as plainly correct at least with respect to the Fourth Amendment challenges. All that the police knew about the hundreds of black males they interrogated in connection with the Oneonta attack was that they were black and male and lived in the same city as the elderly victim. So unable was this combination of facts to amount to reasonable suspicion that it convinced the defendants themselves of the futility of even advancing such a defense. More important for present purposes, *Oneonta* shows that police action based on racially-specific information provided by a victim cannot always be constitutionally defended.

Situation #3—No Victim Specification of Offender's Race— "Racial Profiling."

A third way in which officers used race or ethnicity in detention decisions prior to September 11 was disfavored by the courts and is what critics refer to when they used the term "racial profiling." Generally speaking, racial profiling occurs when an officer's decision of whom to stop and question for suspected criminal activity proceeds from the individual's race or ethnicity itself. In such a case, it is the individual's race or ethnicity that attracts the officer's interest or suspicion. From that point of suspicion the officer may then be motivated to engage in pretextual behavior to justify the individual's stop or arrest.

To see the difference between this type of use of race or ethnicity and that in the previous scenario, let us hypothesize a criminal investigation of an entirely different sort, namely, the investigative work of a Special Agent of the Drug Enforcement Administration (DEA) in connection with the so-called "war on drugs." Suppose our DEA Agent is aware that the vast majority of drug arrests made by members of his unit have involved African American and Latino males between the ages of 17 and 25, despite the fact that they represent only a minority of the resident population. He also knows that many of his department's recent drug arrests have involved males driving flashy, late-model luxury vehicles. Based on the collective experiences of his department, the DEA Agent is more suspicious of, and therefore more likely to stop, a minority male driving a luxury vehicle than a non-minority male driving the same kind of car. Put slightly differently, he factors the race or ethnicity of those with whom he comes into contact into his assessment of whether to detain them for questioning about suspected drug trafficking activities. Is this a valid use of race?

The argument that minorities were more likely than non-minorities to be found in possession of drugs was the most common justification offered in support of this type of use of race or ethnicity.... Empirical evidence did much to discredit the law enforcement justification that minorities were disproportionate possessors of controlled substances, however, and suggested instead that minority drug arrest rates might have more to do with flawed police assumptions than disproportionate minority criminality. On the basis of this and other evidence, prior to September 11, most observers concluded that the racial profiling of Blacks and Hispanics in drug interdiction efforts was constitutionally indefensible.

*   *   *

IV. THE USE OF ETHNICITY IN
TERROR INVESTIGATIONS—PROFILING TERROR

We are now in a position to examine the merit of claims made after September 11 that persons of Middle Eastern descent or origins can and should be made to submit to greater law enforcement intrusions than others in order to provide for the nation's security and bring those responsible for the attacks to justice. As in Part II, it is possible to express the implicit suggestion of ethnic suspicion that lies at the center of such claims in deductive or syllogistic form. It would go loosely something like this:

1. Persons of Middle Eastern origins are more likely to commit (or know of the threat of) an act of terrorism against the United States than persons of non-Middle Eastern origins;
2. X is a person of Middle Eastern origins;
3. Therefore, X is more likely to commit (or know of the threat of) an act of terrorism against the United States than a non-Middle Easterner.

The suggestion embodied within the syllogism (X is a more likely terrorist) is deductively sound only if its principal premise is correct (Middle Easterners are more likely to commit an act of terrorism against the United States).... [U]nless it is true that Middle Easterners are more likely to commit terrorist acts against the United States than non-Middle Easterners, the principal premise is fallacious, and the syllogism topples like a house of cards. Accordingly, to evaluate the validity of this deductive syllogism we would want to know two things. First, what evidence is there to support the premise that persons of Middle Eastern origins are more likely terrorists than persons of other origins? Second, even if the premise is true, can the fact that a particular individual shares that group characteristic fairly lead to the conclusion that he is a more likely terrorist than someone outside that group?

As to the first, the evidence to support the initial premise apparently lies in the events of September 11 themselves. When one examines the comments of those advocating the ethnic profiling of persons of Arab descent post–September 11, the advocates use the horrible acts committed by the 19 hijackers to support their claims that it was fair thereafter to be more suspicious of others ethnically like them. As put by Floyd Abrams, the fact that "all the hijackers [were] from abroad, all were from the [Middle East] and all [were] Arabic speaking," could make it appropriate "to look harder" at others with the same characteristics. Because the logic of those subscribing to this view would dump a very weighty burden on the members of the targeted group, it is deserving of close examination.

The collection of terrorist acts that have occurred on American soil should make any careful thinker hesitate before concluding that persons of Middle Eastern origins are in fact more likely to be terrorists than others. Several "home-grown" terrorists belie this claim. Timothy McVeigh, a white male from upstate New York, committed an act of terrorism responsible for the loss of 168 innocent lives, and over 500 injuries. Had he had his way, the death toll would have been much higher. It was purely and simply a fortuity not in any way creditable to him that more people were not killed when he detonated the bomb outside the Murrah Federal Building. When asked if he had any regrets, McVeigh replied that his only regret was that the building had not collapsed completely. Before the events of September 11, McVeigh's malicious and premeditated crime was frequently referred to as "the deadliest act of terrorism ever committed on American soil." Nevertheless, no one suggested after the bombing of the Alfred P. Murrah Federal Building in Oklahoma City that the effort to bring to justice those responsible for that bombing and the deaths of 168 innocents could properly involve acts of police profiling that would subject to extra scrutiny young, closely-cropped, white males simply because they shared those physical characteristics with McVeigh. And why not? I suspect that it is because, when we are faced with the criminality of a white suspect who may have accomplices, we do not fall prey to the same tortured reasoning to which we seem so easily to fall prey when we are faced with a minority suspect. In such a setting, we seem instinctively to know that the odds of capturing additional culprits by treating all young, white males with suspicion are so astronomically small, and the burdens we place on innocent white males in the process are so astronomically large, that it is a course of investigative conduct that makes no logical sense.

Additional examples provide further reason to doubt the first premise of the syllogism posed above. Like Tim McVeigh, Ted Kaczynski also fails to fit the currently popular stereotype of the Arab or Muslim terrorist. Kaczynski, another native of upstate New York and a White American, was responsible for a string of bombings occurring over the course of seventeen years which resulted in the deaths of three people and injuries of twenty-three others. Unlike the post-9/11 reaction, however, one would search in vain for calls for increased surveillance of scrubby, white male recluses after Kaczynski's reign of terror. And rightly so.

This collection of home-grown terrorist acts should reveal the vacuousness of the initial premise underlying the syllogism stated above (Middle Easterners are more likely to commit acts of terror than non-Middle Easterners). Moreover, even were we to assume the validity of that premise *arguendo*, we would still have to answer a second question, to wit, is it just to target an individual having Middle Eastern origins purely on the basis of that shared ethnic characteristic? The answer suggested by the discussion in Part II is no. In that Part we learned that while race or ethnicity can sometimes play a valid role in a criminal investigation, its value (when used) is extremely limited. The question then becomes: does the post-September 11 ethnic profiling of Arabs and Muslims fit within the categories discussed in Part II which justify the consideration of race or ethnicity? And even if it does, are law enforcement agents utilizing the ethnic marker in an appropriate way?

It should be plain that the bulk of the investigative action following the attacks was not pursuant to a report of a crime by a victim who provided an ethnic description of the perpetrator. With the possible exception of Zacarias Moussoui, whom prosecutors allege was the intended "twentieth" hijacker, the persons most directly involved in the September 11 attacks died while committing them. While it would be folly to assume that all those responsible for the attacks are now either dead (the 19 hijackers) or being detained (Moussoui), neither does the search for additional co-conspirators fit the "Situation #1" mold.

Even if it did, there are reasons to question the legitimacy of an investigative effort that would consider and treat the national community of Arabs and Muslims as suspicious purely on the basis of ethnicity. The lessons of *Oneonta*, where officers targeted an entire African American community (and other persons of color) based on a victim's claim that her attacker was black, should make us hesitate before throwing our support behind a law enforcement operation that would rely on similar discriminatory reasoning on a much broader scale. Even were federal investigators focused on additional co-conspirators in the September 11 attacks themselves, there is in fact no important difference between the reasoning of the Oneonta police (a black man committed this crime, so it is appropriate to target all black men within the city confines in our investigation) and the reasoning of those who support the post-9/11 profiling of Arabs and Muslims (a group of Middle Easterners committed this crime, so it is appropriate to target all Middle Easterners within the country in the government's investigation).

* * *

Chapter 6

THE EXCLUSIONARY RULE

INTRODUCTION

When the police violate the commands of the Fourth Amendment—when they engage in warrantless searches and seizures—any evidence they discover ordinarily must be excluded at trial under the exclusionary rule. Originally, the exclusionary rule operated only in the federal courts. This created the anomalous situation wherein evidence obtained in violation of the Fourth Amendment was frequently admitted in state court while being excluded across the street in federal court. In *Wolf v. Colorado*, 338 U.S. 25 (1949), the Court upheld the constitutionality of this state of affairs, holding that there is no violation of due process when evidence obtained in violation of the Fourth Amendment is admitted into evidence at a state criminal trial. The *Wolf* Court refused to apply the exclusionary rule to the states through the Fourteenth Amendment's Due Process Clause.

In 1961, the Court reversed course. In *Mapp v. Ohio*, 367 U.S. 643 (1961), the Court held that the exclusionary rule is part and parcel of the Fourth Amendment and is incorporated by the Fourteenth Amendment's Due Process Clause. Accordingly, evidence obtained in violation of the Fourth Amendment must be excluded in both federal and state court. In "The Road to *Mapp v. Ohio* and Beyond: The Origins, Development and Future of the

194

Exclusionary Rule in Search-and-Seizure Cases," former Supreme Court Justice Potter Stewart, who disagreed with the decision to overrule *Wolf v. Colorado* in *Mapp v. Ohio*, defends the *Mapp* decision, arguing that the exclusionary rule is constitutionally required because the available alternatives are insufficient to reduce the likelihood of the vast majority of Fourth Amendment violations.

Since *Mapp*, the Court has pulled back its support for exclusion as the remedy for violations of the Fourth Amendment. The Court has permitted the use of illegally seized evidence at grand jury proceedings and in federal civil tax proceedings. The Court has allowed prosecutors to use information derived from an illegal search to impeach a defendant who takes the stand at his own criminal trial. In *United States v. Leon*, 468 U.S. 897 (1984), the Court held that evidence obtained by police relying in objective good faith on a search warrant later deemed invalid may be admitted in the prosecution's case-in-chief. Silas Wasserstrom and William J. Mertens critique the *Leon* decision in "The Exclusionary Rule on the Scaffold: But Was It a Fair Trial?" In the next excerpt, "The End of the Exclusionary Rule, Among Other Things: The Roberts Court Takes on the Fourth Amendment," David A. Moran discusses the Court's refusal in *Hudson v. Michigan*, 547 U.S. 586 (2006), to apply the exclusionary rule to violations of the knock-and-announce rule. Moran warns that if just one more conservative justice is added to the Court, the Court may eliminate the exclusionary rule in its entirety.

In the last excerpt, "The Exclusionary Rule," the Honorable Guido Calabresi proposes a way to deter police from violating the Fourth Amendment without excluding relevant evidence at trial. Judge Calabresi would allow evidence of police impropriety to be considered as a mitigating factor at sentencing and impose automatic police punishment calibrated to whether the police misconduct leading to the illegal search or seizure was negligent, grossly negligent, or intentional.

THE ROAD TO *MAPP V. OHIO* AND BEYOND: THE ORIGINS, DEVELOPMENT AND FUTURE OF THE EXCLUSIONARY RULE IN SEARCH-AND-SEIZURE CASES

POTTER STEWART

I. WHO FREED DOLLREE MAPP? A CASE STUDY IN THE EVOLUTION OF CONSTITUTIONAL LAW

Let us pick up the threads of our story at the home of Dollree Mapp, in Cleveland, Ohio, on May 27, 1957. Mapp lived on the second floor of a two-family brick house and rented out rooms to boarders. In mid-May, three police officers appeared at her home and demanded entrance, explaining that they were searching for a man in connection with a recent bombing. After consulting by telephone with her attorney, Mapp refused to admit them without a search warrant. The officers returned later, with others, and forced their way in. After Mapp asked to see the officers' search warrant, the officers produced a piece of paper, which Mapp grabbed and placed down the front of her blouse. A fracas ensued when one of the officers tried to retrieve the piece of paper. After handcuffing Mapp, the officers searched the house. No bombing suspect was ever found and no search warrant was ever produced. The officers did, however, find four books—*Affairs of a Troubadour, Little Darlings, London Stage Affairs,* and *Memories of a Hotel Man*—as well as a hand-drawn picture described in the state's brief as being "of a very obscene nature."

Dollree Mapp was arrested, tried for and convicted of possession of obscene materials. After the Ohio Court of Appeals and the Supreme Court of Ohio affirmed her conviction, Mapp appealed to the United States Supreme Court.

The jurisdictional statement in *Mapp v. Ohio* raised questions as to the constitutionality of the instructions to the jury, the sentence imposed, the statute upon which the conviction was based, and, finally, the conduct of the police. This last issue was limited solely to the constitutionality of the police behavior under the "shock the conscience" standard delineated in the 1952 stomach pump case, *Rochin v. California.* The substantial federal question that prompted the Supreme Court to hear the appeal was whether the Ohio statute was vague and overbroad in violation of the first and fourteenth amendments' free press guarantee; the overwhelming portion of the briefs and virtually all of the oral argument were devoted to this issue.

In fact, until the circulation of the first draft of the majority opinion, the issue that the Court ultimately was to decide had been mentioned only by an amicus curiae, the ACLU. Its twenty-page brief included only a three-sentence paragraph at the very end asking the Court to overrule its 1949 decision in *Wolf v. Colorado,* which had held that state courts were not required to exclude evidence seized in violation of the fourth and fourteenth amendments. That the ACLU's argument was not regarded by the parties as even a remotely important issue in the case was made clear at the oral argument. The appellant's lawyer was asked whether he was requesting the Court to overrule the *Wolf* case and, thus, to exclude the fruits of an illegal search at a state trial. He answered, quite candidly, that he had never heard of the *Wolf* case.

In any event, Dollree Mapp was to go free. At the conference following the argument, a majority of the Justices agreed that the Ohio statute violated the *first* and fourteenth amendments. Justice Tom Clark was assigned the job of writing the opinion of the Court.

What transpired in the month following our conference on the case is really a matter of speculation on my part, but I have always suspected that the members of the soon-to-be *Mapp* majority had met in what I affectionately call a "rump caucus" to discuss a different basis for their decision. But regardless of how they reached their decision, five Justices of the Court concluded that the fourth and fourteenth amendments required that evidence seized in an illegal search be excluded from state trials as well as federal ones. *Wolf* was to be overruled.

I was shocked when Justice Clark's proposed Court opinion reached my desk. I immediately wrote him a note expressing my surprise and questioning the wisdom of overruling an important doctrine in a case in which the issue was not briefed, argued, or discussed by the state courts, by the parties' counsel, or at our conference following the oral argument. After my shock subsided, I wrote a brief memorandum concurring in the judgment on first and fourteenth amendment grounds, and agreeing with Justice Harlan's dissent that the issue which the majority decided was not properly before the Court. The *Mapp* majority stood its ground, however; only Justices Frankfurter and Whittaker joined Justice Harlan's dissent.

The case of *Mapp v. Ohio* provides significant insight into the judicial process and the evolution of law—a first amendment controversy was transformed into perhaps the most important search-and-seizure decision in history.

*   *   *

B. The Development of the Exclusionary Rule

Since the fourth amendment itself says nothing about the exclusion of illegally obtained evidence, and none of the events leading to its adoption involved pleas that such evidence be excluded, one might expect that the early decisions articulating the rule would have supplied a clear explanation for its creation. Unfortunately, the early cases fail to provide insight and guidance into the constitutional underpinnings for the exclusionary rule. In fact, no decision by the Court has ever fully explored the possible alternative doctrinal bases for the rule, and the justifications for the rule seem to have changed subtly over time—usually without any explicit recognition by the Justices involved.

*   *   *

The first case associated with the development of the exclusionary rule is *Boyd v. United States*. Yet the *Boyd* case was a civil case, not a criminal case; no police were involved, and no search or seizure ever took place. It arose when the government initiated a forfeiture proceeding against two New York businessmen for importing thirty-five cases of plate glass in violation of import and revenue laws. During the course of the civil forfeiture trial, the government sought discovery of invoices for the goods in order to prove the quantity and value of the cases of plate glass. The subpoena served upon the defendants declared that if they did not produce the requested books and papers, "the allegations which it is affirmed they will prove shall be taken as confessed." The defendants produced the invoices, but following a verdict for the government, they appealed the judgment on the grounds that the compelled production of the invoices violated the fourth and fifth amendments.

From the facts, it is hard to find a fourth amendment issue in the case; there was no search or seizure—at least, given the modern view of that amendment. But with a few clever maneuvers, Justice Bradley converted the issue in the case into a fourth amendment question. He reasoned that, because the allegations in the subpoena were to be taken as true if the subpoena was not complied with, the subpoena was "tantamount" to compelled production of the sought-after materials. He concluded that the compulsory production of private papers fell within the scope of the fourth amendment because it "effect[ed] the sole object and purpose of [a] search and seizure." After reviewing the events that gave rise to the adoption of the fourth amendment, including the *Wilkes* case and James Otis's attack on writs of assistance, Justice Bradley found that the search was "unreasonable" because it sought not contraband, such as weapons or stolen goods, but private papers—items that could not even have been obtained through the use of the dreaded writs of assistance.

Having established the fourth amendment violation, Justice Bradley's Court opinion injected exclusion into the picture by noting the "intimate relation" between the fourth and the fifth amendments. He stated that the two amendments "run almost into each other." An unreasonable search violative of the fourth amendment is undertaken in order to compel a man to give evidence against himself. Seizing private books and papers, according to Justice Bradley's opinion, was substantially the equivalent of compelling the owner of the papers to give the testimony contained in the papers. The Court's opinion concluded that to admit into evidence in forfeiture proceedings—described by the Court as "civil in form, [but] ... in their nature criminal"—papers that had been acquired through an illegal search and seizure would constitute a second and independent violation of the Constitution, a violation of the fifth amendment's guarantee against compulsory self-incrimination. Thus, in the *Boyd* case, the exclusion of evidence was not declared to be necessary to remedy the fourth amendment violation. Rather, the concept of excluding evidence was born out of the belief that to admit papers and books would violate the fifth amendment—an amendment which was specially intended to protect a defendant's rights at a trial.

The second of the three cases indentified as the source of the exclusionary rule, *Adams v. New York*, was a criminal case. In 1903, Albert Adams was arrested and convicted for illegal gambling. His conviction was obtained in part because of the admission into evidence of private papers seized by the police while searching for gambling paraphernalia. Relying on the *Boyd* case, Adams's counsel appealed the conviction, arguing that the papers had been seized in violation of the fourth and fourteenth amendments, and that their admission into evidence violated the fifth and fourteenth amendments.

Writing for the Court, Justice Day found no fourth or fifth amendment violation in the introduction of the papers; he therefore did not reach the question of whether those provisions were binding on the states through the fourteenth amendment. His opinion characterized the question raised as an issue of evidence and not as one of constitutional law. . . . Justice Day distinguished the *Boyd* case by reading that opinion merely to hold that the compulsory production of documents violated the fourth and fifth amendments. With that, he seemed to bury the exclusionary rule—even before its birth was recognized.

Ten years later, however, it became clear that the *Adams* case was just a wild turn in the exclusionary rule roller coaster track. In the third case, *Weeks v. United States*, the defendant Weeks, like Adams, was tried for and convicted of illegal gambling. Once again, the conviction was appealed on the ground that papers admitted into evidence had been illegally seized in violation of the fourth amendment. The government brief was short—less than three pages long—and its position was clear: "The question is no longer open." The *Adams* case controlled and thus, in the government's view, the competent evidence, regardless of how it was secured, was admissible. Once again, Justice Day was assigned the task of writing the Court opinion. The Court was unanimous, but this time the conviction was reversed.

Justice Day discussed both the history of the fourth amendment and the language from the *Boyd* case. He distinguished the case at bar from a search for the fruits or evidence of crime, noting that the fourth amendment specifically protected papers and, therefore, letters. Then he referred to the single fact in the case that distinguished it from *Adams*—a single fact that brought the exclusionary rule back to life: Adams's attorney had objected *at trial* to the introduction of evidence because of the means by which it was secured, while Weeks's attorney had filed a petition *before* trial for the return of his private papers and property. In his appeal, Weeks's lawyer cited the refusal to grant his petition as reversible error. The Court agreed, holding that because Weeks had moved for the return of the papers before trial, the fourth amendment required the government to return the illegally seized property. Because the government was required to return the papers before trial, and was unable by virtue of the fifth amendment to subpoena their production, the government could not produce the evidence at trial. Thus, exclusion was required by the hypothetical unavailability of the evidence.

*   *   *

II. THE CONSTITUTIONAL BASES FOR THE EXCLUSIONARY RULE

*   *   *

The Bill of Rights is but one component of our legal system—the one that limits the government's reach. The primary responsibility for enforcing the Constitution's limits on government, at least since the time of *Marbury v. Madison*, has been vested in the judicial branch. In general, when law enforcement officials violate a person's fourth amendment rights, they do so in attempting to obtain evidence for use in criminal proceedings. To give effect to the Constitution's prohibition against illegal searches and seizures, it may be necessary for the judiciary to remove the incentive for violating it. Thus, it may be argued that although the Constitution does not explicitly provide for exclusion, the need to enforce the Constitution's limits on government—to preserve the rule of law—requires an exclusionary rule. Under this third "doctrinal" basis for the exclusionary rule, which has been described as "constitutional common law," the exclusion of unconstitutionally obtained evidence is not a constitutional *right* but a constitutional *remedy*. It is a right only in the sense that every remedy vests a right in those who may claim it.

Under such an approach, the determination whether the exclusionary rule is constitutionally required turns on whether there are other adequate remedies available to ensure that the government does not violate the fourth amendment at its pleasure. The Supreme Court made just such an inquiry in the *Wolf* case. Writing for the Court, Justice Frankfurter referred to the alternatives to exclusion—criminal prosecutions and civil actions—and concluded that "it is not for this Court to condemn as falling below the minimal standards assured by the Due Process Clause a State's reliance upon other methods which, if consistently enforced, would be equally effective."

*   *   *

... [T]he Constitution requires only that there be some *effective* remedy to ensure that agents of the government obey the fourth amendment. Thus exclusion is constitutionally required only if without it there would be no adequate means to ensure that the government obeys the fourth amendment. I turn now to that question.

*   *   *

b. *Other Remedies.* In addition to the exclusionary rule, there are several other remedies currently available for fourth amendment violations. A federal statute makes it a crime for anyone acting under color of law to deprive a person of rights protected by the Constitution, including the right to be free from unreasonable searches and seizures. But under the Supreme Court's decision in *Screws v. United States*, only "willful" deprivations of constitutional rights may serve as the basis of a valid criminal prosecution. Though this is as it should be—criminal sanctions are too great a penalty and too strong a deterrent to effective law enforcement to be applied whenever a police officer inadvertently or negligently violates the fourth amendment—it does dilute the efficacy of this remedy. Moreover, in practice, the harshness of the sanction is also an obstacle to its effective enforcement. Because the vast majority of police officers are law abiding, juries are inclined to credit the testimony of those few who are not. As a result, it is difficult to obtain a conviction for willful deprivation of fourth amendment rights, and hence, criminal prosecutions are rare.

Another infrequently invoked remedy is an action in federal court seeking an injunction against fourth amendment violations by a law enforcement agency. In light of the Court's decision in *Rizzo v. Goode*, a party seeking to obtain such an injunction bears a heavy burden in establishing that widespread constitutional violations result from a *policy* of the agency being sued. In *City of Los Angeles v. Lyons*, the Supreme Court held just last Term that a victim of unconstitutional police practices cannot maintain an action for an injunction against such practices unless he can establish that he is likely to be injured by the practices again in the future. Thus, this alternative as well can hardly be considered an effective surrogate for the exclusionary rule.

A far more common alternative remedy is an action for damages against federal officials directly under the fourth amendment. The analogous damage action against persons acting under color of *state* law may be brought under section 1983. In certain circumstances a damage action may also be brought directly against the governmental body that employs an officer who violates the fourth amendment. Under the Supreme Court's decision in *Monell v. Department of Social Services*, a municipality or other local governmental body may be held liable where the unconstitutional act implements or executes an official governmental policy.

As will be spelled out in greater detail later, the advantages of a damage action over the exclusionary rule are threefold: first, it compensates the innocent victims of a fourth amendment violation as well as those victims accused of criminal offenses; second, it has an element of proportionality because the amount of a judgment may be varied to reflect the egregiousness of the constitutional violation; and third, by imposing a sanction directly upon the individual violator, it produces a measure of what is frequently described as "specific deterrence."

But a host of problems suggests that a damage action, although necessary to ensure that the fourth amendment is not merely hortatory, is not by itself sufficient. First, as noted above, juries are inclined to believe the testimony of law enforcement officials because the vast majority of them *are* honest and endeavor to perform their jobs in accordance with the Constitution. This fact, when coupled with the immunity from liability for actions reasonably taken in good faith, makes it very difficult to obtain a judgment against a police officer. Second, despite the availability of attorney's fees for prevailing litigants, it is often difficult to obtain competent counsel to prosecute such an action. Finally, if a money judgment *is* won, many officers do not have the resources to satisfy a judgment necessary to compensate the victim of a heinous fourth amendment violation.

Although government bodies are rarely, if ever, judgment-proof, some of the same problems—and others—attend damage actions against governmental entities. Since the same police officers are likely to be called to testify in a damage action brought against the government, the credibility problems already discussed are likely to arise in such cases. Although the Court has held in *Owen v. City of Independence* that municipalities do not enjoy the same good-faith immunity afforded to individual police officers, other decisions make clear that a local governmental body may be held liable under section 1983 only when its *policies* give rise to the constitutional violation. Since most fourth amendment violations are the result of wrongful actions by individual law enforcement officials, not of unlawful governmental policies, the circumstances under which a governmental body will be held liable for a fourth amendment violation are likely to be rare, indeed.

*   *   *

In sum, the most "powerful" remedies, criminal prosecutions for willful violation of the fourth amendment and actions for injunctions against large-scale violations, are rarely brought and rarely succeed. Damage actions for fourth amendment violations serve the salutary objective of compensating all victims of fourth amendment violations to a degree reasonably related to the harm resulting from the infringement. But damage actions are also expensive, time-consuming, not readily available, and rarely successful. As a result, the deterrent effect of these actions can hardly be said to be great, since the prospect of a judgment for money damages is extremely remote.

Taken together, the currently available alternatives to the exclusionary rule satisfactorily achieve some, but not all, of the necessary functions of a remedial measure. They punish and perhaps deter the grossest of violations, as well as governmental policies that legitimate these violations. They compensate some of the victims of the most egregious violations. But they do little, if anything, to reduce the likelihood of the vast majority of fourth amendment violations—the frequent infringements motivated by commendable zeal, not condemnable malice. For those violations, a remedy is required that inspires the police officer to channel his enthusiasm to apprehend a criminal toward the need to comply with the dictates of the fourth amendment. There is only one such remedy—the exclusion of illegally obtained evidence.

It was with that in mind that I wrote in the Court's opinion in the *Elkins* case that "[t]he rule ... compel[s] respect for the constitutional guaranty in the only effectively available way—by removing the incentive to disregard it." I believed then, and I believe now, that the exclusionary rule *is* constitutionally required, not as a "right" explicitly incorporated in the fourth amendment's prohibitions, but as a remedy necessary to ensure that those prohibitions are observed in fact. Thus, although I did not join in the Court's opinion in the *Mapp* case—because it decided an issue that was not before the Court— I agree with its conclusion that the exclusionary rule *is* necessary to keep the right of privacy secured by the fourth amendment from "remain[ing] an empty promise."

*   *   *

THE EXCLUSIONARY RULE ON THE SCAFFOLD: BUT WAS IT A FAIR TRIAL?

Silas Wasserstrom and William J. Mertens

Seventy years ago, the Supreme Court unanimously held that evidence seized in violation of the fourth amendment is inadmissible in federal criminal prosecutions. When it was first formulated, this doctrine, which later became known as the exclusionary rule, rested on a constellation of related, but not very clearly articulated principles: (1) that it is simply unfair to convict a defendant on the basis of evidence unlawfully seized from him; (2) that it is an additional unlawful invasion of his privacy to admit tainted evidence at trial; (3) that it is wrong for the courts to allow the government to profit from the wrongdoing of its own agents; and (4) that the integrity of the federal courts would be compromised if they became accomplices to governmental lawlessness by admitting illegally seized evidence.

From its inception, the rule was bitterly attacked by many commentators, but... the Warren Court never questioned the rule's constitutional basis or its importance. As the Court proclaimed in *Terry v. Ohio*, "[c]ourts which sit under our Constitution cannot, and will not, be made parties to lawless invasions of constitutional rights of citizens by permitting unhindered governmental use of the fruits of such invasions."

Over the past ten years, however, the Burger Court has taken a considerably less exalted view of the exclusionary rule. In a series of decisions beginning with *United States v. Calandra* in 1974, the Court has robbed the rule of the various normative principles which were its original support and has repeatedly asserted that the "sole purpose" of the rule is an instrumental one: "to deter future unlawful police conduct and thereby effectuate the guarantee of the Fourth Amendment against unreasonable searches and seizures." The rule does not, the Court said in *Calandra*, vindicate the constitutional rights of the accused, but rather is a "judicially created remedy" which should be "restricted to those areas where its remedial objectives are thought most efficaciously served." Thus, according to the Court, the question of whether the rule should apply in a particular context is to be determined by balancing the marginal increment in deterrence achieved by excluding the evidence at issue against the putative social costs of the rule's application.

While this cost-benefit analysis appears neutral and detached, the Court balances with its thumb on the scale. To begin with, the Court has no reliable way to quantify and assess either the costs which the rule exacts by impeding the search for truth, or the benefits which the rule provides by deterring police misconduct. Furthermore, these putative costs and benefits measure incommensurables: How much privacy should be sacrificed to achieve more accurate fact finding in a relatively small number of cases? "Balancing," therefore, can be attempted only by imposing a value judgment which is concealed by the illusory precision of cost-benefit analysis. The result of this seemingly neutral procedure, then, is largely preordained by the values which the Justices bring to the process.

*   *   *

...In subsequent cases the Court has balanced costs and benefits and ruled that illegally seized evidence is admissible to impeach the defendant's testimony at his criminal trial, in civil proceedings to collect federal wagering taxes, in deportation proceedings, and in the trials of defendants who are the targets, though not the victims, of illegal searches. This same mode of analysis has also led the Court to rule that federal habeas corpus relief is unavailable to a state prisoner who had an opportunity to litigate his fourth amendment claim in the state courts.

In these decisions, most of which involved the admissibility of illegally seized evidence in proceedings collateral to the criminal prosecution itself, the Burger Court steadily whittled away at the exclusionary rule. Nevertheless, until last Term, the Court had been willing simply to assume that the benefits of excluding illegally seized evidence from the prosecution's case-in-chief outweighed the costs. The Court left intact the application of the rule in this, its paradigmatic setting. Last Term, however, the Court put aside its whittling knife, and went after the exclusionary rule with a machete. In *United States v. Leon,* ... the Court reached out to adopt ... the so-called "good faith" exception to the exclusionary rule. The Court, for the first time, engaged in a cost-benefit analysis of the admissibility of illegally seized evidence in the government's case-in-chief and concluded that where the police rely reasonably and in good faith on an invalid warrant, the fruits of their illegal search or seizure are admissible for all purposes.

*   *   *

In *Leon,* the police initiated a narcotics investigation after receiving information from an informant. Based on their observations of the suspects' suspicious comings and goings and on information from an informant, the police secured warrants from a state court judge to search residences and automobiles belonging to, or used by, the suspects. These searches uncovered illegal drugs and drug paraphernalia, and the respondents were charged in federal court with various federal drug offenses. The District Court found that the affidavit in support of the warrant did not establish probable cause and ordered much of the evidence seized in the searches suppressed. A divided panel of the Ninth Circuit affirmed, ruling that the affidavit did not establish the informant's credibility or basis of knowledge as required by the two-pronged test of *Aguilar-Spinelli.* ...

The Ninth Circuit decided *Leon* before the Supreme Court decided *Gates.* It invalidated the warrant because the supporting affidavit failed the two-pronged test which the Court in *Gates* was soon to repudiate. Consequently, no lower court had reviewed the magistrate's decision to issue the warrant challenged in *Leon* under *Gates'* totality of the circumstances approach and deferential standard of review. Therefore the Court should have remanded the case to the Ninth Circuit for reconsideration in light of *Gates.* Or the Court might have reviewed the sufficiency of the affidavit itself. Had it done so, it doubtless would have found the warrant valid under *Gates* and the search lawful.

The Court, however, neither remanded nor reviewed the affidavit. In its zeal to modify the exclusionary rule, the Court brushed aside the traditional strictures against deciding important constitutional issues except where necessary for resolution of the case.

*   *   *

In his opinion for the Court, Justice White argues that the exclusionary rule will not deter fourth amendment violations when it is applied to suppress evidence seized by police who have reasonably relied on an invalid warrant. And, according to Justice White, police reliance on an invalid warrant is almost always reasonable, for ordinarily the error leading to the issuance of an invalid warrant should be attributed to the magistrate, not the police. The exclusionary rule, the argument continues, cannot be used to deter the errors of magistrates. Justice White thus concludes that the exclusionary rule should not ordinarily be applied where the police have made an unconstitutional search or seizure pursuant to an invalid warrant.

*   *   *

In short, Justice White's argument draws three conclusions: (1) the exclusionary rule was not designed to affect the behavior of magistrates; (2) magistrates are now performing well; and (3) to the extent that some magistrates are not performing well, the exclusionary rule will not improve their performance. Each of these points will be considered in turn.

The rule is "designed to deter police misconduct" rather than to affect the behavior of magistrates. It is hard to know just what Justice White means by "designed" here. In the first place, it is only in recent years that the exclusionary rule has been viewed as intended to deter anyone. When it was initially "designed," it was seen as a constitutional requirement which vindicated the personal rights of the accused and preserved the integrity of the federal courts. Indeed, in *Boyd v. United States*, the Court's first application of the exclusionary sanction, there was no police misconduct whatsoever, and the evidence suppressed had been obtained pursuant to a court-ordered subpoena. Moreover, it is somewhat odd to suppose that the exclusionary rule was not designed to deter the issuance of invalid warrants. When the fourth amendment was adopted, its purpose plainly was to prohibit the issuance of warrants that did not satisfy its requirements of probable cause and particularity. And if there is one thing clear from the cryptic language of the fourth amendment, it is that "no warrant shall issue but upon probable cause." It is at least anomalous, then, to hold as the Court did in *Leon*, that what is now the primary remedy for fourth amendment violations—and in warrant cases probably the only remedy—should not apply to what the framers viewed as the quintessential fourth amendment violation.

*   *   *

Magistrates are performing well. In text, Justice White boldly declares that there is "no evidence suggesting that judges and magistrates are inclined to ignore or subvert the Fourth Amendment...." Then, in a footnote, he acknowledges that "there are assertions that some magistrates become rubber stamps for the police and others may be unable effectively to screen police conduct." He then dismisses these "assertions" with one of his own: "[W]e are not convinced that this is a problem of major proportions."... [However], there is substantial evidence, not merely "assertions," that some magistrates do in fact "serve as rubber stamps for the police" while others "may be unable effectively to screen police conduct." The Van Duizend Study reports that some of the magistrates interviewed "expressed reluctance to substitute their judgment for that of investigating officers," and other researchers have reported similar findings. Indeed, in *Gates*, the Supreme Court itself acknowledged that search and arrest warrants are often issued "by persons who are neither lawyers nor judges and who certainly do not remain abreast of each judicial refinement of the nature of probable cause...."

The real issue, however, is not how well magistrates are performing now, but whether their performance is likely to deteriorate if their errors will no longer result in suppression. If the warrant issuing process is functioning as well as Justice White says it is, this is a reason for retaining the exclusionary rule in warrant cases, not a reason for abandoning it, for it is under an exclusionary rule regime that this well-functioning system has evolved. One would have thought that the old adage, "if it ain't broke don't fix it," would have had some appeal to the conservatives on the Burger Court. For if we have such competent magistrates, this may be in no small part because the exclusionary rule gives legislatures an incentive to finance a system of professional magistrates who are capable of making probable cause determinations. If we do have such capable magistrates, it is certainly *not* because the Supreme Court has imposed demanding qualifications for those authorized to issue warrants. In *Shadwick v. City of Tampa*, the Court ruled that untrained court clerks, with no other judicial authority, qualify as neutral and detached magistrates for fourth amendment purposes. Now that the errors of magistrates will no longer result in exclusion, more jurisdictions may well entrust the warrant issuing process to such untrained court clerks.

Magistrates will not be deterred by the threat of exclusion. According to Justice White, the threat of exclusion cannot significantly deter magistrates because they are not "adjuncts to the law enforcement team," but "neutral judicial officers [who have] no stake in the outcome of particular criminal prosecutions." To begin with, however, the evidence shows that some magistrates do see themselves as adjuncts to the police. And, again, it is important to remember that the good faith exception of *Leon* will apply only where evidence has been seized pursuant to a warrant that fails to satisfy the very lax standards of *Gates*. A warrant that cannot survive scrutiny after *Gates*, then, must be a bad warrant indeed. It would seem that those magistrates who do see themselves as part of the "law enforcement team" would be tempted to issue exactly that sort of bad warrant. Thus, after *Gates*, the threat of exclusion would be aimed at precisely those zealous magistrates who, because they care about convictions, might well have been deterred by that threat. The good faith exception removes that deterrent, for the evidence will come in even where partisan magistrates aid the police by issuing warrants which cannot be upheld even under the *Gates* standard.

The more important issue, however, is not the deterrent effect of the exclusionary rule on the conduct of individual magistrates, but the extent to which the rule helps preserve the integrity of the warrant issuing process as a whole. Thus, the Court should have taken a more serious look at the process' potential flaws and unhealthy tendencies rather than just focusing on how well the process is functioning now. Viewed from this perspective, the fact that only "some" magistrates become "rubber stamps for the police" or are "unable effectively to screen police conduct" cannot be brushed aside so cavalierly. Empirical studies can confirm what common sense would lead us to expect: even with the exclusionary rule in place, police sometimes engage in magistrate shopping, seeking out those magistrates who are most accommodating. Police officers quickly learn who these indulgent magistrates are. And because in most jurisdictions no record is made when an application for a warrant is turned down, the police can simply present the same affidavit to other magistrates, hoping to find one who is less scrupulous about probable cause.

Although the exclusionary rule does not prevent magistrate shopping, it does help to contain it. With the rule in place, the police know that if a reviewing court finds the warrant invalid, it will suppress the evidence seized pursuant to the warrant. Under the good faith exception, however, even evidence seized under an invalid warrant will generally be admissible. The police need concern themselves only with getting a warrant and not with getting a warrant that will hold up on review. Consequently, under the good faith exception, we can expect a variation of Gresham's Law to operate; "bad" warrants—those issued by the most indolent, incompetent, and indulgent magistrates—will effectively drive out "good" warrants. As a practical matter, the standard of probable cause will be established by the least demanding official authorized to issue warrants, even if this standard falls below the already diluted standard of probable cause established by the Court in *Gates*. This standard, it is important to remember, need not be set by a judge, a lawyer, or even by an experienced or knowledgeable layman. Instead, as the Court ruled in *Shadwick*, this standard can be set by a low-level, untrained civil servant whose desk happens to be in the courthouse.

*   *   *

While the Court in *Leon* insisted that the exclusionary rule has no impact on the behavior of magistrates, it grudgingly assumed—at least "in the absence of a more efficacious sanction"—that the rule deters police misconduct. But, according to the Court, the rule should not be applied where the police have acted reasonably and in good faith:... Where a police officer acting "with objective good faith" obtains a search warrant from a judge or magistrate and acts within its scope, ... "there is no police illegality and thus nothing to deter." Ordinarily, the officer "cannot be expected to question the magistrate's probable cause determination or his judgment that the form of the warrant is technically correct." Therefore, "penalizing the officer for the magistrate's error, rather than his own, cannot logically contribute to the deterrence of Fourth Amendment violations."...

To make this argument the Court sharply bifurcates the warrant process; magistrates play one role—they issue warrants—and the police play a second role—they execute warrants. Indeed, portions of the *Leon* opinion read like a description of the warrant process as it functioned two hundred years ago when police departments did not exist, and constables executed warrants on the complaint of private citizens: "'[O]nce the warrant issues, there is literally nothing more the policeman can do in seeking to comply with the law...' Penalizing the officer for the magistrate's error, rather than his own, cannot logically contribute to the deterrence of Fourth Amendment violations."

The modern police force does not, however, function like an eighteenth century constabulary. Present-day magistrates do not issue warrants sua sponte or on the complaint of private citizens, but at the behest of the police. Where a warrant is invalid, it is usually because the supporting police affidavit failed to establish probable cause. And it is not as though we cannot expect the police to make accurate assessments of probable cause without the help of a magistrate, for we expect them to make such assessments whenever they search or seize without a warrant, something they do far more often than search or seize with warrant in hand. Consequently, it is not "illogical" to suppose that the exclusionary rule, without a good faith exception, provides an incentive to law enforcement agencies to make sure that their warrant applications establish probable cause. The rule ensures that if the magistrate "takes the bait" and issues an invalid warrant, any evidence which the police seized pursuant to the warrant will be lost. Under the good faith exception of *Leon*, however, the magistrate's mistake in issuing an invalid warrant effectively insulates the police officer's error in seeking the warrant on an insufficient basis. Because magistrates' errors will not result in suppression, the police need not worry about their own.

Moreover, the Court again fails to recognize that the exclusionary rule works as a systemic deterrent affecting a wider audience than just police and magistrates. Prosecutors obviously want to assure that evidence seized by the police will be admissible at trial. This is why many state and federal prosecutors take an active role in reviewing, or even preparing, warrant applications before they are presented to a magistrate. In both *Leon* and *Sheppard*, for example, prosecutors had reviewed and approved the affidavits which the police had submitted. The Van Duizend Study reports that local prosecutors frequently become involved in the warrant issuing process. All twenty-five U.S. Attorneys that responded to a letter that we sent out this summer reported that they regularly screen both search and warrant applications. Virtually all said that a primary reason for doing so was to "avoid possible suppression of evidence at trial due to an invalid warrant." Several replied that this was their only purpose.

Several U.S. Attorneys also emphasized that this screening process was time-consuming both for prosecutors and for the agents involved, but that it was still worthwhile. One office expressed pride in the fact that its procedures had "resulted in a virtually 100 percent record of valid warrants."

The good faith exception reduces, if it does not eliminate altogether, the incentive for prosecutors to assure that warrant searches comply with the requirements of the fourth amendment. Indeed, the exception may provide a *disincentive* to the conscientious screening of warrant applications, for when the police obtain an invalid warrant on the basis of an affidavit that a prosecutor has disapproved, this might well count against the officer's claim of reasonable reliance.

*   *   *

THE END OF THE EXCLUSIONARY RULE, AMONG OTHER THINGS: THE ROBERTS COURT TAKES ON THE FOURTH AMENDMENT

DAVID A. MORAN

* * *

III. *HUDSON*: THE COURT KILLS THE KNOCK-AND-ANNOUNCE RULE AND PUTS THE EXCLUSIONARY RULE ON LIFE SUPPORT

I must confess that I really never saw it coming. When an attorney named Richard Korn telephoned me out of the blue in February 2005 to ask if I would take a look at a case, *People v. Hudson*, that he had just lost in the Michigan courts and assess whether it would make a good vehicle for challenging the Michigan Supreme Court's 1999 decision in *People v. Stevens*, I did not hesitate. After all, I had long been critical of *Stevens*, which had held that

215

exclusion of evidence was not an appropriate remedy for a Fourth Amendment knock-and-announce violation. *Stevens*, in effect, gave the Michigan police carte blanche to violate the knock-and-announce rule, the ancient common law requirement that the police must knock and generally allow residents to open their doors, thereby sparing residents a forcible and terrifying police entry. The Michigan Supreme Court's decision seemed especially vulnerable given that the United States Supreme Court had twice suppressed evidence seized after knock-and-announce violations, and had, just eleven years ago, unanimously held that the knock-and-announce rule was part of the Fourth Amendment in *Wilson v. Arkansas.*

Since the Michigan Supreme Court's refusal to suppress evidence seized after a knock-and-announce violation was out of step with the U.S. Supreme Court's ruling in *Wilson* and with the rule followed in every other state and federal circuit, except one, I felt confident that the Court, if it granted certiorari, would pull Michigan back into line.... While I certainly realized that it was possible I could somehow lose *Hudson*, it never occurred to me that I could effectively kill an 800-year-old rule protecting personal privacy and simultaneously put the entire exclusionary rule at risk.

But that is exactly what happened. Now that I have recovered from the shock, it is time to do the post-mortem. I will begin by discussing the case itself and the opinions it produced. I will then turn to what the decision means for the knock-and-announce rule. Finally, I will discuss the implications for the exclusionary rule.

A. THE CASE AND JUSTICE SCALIA'S MAJORITY OPINION

After reviewing the case file, I immediately recognized that *Hudson* was an ideal vehicle for challenging *Stevens*. First, there was never any dispute that a knock-and-announce violation had occurred when police officers with a search warrant raided the home that Booker T. Hudson, Jr., shared with his wife in Detroit. Indeed, the police officer in charge of the raid candidly testified at a suppression hearing that, despite having no grounds to dispense with the knock-and-announce requirement, he and the other six officers burst through the front door only three to five seconds after yelling, "Police, search warrant!" This testimony clearly established a knock-and-announce violation because the Court had earlier held in *Richards v. Wisconsin* that the police may force their way inside only after announcing their presence and waiting a reasonable amount of time, unless they have specific reasons to believe that the delay would frustrate the purpose of the search or endanger them. Faced with this testimony, the prosecutor at Hudson's suppression hearing conceded that the officers had violated the knock-and-announce rule. That concession was justified because, even though it is not clear exactly how long the police are supposed to wait before performing a forcible entry, three to five seconds is clearly not enough.

The second reason why *Hudson* struck me as a good vehicle to challenge *Stevens* was that Hudson had been convicted of a relatively minor crime. The police found some seven people in the house who had, between them, approximately twenty rocks of crack cocaine. At his bench trial, the judge, finding no reason to believe that all, or even most, of the cocaine rocks belonged to Hudson, convicted him of possessing only the five rocks that the police found in his pants. For this minor offense, the judge sentenced Hudson to probation.

The legal issue in the case was straightforward, or so I thought. According to the Michigan Supreme Court, evidence found inside a home following a knock-and-announce violation should not be suppressed because such evidence should always be regarded as "inevitably discovered"; that is, the police still would have discovered the same evidence had they complied with the knock and announce requirement. The Court had adopted the inevitable discovery doctrine as an exception to the exclusionary rule in *Nix v. Williams,* but the Michigan Supreme Court's approach amounted to a massive expansion of the doctrine for two interrelated reasons. First, the Court had stressed that the inevitable discovery doctrine applies only when the prosecution can demonstrate that evidence would have been discovered by means "wholly independent" of the unconstitutional police conduct. *Stevens,* however, did not require the existence of any independent means of discovery at all. Second, the Court in *Nix* specifically recognized that the inevitable discovery doctrine would not undermine the deterrence rationale of the exclusionary rule because the officer who engaged in the violation would not normally know whether the same evidence would inevitably be found by independent means. By contrast, after *Stevens,* police in Michigan knew to a certainty that any evidence they found after knock-and-announce violations would always be regarded as "inevitably" discovered. For these reasons, every state and federal court to consider the argument that the inevitable discovery doctrine created a per se exception to the exclusionary rule for knock-and-announce violations, except the Michigan Supreme Court and the Seventh Circuit, had rejected it.

Therefore, I thought *Hudson* was about two things: the importance of maintaining an effective deterrent so that police would respect the knock-and-announce rule; and, more abstractly, the proper scope of the inevitable discovery exception to the exclusionary rule. What I did not realize was that the case would put the exclusionary rule itself into play.

But for some bad timing, my understanding of the case almost certainly would have prevailed. When the case was first argued on January 9, 2006, it seemed clear that at least five members of the Court agreed that *Stevens* represented an indefensible extension of the inevitable discovery doctrine that would, if accepted, render the knock-and-announce rule meaningless. Unfortunately, one of those five justices was Sandra Day O'Connor, who was replaced by Samuel Alito in February. Two months later, the Court ordered the case reargued.

At the re-argument on May 18, 2006, it became clear to me for the first time that the case was no longer about the knock-and-announce rule or the inevitable discovery doctrine when Justice Scalia asked me, in a series of questions, why the threat of internal police discipline would not convince officers to comply with the knock-and-announce rule. When I responded that such a notion contradicts the very premise of *Mapp v. Ohio*, the seminal 1961 case in which the Court extended the exclusionary rule to the states because other remedies had proven worthless at deterring Fourth Amendment violations, Justice Scalia replied, "*Mapp* was a long time ago. It was before section 1983 was being used, wasn't it?"

Less than a month later, the Court issued its decision in *Hudson*. Writing for five members of the Court, Justice Scalia began his analysis with a lengthy discussion of the history of the exclusionary rule and its "costly toll upon truth-seeking and law enforcement objectives." Turning to the knock-and-announce rule, the Court noted that the rule protects residents and police from violence that may occur when residents mistake the police for criminals, preserves private property from unnecessary destruction, and allows residents an opportunity to compose themselves and prepare for a police entry. After reciting these interests, however, Justice Scalia concluded, "What the knock-and-announce rule has never protected, however, is one's interest in preventing the government from seeing or taking evidence described in a warrant. Since the interests that *were* violated in this case have nothing to do with the seizure of the evidence, the exclusionary rule is inapplicable."

A moment's thought should reveal just how jaw-dropping this statement is. *None* of the interests protected by the Fourth Amendment is about preventing the government from seizing one's contraband or criminal evidence. Indeed, by definition, a person has no right to keep contraband or criminal evidence. Instead, the very point of the exclusionary rule is to safeguard the interests that are protected under the Fourth Amendment by taking away the incentive the police would have to violate those interests in order to obtain contraband or evidence. Thus, under Justice Scalia's reasoning, drugs seized from a person who has been illegally detained and searched should not be suppressed because the rules governing lawful arrest are designed to protect people from the indignities and inconvenience of arrest, not to protect anyone's possessory interest in narcotics. Similarly, obscene material seized from a home following a warrantless entry should not be suppressed because the warrant requirement protects a homeowner's right against unlawful intrusions, but not his right to possess obscenity.

Having completely recast the exclusionary rule as a narrow remedy that applies only when the evidence seized is of the type that the constitutional protection was designed to protect, Justice Scalia then turned squarely to the argument that exclusion is necessary to deter officers from routinely violating the knock-and-announce rule. With a reference to *Mapp*, he wrote, "We cannot assume that exclusion in this context is necessary deterrence simply because we found that it was necessary deterrence in different contexts and long ago. That would be forcing the public today to pay for the sins and inadequacies of a legal regime that existed almost half a century ago."

So, exactly how have times changed since 1961, when *Mapp* was decided? In two key respects, according to Justice Scalia. First, it is easier to sue the police than it was in those days because of the availability of statutory remedies such as 42 U.S.C. § 1983. In response to the fact that none of the parties in *Hudson* had found a single case in either state or federal court in which anyone recovered anything other than nominal damages for a knock and announce violation, Justice Scalia wrote, "we do not know how many claims have been settled, or indeed how many violations have occurred that produced anything more than nominal injury." Thus, having assumed away the inconvenient lack of evidence that the police have ever been successfully sued for a knock and announce violation, Justice Scalia concluded, "As far as we know, civil liability is an effective deterrent here, as we have assumed it is in other contexts."

Justice Scalia's second important post-*Mapp* change "is the increasing professionalism of police forces, including a new emphasis on internal police discipline." Without a trace of irony, Justice Scalia proceeded to cite a study from criminologist Samuel Walker for the proposition that there have been "wide-ranging reforms in the education, training, and supervision of police officers" since the days of *Mapp*.

It was left to Professor Walker to point out in an op-ed article that Justice Scalia "twisted my main argument to reach a conclusion the exact opposite of what I spelled out in this and other studies." Professor Walker explained:

> [T]he Warren court in the 1960s played a pivotal role in stimulating these reforms. For more than 100 years, police departments had failed to curb misuse of authority by officers on the street while the court took a hands-off attitude. The Warren court's interventions (*Mapp* and *Miranda* being the most famous) set new standards for lawful conduct, forcing the police to reform and strengthening community demands for curbs on abuse. Scalia's opinion suggests that the results I highlighted have sufficiently removed the need for an exclusionary rule to act as a judicial-branch watchdog over the police. I have never said or even suggested such a thing. To the contrary, I have argued that the results reinforce the Supreme Court's continuing importance in defining constitutional protections for individual rights and requiring the appropriate remedies for violations, including the exclusion of evidence.

For the reasons stated by Professor Walker, Justice Scalia's argument that increased police professionalism obviates the need for the exclusionary rule is equivalent to a claim that we should dismantle the gun towers at the state prison because escape attempts have dropped dramatically since the towers were built.

*   *   *

It was, of course, the evident hostility to the exclusionary rule permeating Justice Scalia's opinion for the Court that attracted the most attention to the decision in *Hudson*. If, as Justice Scalia claimed, *Mapp* is merely a relic from "a legal regime that existed almost half a century ago," and the police today reflexively respect constitutional rights because of "increasing professionalism" and an "effective regime of internal discipline," then the exclusionary rule would seem to be an unnecessary and excessive remedy for any kind of constitutional violation.

Until *Hudson* was decided, I am not aware of any scholar who seriously believed that the exclusionary rule was in danger of being overruled. In the weeks since that decision, everyone in the field believes that it is now crystal clear that the rule will become a historical relic if one more like-minded justice joins the Court.

Indeed, it even seems possible that the Court could overrule the exclusionary rule with its current composition. Although Justice Kennedy insisted in the first paragraph of his concurring opinion that the "continued operation of the exclusionary rule, as settled and defined by our precedents, is not in doubt," he joined the very parts of Justice Scalia's opinion that cast doubt on the exclusionary rule. If he really believes in the continuing vitality of the exclusionary rule, it is an absolute mystery to me why he would cast the crucial fifth vote for an opinion that openly declared war on the exclusionary rule.

The hot question that is being asked in the solicitor general's office and in state attorney general offices across the country is: "when will the time be ripe to take down the exclusionary rule in *toto*?" To put it more concretely, if a challenge is brought now, which Justice Kennedy will be there? The Justice Kennedy who signed on to Justice Scalia's opinion denigrating the exclusionary rule, or the Justice Kennedy who tried (but failed) to take it all back in his concurrence? Will there be a retirement among the *Hudson* dissenters so that President Bush (or, perhaps, his successor) can appoint another justice hostile to the exclusionary rule?

I am quite confident that a state prosecutor or attorney general will bring a direct challenge to the entire exclusionary rule to the Court within the next year. That is, a certiorari petition will be filed in a state criminal case that will concede that a clear constitutional violation occurred, such as failure to obtain a warrant before searching a house, but that will argue that *Mapp* should be overruled and that the evidence found after the violation should therefore be admitted.

*   *   *

There are, in short, a lot of variables that make it impossible to predict the future of the exclusionary rule. But there is no doubt after *Hudson* that the exclusionary rule is back in play and could well be overruled within the next few years.

Like I said, I never saw it coming.

THE EXCLUSIONARY RULE

Guido Calabresi

If there is a litmus test to distinguish between so-called liberals and so-called conservatives in the United States, it is the exclusionary rule. More than one's views on abortion, more than one's views on law and economics, more than one's views on *Bush v. Gore*, one's position on the exclusionary rule is viewed as a reliable indicator of the side on which one is situated. To liberals, it is a pillar of privacy; it is essential to protect individuals from predations on the part of the police. To conservatives, it is an absurd rule through which manifestly dangerous criminals are let out because the courts prefer technicalities to truth.

Of course, I am not talking about evidence whose veracity is made doubtful as a result of the means by which it was obtained, such as confessions extracted through physical or psychological torture. Rather, I am talking about evidence whose validity or "truthfulness" is unaffected or actually increased as a result of how it was gathered, yet where the method of obtaining the evidence ostensibly violates constitutional or other legal commands. Consider, for example, illegal wiretapping, warrantless searches, and stops that do not meet even the requirements of *Terry v. Ohio*.

222

The interesting paradox is this: liberals ought to hate the exclusionary rule because the exclusionary rule, in my experience, is most responsible for the deep decline in privacy rights in the United States. Indeed, the existence of the exclusionary rule has been the reason for more diminutions in privacy protection than anything else going on today. Why is this? Well, the dynamics of this process are very easy to understand.

What, for instance, qualifies as a reasonable search (the Constitution's reference point) is frequently a close question. On the one hand, the police must protect society by catching criminals and by using a variety of means to gather evidence. On the other hand, individual privacy interests may be infringed upon by those means. The judge who seeks to balance these conflicting values in determining whether a search is reasonable, however, finds that there is frequently an enormous thumb on the scale. If the judge holds the search to be unreasonable and therefore excludes the evidence, someone who is manifestly guilty of a very serious crime will be released.

Judges—politicians' claims to the contrary notwithstanding—are not in the business of letting people out on technicalities. If anything, judges are in the business of keeping people who are guilty *in* on technicalities. Regardless of who appointed her, the judge facing a clearly guilty murderer or rapist who makes a Fourth Amendment or other constitutional claim will do her best to protect the fundamental right *and* still keep the defendant in jail. It is perfectly obvious: the judge will do so simply because she does not like the idea of dangerous criminals being released into society.

This means that in any close case, a judge will decide that the search, the seizure, or the invasion of privacy was reasonable. That case then becomes the precedent for the next case. The next close case comes up and the precedent is applied: same thing, same thumb on the scale, same decision. The hydraulic effect, as Chief Judge John M. Walker, Jr. has sometimes called it, or the slippery slope, means that courts keep expanding what is deemed a *reasonable* search or seizure.

You can look around and see how often this has happened. Exigent circumstances, which used to be relatively uncommon, are now everywhere. What was enough to permit a *Terry* stop used to be quite limited. Today, however, almost anything a policeman says to justify a search is acceptable—and for good reason—because, case-by-case, the precedents have broadened the reasonable search doctrine.

On a side note, it is also my sense that this situation has led police to lie in order to prevent certain evidence from being excluded. Indeed, Chief

Judge Walker has taught me that such perjury is not infrequent in this kind of case. One may ask, "Why can't the courts stop this?" But again, the question of fact as to whether the police are lying, or whether the evidence was properly obtained, is often close. If it is a close question and a judge finds that the police did not tell the truth, then—given the exclusionary rule—a murderer or rapist will be released. As a result, when in doubt a judge will say, "Maybe they are telling the truth." The hydraulic effect is at work here as well.

Of course, the standard liberal response to this argument is to question how the police can be controlled in the absence of a robust exclusionary rule. "Without the rule," they say, "how can there be anything to stop the police from invading privacy?" These scholars often point to history in arguing that the lack of an exclusionary rule would result in little or no protection for privacy rights. They contend that though perhaps the rule does not work very well, it is better than anything else. And, of course, there is a lot to be said for this position because—aside from the exclusionary rule—most, if not all, of the suggestions for controlling the police in this area simply do not work.

…Currently, absent the exclusionary rule, there are almost no incentives for the police to be good actors, and in the absence of such incentives, teaching and preaching are not going to have much of an effect. Another standard suggestion often made by conservatives is to punish the police officers individually. Though such punishment, if it were imposed, might well prompt the police to refrain from unreasonable searches, there is a fundamental incentive problem with this solution as well. Who is going to tell us that the police did something wrong if there is no incentive for a defendant to report what happened? Why should a criminal accuse the police of engaging in misconduct, and thereby incur the possible wrath of the police, unless he has something to gain from it?

More sophisticated people such as Akhil Amar have suggested that tort suits may resolve this problem. It is true that, nominally, the tort regime does include the right incentives for the detained criminal to make known police misconduct. The criminal receives the tort verdict, and the misbehaving cop can thereafter be punished.

There are, however, two major problems with using tort law in this manner. The bigger problem is that it does not take into account how juries actually work in tort cases. The reason that tort suits—that great American pastime—work the way they do in most civil cases is because juries identify with the plaintiff. They see the plaintiff as someone like themselves and consequently decide in favor of the plaintiff.

Jurors are considerably more reluctant to identify with a criminal defendant who brings a tort action against the police for violation of his rights. In these cases, the plaintiff is a criminal and the jurors do not see themselves in that way. Of course, the mechanism works a little bit better when the illegal search was of innocent people. Even there, however, the jurors tend not to identify with the people searched. All too often, jurors think those people are the sort likely to be criminals even if they have not committed a crime in the case at hand. Hence, they view the plaintiffs as different from themselves. The result is that plaintiffs bringing tort actions against the police often fail to get jury verdicts.

*   *   *

So, in the words of that celebrated "scholar" Lenin, "What is to be done?" Well, I have my own half-baked solution to the exclusionary rule problem. One of the things I have noticed as a judge is that even when people have been sentenced to thirty or forty years in jail, they fight desperately to get two points down on the sentencing guidelines. Now at first, I wondered why the difference between a jail term of thirty-five years and one of forty years mattered so much to somebody. After further thought, I realized that many of the people who are sent to jail are sexually active people in their early twenties. The difference between getting out at my age and getting out at Judge Walker's age may be very significant indeed. As a result, the possibility of moving a few points down on the sentencing guidelines may act as a strong incentive for criminal defendants to argue that evidence was improperly obtained.

Let us consider a system where questions about the propriety of evidence could be raised after the trial's conclusion and the defendant's conviction. At that point, there would be no incentive for the prosecutor to charge more *ex ante*. At the same time, the convicted defendant would have a real incentive to argue that evidence was improperly introduced. Under such a system, there would be a hearing at which the court would determine whether the evidence was obtained wrongfully through negligence, gross negligence, or wanton and willful behavior. On that basis, a judge would come down two, three, or four points on the sentencing guidelines. (I am not interested in the calibration of the numbers themselves at this point. That is something to be worked out later, namely, by figuring out what "price" suffices to provide the right incentives.)

If this system were instituted, I think defendants would readily report any improper collection of evidence. While judges may be tempted to place a thumb on the scale in the context of criminal punishment, just as they are tempted to do in the context of admitting evidence and testimony at trial, the effect is counteracted by the fact that many judges find even the sentences at the lower end of the existing sentencing scale to be more than adequate. Because the sentencing guidelines are so severe, judges are not unduly worried about whether a criminal goes to jail for thirty-five years as opposed to forty. As a result, I do not think that the thumb on the scale would operate anywhere near as strongly in the sentencing area as it does when the issue is the suppression of evidence.

*   *   *

Though such a system gives defendants an incentive to inform courts about police misconduct, it still provides little deterrence for potential bad actors in law enforcement. But this can be readily cured. One could imagine a system that punished individual policemen when it was discovered that the cops had acted with negligence, with gross negligence, or willfully and wantonly. If the search or seizure was simply negligent, the punishment might be very slight. If the police behavior was grossly negligent, the punishment might be greater. If there was an intentional wrong, the penalty might be much more severe.

Again here, I am not interested in the calibration. But I do believe that by pairing an automatic police punishment with a sentencing procedure that provides an incentive for criminals to disclosure police misconduct, we would have a system that would be far more effective in controlling the police than anything we have now, or would have even with a mechanism based on tort suits combined with multipliers. This is especially so because my suggested approach addresses a major incentive problem with the use of tort damages, which, as Peter Schuck pointed out in his book on suits against the government, are usually paid by a totally different part of the government than that for which the "wrongdoer" works.

Similarly, this approach addresses a major problem with the use of the exclusionary rule: excluding evidence fails to affect the "cowboy" cop very much. The cowboy has gathered the evidence, arrested the criminals, and received all the publicity: "I've caught the perps. I did my job, and then these crazy judges let the person out." That the criminal was let off does not greatly deter the cowboy, who will be affected only by a punishment that is directed specifically at him.

*   *   *

Part III

THE FUTURE OF THE FOURTH AMENDMENT

Chapter 7

THE FOURTH AMENDMENT AND NEW TECHNOLOGIES

INTRODUCTION

The world as we know it today looks a lot different from the world known to the Framers of the Fourth Amendment. Advances in technology have enabled the government and private parties to compile vast amounts of information about where we shop, what we like to eat, which movies we like to watch, and where we travel. New technologies make it possible to record every keystroke one types on one's computer. New technologies enable airport screeners to "see" what is underneath one's clothing without requiring a strip search. Whether and how the Court should deal with the intrusions on privacy that accompany the advent of new technologies is the subject of this chapter.

In "The Fourth Amendment and New Technologies: Constitutional Myths and the Case for Caution," Orin S. Kerr argues that legislatures are better equipped than courts to respond to intrusions of privacy resulting from technological advances. Kerr suggests that courts should therefore defer to legislatures when it comes to dealing with privacy concerns regarding rapidly changing technologies. In "A World without Privacy: Why Property Does Not Define the Limits of the Right against Unreasonable Searches and Seizures," Sherry F. Colb argues that Kerr offers a false choice between courts and legislatures. Colb argues that courts should not defer to legislatures, but should work in tandem with legislatures to protect individuals from privacy intrusions caused by technological advances.

In addition to the question of which institutional actor is best equipped to deal with these questions is whether sufficient attention is being paid to the significant constraints on liberty brought about by the government's use of new technologies. In "Paradigms of Restraint," Erin Murphy warns that courts are overlooking the significant threat to liberty posed by technological measures such as GPS tracking bracelets, biometric scanners, online offender indexes, and DNA databases. Murphy argues that while physical incapacitation of dangerous persons has always invoked some measure of constitutional scrutiny, virtually no legal constraints circumscribe the use of technologies to achieve similar goals.

In *Kyllo v. United States*, 533 U.S. 27 (2001), the Court addressed whether the use of a thermal imaging device aimed at a home constitutes a "search" within the meaning of the Fourth Amendment. Acknowledging that the degree of privacy secured to citizens by the Fourth Amendment has been affected by advances in technology, the *Kyllo* Court held that "obtaining by sense-enhancing technology any information regarding the interior of the home that could not otherwise have been obtained without physical 'intrusion into a constitutionally protected area' constitutes a search at least where (as here) the technology in question is not in general public use." *Id.* at 34.

In "Peeping Techno-Toms and the Fourth Amendment: Seeing Through *Kyllo*'s Rules Governing Technological Surveillance," Christopher Slobogin critiques the *Kyllo* decision. Slobogin argues that making Fourth Amendment protection turn on whether or not a given technology is in general public use threatens to erode privacy protections as new sense-enhancing technologies become more readily available to the public.

In "Discretionless Policing: Technology and the Fourth Amendment," Elizabeth E. Joh proposes the use of technology to deal with the problem of racial profiling discussed in chapter 5. Joh suggests that the government should increase the use of automated enforcement mechanisms such as speeding cameras, red-light cameras, and factory-installed transponders in cars that record all occurrences of speeding. Given the attractiveness of such technologies to municipalities seeking an easy source of revenue, Joh's proposal should be carefully examined by those concerned with increasing intrusions on the privacy of motorists.

THE FOURTH AMENDMENT AND NEW TECHNOLOGIES: CONSTITUTIONAL MYTHS AND THE CASE FOR CAUTION

ORIN S. KERR

* * *

In the context of the Fourth Amendment, technological change often upsets preexisting associations between law enforcement investigative steps and their privacy implications. Some new technologies make preexisting forms of surveillance more intrusive; others have the opposite effect....

Consider the following example: A police officer stands on the public street outside a home and tries to peer inside, hoping to collect clues of criminal activity. How much can he learn about what is going on inside? The answer depends heavily on existing technologies. At a basic level, corrective eyeglasses may allow the officer to see through the windows of the home more clearly. Give the officer a flashlight, and he will be able to peer into the house through a window at night. Let the officer use an infrared imaging device, and he will be able to see a thermal image of the exterior of the home. Give him a shotgun microphone, and he may be able to hear communications

230

inside. All of these new technologies allow the officer to gather more evidence than before.

The dynamic works both ways, of course. People inside the home could take defensive measures against each of these technologies. For example, they could close the shutters or use tinted windows to block the flashlights and glasses. They could use thermal insulators to defeat the thermal imager. They could use soundproofing or white-noise generators to counter the shotgun microphone. All of these technologies block the surveillance. How much information can the police officer glean about the house from the public street? It depends on the technologies in use by both the police and the targets of the surveillance.

*   *   *

The social importance of technologies can also change as related technologies develop. The public telephone provides an interesting example. In the 1960s, public telephones provided a vital means of communication for many Americans. *Katz v. United States* gave this role constitutional significance: in support of the Court's conclusion that the Fourth Amendment protected Charles Katz while he used the pay phone booth, the Court added a single line of explanation: "To read the Constitution more narrowly is to ignore the vital role that the public telephone has come to play in private communication." Perhaps the Court did not mean this literally; perhaps it is rhetorical fluff. But if taken at face value, it would create a serious question as to the continuing vitality of *Katz*. The reason is that public telephones no longer play a vital role in private communication. The pay telephone has been largely eclipsed by the cell phone. Since the mid-1990s, over 100 million Americans have purchased cell phones, and the number of public telephones in the United States has dropped by more than 30%. Existing pay phones are used about half as much today as they were in 1996. As a *Chicago Tribune* headline recently announced, "Pay Phones May Go the Way of Dinosaurs." The Supreme Court could reasonably declare the public telephone "vital" in 1967; today it could not.

These examples highlight how technological change complicates the creation of Fourth Amendment–like rules. The privacy implications of a rule at one time may be quite different from the implications of the rule at another time. The rules are based on often-unstable assumptions, and the law's challenge is to respond to the changing facts. The question is, which branch of government is best equipped to respond to these difficulties? Legislatures or courts?

C. THE CHALLENGE OF EX POST DECISIONMAKING

Courts and legislatures generate rules of criminal procedure in somewhat different ways, subject to different constraints....I will sketch the three basic differences critical to a comparison of the institutional competence of courts and legislatures in this context: ex ante versus ex post decisionmaking, flexibility, and the information environment of judicial versus legislative rules.

The first difference is that legislatures typically create generally applicable rules ex ante, while courts tend to create rules ex post in a case-by-case fashion. That is, legislatures enact generalized rules for the future, whereas courts resolve disputes settling the rights of parties arising from a past event. The difference leads to Fourth Amendment rules that tend to lag behind parallel statutory rules and current technologies by at least a decade, resulting in unsettled and then outdated rules that often make little sense given current technological facts.

Consider the hurdles that must be overcome before the courts resolve how the Fourth Amendment applies to a new technology. Because the Fourth Amendment applies only to actual searches, not to technologies that merely have the potential to conduct searches, courts generally cannot pass on how the Fourth Amendment applies to a technology until long after a technology has been introduced. For a trial court to address the Fourth Amendment implications of a technology, the technology must be used by the government in the course of investigating a criminal offense; the use of the technology must yield evidence of a crime; it must lead to an arrest; and then it must lead to a constitutional challenge requiring judicial resolution. Appellate decisions come only much later. Because plea agreements usually require a defendant who pleads guilty to waive a right of appeal, and the overwhelming majority of cases end in a plea, appellate decisions come only in the rare case in which a defendant has been convicted at trial and then appeals, or else signs a conditional plea allowing an appeal. When an appeal is heard, it is usually decided more than a year after the initial trial court's decision. Very few appeals lead to published, precedential opinions. Even if the issue does lead to a published decision of an appellate court, Supreme Court review is not likely; the Court hears only about 80 or 90 cases a year. If the Supreme Court does agree to resolve the case eventually, it is likely to happen several years after the circuit courts have first addressed the issue.

The history of Fourth Amendment law reflects this gap. The Supreme Court first considered the Fourth Amendment implications of wiretaps almost six decades after the invention of the telephone. Pen registers were in widespread use by the 1960s, but the Supreme Court did not pass on whether their use violated the Fourth Amendment until 1979. Even today, no Article III court at any level has decided whether an Internet user has a reasonable expectation of privacy in their e-mails stored with an Internet service provider; whether encryption creates a reasonable expectation of privacy; or what the Fourth Amendment implications of the "Carnivore" Internet surveillance tool might be. The technologies exist, and in the case of encryption and e-mail, are used by millions of Americans everyday. But no one really knows how the Fourth Amendment applies to them.

*   *   *

Legislative rules are different. Legislatures can act at any time, even when a technology is new.... [R]ecent history suggests that legislatures usually act at a surprisingly early stage, and certainly long before the courts. For example, while the courts have not yet decided how the Fourth Amendment protects stored e-mails, Congress enacted a comprehensive regime to protect the privacy of e-mails *in 1986* in the form of the Electronic Communications Privacy Act. Congress regulated the privacy of e-mail before most Americans had even heard of e-mail. Similarly, Congress enacted laws to regulate the "Carnivore" Internet surveillance system in 2001 before any Fourth Amendment challenges were raised to its use.

*   *   *

D. THE NEED FOR FLEXIBILITY
IN LIGHT OF CHANGING FACTS

A second difference between judicial and legislative rulemaking concerns their operative constraints. Judicial rulemaking is limited by strong stare decisis norms that limit the ability of judicial rules to change quickly; in contrast, legislatures enjoy wide-ranging discretion to enact new rules. The difference favors legislatures when technology is in flux because the privacy implications of particular rules can fluctuate as technology advances. To ensure that the law maintains its intended balance, it needs mechanisms that can adapt to technological change. Legislatures are up to the task; courts generally are not. Legislatures can experiment with different rules and make frequent amendments; they can place restrictions on both public and private actors; and they can even "sunset" rules so that they apply only for a particular period of time. The courts cannot. As a result, Fourth Amendment rules will tend to lack the flexibility that a regulatory response to new technologies may require.

The statutory framework that governs Internet privacy demonstrates the flexibility and creative potential of legislative approaches. Congress enacted the Electronic Communications Privacy Act ("ECPA") in 1986 to regulate the privacy of Internet communications. Since that time, Congress has amended the framework no less than eleven times.... [L]egislative rules can impose creative and flexible regulatory regimes involving new technologies. For example, Congress opted to regulate both public and private parties to best protect privacy. This would be difficult if not impossible under the Fourth Amendment, which regulates only the government and private parties acting on the government's behalf. But ECPA recognizes that private parties acting on their own can pose a serious threat to Internet privacy: if America Online can look through the e-mails of its 30 million subscribers and disclose the evidence to the police without restriction, this would gut Internet privacy protections. The Fourth Amendment does not restrict this disclosure, but ECPA does: in addition to restricting the ability of law enforcement to order private ISPs to disclose communications to law enforcement, the law also restricts the ability of private ISPs to disclose communications to law enforcement voluntarily.

*   *   *

It is far harder for the courts to adopt such flexible rules under the Fourth Amendment.... To allow the governing rules to change as needed over time, courts would be forced either to expressly change the governing rules at regular intervals or else articulate the governing rule using a standard that keeps the result unclear to incorporate changed circumstances. Stare decisis norms make the first option unrealistic; it's hard to imagine the courts creating new rules every few years to keep the law up to date. But the latter option leads to intolerable uncertainty....

We can see the challenge of changing facts in Justice Scalia's effort to craft a rule for sense-enhancing devices in *Kyllo v. United States*. Justice Scalia recognized the key difficulty: thanks to technological change, use of a particular sense-enhancing device might seem objectionable in one era but routine in another. He thus tried to craft a rule that would apply across time, producing different results at different times. Recall the Court's holding in that case: "[w]here...the Government uses a device that is not in general public use, to explore details of the home that would previously have been unknowable without physical intrusion, the surveillance is a 'search' and is presumptively unreasonable without a warrant." Notably, this rule does not mean that the warrantless use of devices such as thermal imagers directed at the home necessarily violates the Fourth Amendment; rather, the devices will violate the Fourth Amendment *until they enter "general public use."* At some point in the future, thermal imaging devices will likely come into widespread use: they are increasingly used as non-contact thermometers by hobbyists, electricians, and mechanics, and can be purchased on-line for $40. But how can anyone determine when the use of a thermal imaging device is in "general public use" so that the government can use one without a warrant?

*   *   *

E. THE JUDICIAL INFORMATION DEFICIT

The third important difference between judicial rules and legislative rules relates to the information environment in which rules are generated. Legislative rules tend to be the product of a wide range of inputs, ranging from legislative hearings and poll results to interest group advocacy and backroom compromises. Judicial rules tend to follow from a more formal and predictable presentation of written briefs and oral arguments by two parties. Once again, the difference offers significant advantages to legislative rulemaking. The task of generating balanced and nuanced rules requires a comprehensive understanding of technological facts. Legislatures are well-equipped to develop such understandings; courts generally are not.

*   *   *

Up to now, I have focused on the institutional advantages of legislatures over courts. I now turn to the institutional advantages courts may offer over legislatures. Commentators have pointed out two primary advantages of judicial rulemaking in new technologies. The first advantage is that courts can regulate interstitially, making cautious judgments on a case-by-case basis. The second advantage derives from public choice theory; it posits that we cannot trust legislative rules to serve the public interest because legislatures can be captured by special interest groups that engage in rent-seeking....

Consider the argument that the interstitial, case-by-case nature of judicial rulemaking is well-suited to regulate new technologies. Much of the scholarship in this area focuses on applying law to the Internet. Professor Lessig suggested in an early article that "the meandering development of the common law" will lead to the best rules for Internet law.... In contrast, legislative solutions will tend to impose a single approach that will often prove a poor fit for the problem.

* * *

I find this argument persuasive in a civil law context, but not in the context of criminal procedure. The case-by-case approach necessarily leaves questions open, and therefore leaves the law uncertain. While this may facilitate bargaining in the civil context, there is no analogous benefit for criminal procedure. Police officers and suspects do not normally negotiate over the rules the police will follow. Either the police will take certain investigative steps or they won't; it is their decision to make based on existing law, not the suspect's. As a result, interstitial rulemaking that leaves the rules unclear lessens the clarity of the limits on the government's powers to invade privacy, underdeterring police behavior in some contexts and overdeterring it in others. Legal uncertainty may be a benefit in the civil context, but in the criminal context rule-uncertainty is a liability.

* * *

The insights of public choice theory also have only limited force in the context of criminal procedure rules. Public choice theorists have noted that legislative decisions are often influenced by rent-seeking, efforts by interest groups to lobby the government to enact rules that benefit the group at the expense of the public. In contrast, judicial decisionmaking is generally more independent, which in theory can lead to better rules. While these insights have considerable merit in many contexts, they have relatively little force in the context of criminal procedure rules. Privacy and security may be considered public goods, shared equally by the public.... Governments seek reelection from the public, not greater profits: their interest generally lies more in satisfying the public than in fleecing them.

* * *

But what if majoritarian preferences are insufficiently protective of privacy? Donald Dripps has argued that courts must intervene in the area of criminal procedure because statutory criminal procedure rules tend to create intolerable results: in Dripps's words, legislatures "don't...give a damn about the rights of the accused." Dripps argues that legislatures cannot create privacy-protective criminal procedure rules because most voters identify themselves as the potential victims of crime rather than its perpetrators. While those who tend to be targeted by the police as suspects may want greater restrictions on law enforcement, those groups tend to be relatively politically powerless. Because politically powerful majorities are more concerned with making sure that criminals are caught, politicians have little to no incentive to protect the rights of the accused. In such circumstances, Dripps argues, we must rely on courts rather than legislatures to generate balanced rules.

There are two reasons to approach this argument with caution. First, Dripps offers only sparse evidence in support of his claim. Second, the dynamic Dripps observes may be true in some contexts but not others.... New technologies are often used disproportionately by politically powerful groups. Consider the case of the Internet and the "Digital Divide." The Digital Divide exists because use of computers and the Internet is more widespread among affluent white majorities than among minority groups.... [M]any criminal investigations involving new technologies will tend to target users of new technologies. Such users generally will be able to represent their interests before Congress effectively, resulting in a healthy debate and relatively favorable conditions for balanced legislative rules.

* * *

A WORLD WITHOUT PRIVACY:
WHY PROPERTY DOES NOT DEFINE THE LIMITS OF THE RIGHT AGAINST UNREASONABLE SEARCHES AND SEIZURES

SHERRY F. COLB

Imagine for a moment that it is the year 2020. An American company has developed a mind-reading device, called the "brain wave recorder" ("BWR"). The BWR is a highly sensitive instrument that detects electrical impulses from any brain within ten feet of the machine. Though previously thought impossible, the BWR can discern the following information about the target individual: (1) whether he or she is happy, sad, anxious, depressed, or irritable; (2) whether he or she is even slightly sexually aroused; (3) whether he or she is taking any medication (and if so, what the medication is); (4) if a female subject, whether she is pregnant; (5) whether he or she is experiencing a feeling of guilt or remorse; and (6) whether he or she is having aggressive impulses toward another person or persons. At this stage in its development, we do not know whether or not the BWR will advance beyond detection of this information and whether or not it will become generally available to the public. It is currently a technology that belongs exclusively to the government and to extremely wealthy private collectors.

Under Professor Orin Kerr's provocative and interesting thesis, federal or state police could use the BWR on innocent people without implicating their Fourth Amendment rights against unreasonable searches and seizures. To be more concrete, if, for example, the police were to utilize the BWR to determine whether John Doe—a man who neighbors say seems "strange" and doesn't "fit in"—feels sexually aroused when he is in the presence of women, the man could not complain of an invasion of any Fourth Amendment reasonable expectation of privacy.

On Kerr's analysis, while existing Fourth Amendment doctrine nominally protects normatively and empirically reasonable expectations of privacy, in practice, in almost all cases, the doctrine protects only property (in a broad and flexible sense, so that it includes rented spaces, for example) but not privacy.* Because the BWR reads Doe's internal state without physically trespassing on his property, the regulation of its use—as a matter of most of the case law—should be left to Congress. As a normative matter, Kerr proposes that the Supreme Court defer to Congress in the area of handling the privacy implications of evolving technologies.

The Supreme Court and other judicial bodies, according to Kerr, would have a difficult time understanding the mechanics of how the BWR works or the context in which it might be used, whether by private people or by law enforcement. Moreover, the courts would be unlikely even to reach the issue of how the Fourth Amendment applies to the BWR for many years after its appearance on the technological scene. Congress would therefore represent (and has historically represented) a better source of protection for our privacy from hi-tech government intrusion than the judiciary.

In one sense, the source of our privacy does not seem to matter very much. Most people would presumably want to be protected from the use of the BWR, particularly when the government lacks probable cause or some other articulable basis for suspecting the individual targeted. But if we were effectively protected from such intrusion, then the fact that it was Congress

---

*In a part of his *Michigan Law Review* article not reprinted in this book, Kerr argues that the Fourth Amendment largely protects property, not privacy. Orin S. Kerr, "The Fourth Amendment and New Technologies: Constitutional Myths and the Case for Caution," *Michigan Law Review* 102, no. 801, 809 (noting that the "reasonable expectation of privacy" in Fourth Amendment law is not the same as the privacy that a reasonable person would expect, but is largely tied to property law concepts).

doing the protecting rather than the courts would probably not make much of a difference in people's lives. Indeed, most Americans probably do not even know—when they think about particular privacy rights—whether those rights exist as a matter of statutory or constitutional law.

The question for courts, however, and for those like Professor Kerr and myself who study the constitutional law of criminal procedure, is not whether robust privacy protection from Congress is somehow better or worse than what courts can provide. The appropriate question is whether courts have (and whether they ought to have) an obligation to apply the Fourth Amendment to new technologies that could invade privacy without physically trespassing on anyone's private property. Kerr answers this question no, and I answer it yes.

*   *   *

II. NORMATIVE INQUIRY

Normatively, Kerr poses the critical Fourth Amendment question presented by new technologies as involving a choice between judicial protection of privacy and congressional (or state legislative) protection of privacy. Kerr argues that because Congress has so far done a good job of protecting privacy in the area of technology, and because the judiciary has tended to fall behind the curve in protecting privacy (for various institutional reasons), Congress is a sensible repository for our trust in securing privacy, while the judiciary is not.

Yet Kerr offers a false choice between courts and legislatures. Judicial protection of Fourth Amendment privacy from technological intrusion hardly bars similar or additional protection by Congress.... Having two separate government bodies protecting privacy, moreover, does not create conflict, because the roles of the two branches are distinct from each other. It is the courts' job to interpret the Fourth Amendment right against unreasonable searches and seizures. By contrast, Congress may extend protection beyond that covered by the Constitution as a matter of majoritarian preferences.

To be sure, there would be the potential for conflict if the Court systematically overprotected privacy. In those circumstances, as a matter of constitutional law, Congress could not "correct" the Court's errors through ordinary legislation. Kerr's arguments, however, (which I find persuasive on this point) indicate that where the Court errs it will typically err in underprotecting privacy. In those circumstances, Congress can generally provide supplemental protection without any conflict.

*   *   *

Furthermore, and perhaps more importantly, from a practical perspective, Congress does not (as the Court does under the Fourth and Fourteenth Amendments) have the authority to regulate the behavior of state governments without an affirmative grant of power. The Commerce Clause is one such affirmative grant, but not all state and local threats to privacy would trigger application of the Commerce Clause. Thus the Fourth Amendment (as incorporated through the Fourteenth Amendment) could be a crucial source of authority for congressional privacy legislation.

Kerr is correct to suggest that Congress can achieve a great deal by regulating private actors, such as banks and internet service providers, because they are often the source for law enforcement's acquisition of technologically created private material. Congress can regulate *them* as actors in interstate commerce. But when... technologically educated employees who work for the police... invade individuals' privacy in technologically advanced ways, Congress may not have the power to protect privacy from such invasions.

Perhaps most fundamentally, Kerr's argument that Congress alone should be entrusted with protecting privacy because it does a better job than the Court when new technologies are involved is a non sequitur. If in fact the Fourth Amendment provides a constitutional right to privacy, then the Court has an affirmative obligation to apply that right to new contexts.... The Supreme Court and lower federal courts, in other words, are charged with the responsibility of saying what the Constitution means and applying it to factual scenarios presented by litigants. If Congress does a smashing job of protecting privacy, then litigants will have recourse to legislative *and* constitutional arguments when they appear in court. But the availability of one kind of protection does not and should not preclude the availability of the other. To refuse to enter into the thicket of Fourth Amendment rights against new technologies, in other words, would be an abdication of the courts' responsibilities.

*   *   *

PARADIGMS OF RESTRAINT

ERIN MURPHY

Everybody understands, or at least has a glimmering understanding of, what it means to go to jail. Whether from popular media or personal experience, most people imagine imprisonment as the strongest and most singular instrument of state power. And who, accordingly, would not trade nearly anything to avoid incarceration? Faced with a choice between prison and house arrest, global positioning system (GPS) tracking, or even public humiliation, who would not choose any—or even all—of the latter? But reconsider that trade-off when detailed more precisely: for instance, one day in jail versus having to fill out a form at a government office downtown after every hairstyle change or car rental; one week in jail versus a lifetime of GPS tracking; or one month in jail versus never being able to reside in or visit—for any reason—any major American city. Suddenly prison may no longer seem the state's only means of restricting liberty that merits serious consideration.

Physical incarceration has long served as the primary means of incapacitating persons found guilty of committing criminal offenses. Not surprisingly then, it is a power checked and monitored in multifarious ways; a litany of enumerated, entrenched procedural rules circumscribes the use of incarceration as a punitive sanction for wrongdoing in the American legal system. Of course, a criminal conviction is not the only lawful means by which the state imprisons individuals. The state also has at its disposal an array of civil measures for preventive incapacitation of "all of those whom we know (or think we know) to pose a danger of serious harm to others," including commitment of the mentally ill, certain illegal immigrants, pretrial defendants, violent sexual predators, and terrorist suspects. Although fewer rules circumscribe the "civil" or "regulatory" forms of physical incapacitation, in many cases the standards closely approximate those required for penal sanctions.

But if penal incapacitation constitutes the first system of social protection and civil regulatory incapacitation the second, then a third system is emerging—the preventive state has become a technological one. The dawn of the twenty-first century witnessed an explosion in technologies such as GPS tracking bracelets, biometric scanners, online offender indexes, and DNA databases—all adopted as a means of controlling and regulating a particular subset of the population without exerting physical control. Technology permits the government to physically track large numbers of persons in real time; to prove conclusively which person wore a hat or took a sip from a discarded soda can; to electronically zone an individual into or out of designated spaces, or perhaps even to isolate and identify a single face in a ten thousand-person crowd. Regulation of the dangerous, in a technologically advanced society, has become as much about keeping a person out of a place as it used to be about locking a person up in one.

But whereas a rich debate explores the potential for abuse of physical incapacitation, whether as a matter of criminal sanction or "regulatory" control, a corresponding dialogue surrounding the risks posed by nonphysical, technology-based means of control is conspicuously lacking. Essentially no legal structures superintend the use of noncorporeal means of incapacitation, even though their use raises many of the concerns manifest in the use of physical restraints, and even as the advent of technological alternatives has diminished the government's need to rely on conventional forms of incapacitation.

The purpose of this Article is to examine the generally unheeded intersection of two well-documented trends: the state's increasing desire to preventively regulate specified individuals and its increasing ability to use innovative technologies, rather than physical incapacitation, to realize that desire. Many scholars have observed that the government and private entities routinely collect and store large quantities of data about individuals in society. But none have focused on the concerns unique to the use of technological means of exercising control over *specified* persons or populations, in particular those deemed by the state to be "dangerous," in order to regulate or control them.

*   *   *

III. FOUR PHYSICS OF THE NONPHYSICAL WORLD

*   *   *

Technological restraints on liberty characteristically present as substitutes for their physical world counterparts. A typical assessment is that technological advances simply hone otherwise ordinary physical mechanisms and thereby render them more efficient, more accurate, and less intrusive. In this view, the electronic bracelet is the less restrictive alternative to the jail cell or on-site surveillance, the DNA sample or biometric scan a more accurate alternative to the fingerprint or eyewitness, and the online record the more efficient alternative to its paper and file counterpart. Rather than question every fan at the ballpark, officers can sit unobtrusively on the sidelines with their facial scanner or DNA swab. Rather than go downtown to retrieve cumbersome paper documents, an officer can just scan an image remotely or a suspicious neighbor can simply run a web search online.

But technologies of restraint do not simply provide more efficient means to the same end. Technology alters—rather than just mechanizes—the relationship between the individual and the state. By way of illustration, consider a recent study of toll rate changes on the interstate highway system. The researcher found that toll rates increased 20-40 percent on thoroughfares that have adopted electronic toll collection systems, like FasTrak or E-ZPass, when compared to those that still relied on manual collection. She offered the simple explanation that hidden costs are easily hiked costs—automating the activity of toll collection rendered it not just quicker and more efficient, but in fact changed the nature and salience of the tax imposed. Anecdotal observations provide additional support for the idea that technology changes, rather than simply optimizes, such relationships. In San Francisco, FasTrak users have specially designated lanes that allow them to pass through timed traffic lights (aimed at regulating signals) at a more rapid pace. In central Florida, new highway construction presumes that drivers have Sun Pass systems and relies upon sensors on a bar over the highway to collect tolls; to pass through an actual toll booth to pay with cash, drivers must exit into lanes alongside the regular travel lanes (akin to rest stops). Technology, then, does more than just make traveling with FasTrak more efficient—it also makes traveling without it more cumbersome. By comparison, a no-fly database and iris scanning device may mean that some innocent persons will never be intrusively searched at the airport again, but it also may mean that other innocent persons will *always* be subjected to such searches.

These dynamics of highway travel may very well provide insights into the dynamics of noncorporeal incapacitation of dangerous persons. The constraints of the physical world serve as a major curb on the power of the punitive state. A police department faces a wide range of enforcement options and cannot pursue them all; it must task its officers to those assignments perceived most critical. The same limitations confront the correctional system; already the jails and prisons are bursting at the seams. Most ordinary citizens do not worry about the police tailing them or sifting through their curbside trash or peering in their windows—not because the law prevents the police from engaging in such activity, but because simple economics prohibit it from occurring on a wide scale. Resource constraints impose priorities on the exercise of the police power, which in turn curbs excess and abuse. The same constraints restrain private acts of vigilance: many people may have an interest in the criminal histories of all their neighbors, but absent some certain benefit in making the task a priority, they simply will not expend the time and energy necessary to figure it out.

The efficiency gains of technological restraints upset these expectations. The economics of the virtual world, although not cost free, are far less prohibitive. Fewer choices must be made. A GPS tag can generate more information about identity or location on far more individuals than a fleet of officers on the beat. It is much simpler to run DNA samples in a database than to pound the pavement looking for witnesses. A camera affixed near a government landmark can generate far more hits when linked to a database than can a police officer monitoring the same traffic by sight. An online web search or registry can offer up more information in a couple hours than could be obtained the old-fashioned way in a couple weeks.

In short, the economics of technological control enable the regulation of greater numbers of persons under less stringent conditions for a longer period of time and to a greater degree than an equivalent physical intrusion. Even setting aside the capacity to cumulate restraints,... any single technique of restraint can operate far more pervasively, and reach far more extensively, than its physical-world analogue.

Yet because courts ignore the impediments of the physical world, they likewise ignore the "net widening" that is enabled when its constraints are lifted. Appraising the impact of a technological restraint by comparing it to a physical analogue, when the physical world does not dictate the economies of its use, undervalues its potential effect on liberty. To return to the examples given at the start of this Section: the face-scanned ballpark attendees could not all have been individually interrogated—they would have been left undisturbed unless they aroused some suspicion. The net-savvy neighbor never would have gotten around to going downtown to check the records in the first place. The crime scene eyewitness would not have been able to identify every cup from which the suspect sipped or the names of family members, including the suspect's previously unknown biological father. The GPS-tracked individual would not have otherwise gone to jail, but rather would have remained wholly free.

Compare, however, the Supreme Court's assessment of the harm wrought by the online posting of sex offenders' biographical information. The Court, analyzing the intrusiveness of the posting, declared that "[t]he record in this case contains no evidence that the Act has led to substantial occupation or housing disadvantages... *that would not have otherwise occurred* through the use of routine background checks." The Court further reasoned that the process of searching online "is more analogous to a visit to an official archive of criminal records than it is to a scheme forcing an offender to appear in public with some visible badge of past criminality." In assessing the harm, therefore, the Court dismissed as insignificant the possibility of any change in the likelihood or frequency of intrusion; the analysis centered instead upon whether the intrusion could have occurred in the absence of the technology. In the Court's own words, online registration simply "makes the document search more efficient, cost effective, and convenient"; it did not affect the very meaning of the act of retaining a criminal record.

Yet reducing the difficulty of obtaining such records by placing them online dramatically increases the likelihood, frequency, and scope of their access, and in turn dramatically alters their impact. The Internet is open twenty-four hours. It requires no bus fare, no plane ticket, no copy card. It has no lines, or clerks on lunch break. A virtual file cannot be checked out or lost as readily as it can in the real world. And a database can be "trolled" and "fished" for information interminably, whereas the same fishing expedition done in person would likely incur the wrath of everyone else in line as well as the staff.

The "visit to an official archive," in contrast, would likely include all of these impediments. The sheer inconvenience of obtaining paper records thus imposes a de facto screening mechanism: only those individuals deeply invested in obtaining particular information in fact gain access to it. In removing these impediments, the government changes the very meaning of its record keeping. A technically "public record," filed away in a drawer in a clerk's office, is simply not identical to the same record—in terms of its pub-licity—posted online. Whether a record is kept in a drawer at a registry, posted all over town on billboards, or placed on a website largely dictates its publicity—not the label placed on it by law.

*   *   *

This myth that technological restraints simply optimize the conditions of the physical world, rather than enable greater degrees of intrusion, in turn often serves to legitimize a second misconception—that technological restraints are always preferable to physical ones. That is, even assuming that technological restraints did apply only in circumstances identical to a physical-world coun-terpart, they still would not necessarily effectuate an equal, much less smaller, deprivation. Naturally, if asked which is worse, targeted technological surveil-lance or full-fledged incarceration, few would dispute that surveillance pres-ents the less offensive option. Many people may prefer a year under electronic monitoring to a year in jail, or providing a DNA sample or biometric image for search and storage in a national database to being brought in for questioning.

Rephrase the question as a choice between one day of incarceration and a year of intensive technological surveillance, however, and choosing the least offensive option may appear more complicated. Many people would likely trade a year in jail to avoid a lifetime ban from their hometown or the indelible stigma of public registration. And most people would likely accept the possibility that the police may confront them if there is an individualized suspicion of involvement in criminal activity rather than voluntarily con-tribute their biological and biometric samples to a government database so that they can be routinely ruled out as a suspect. There is a value in not having to engage with government officials on a prolonged or regular basis that may, in certain circumstances, transcend even the value of personal physical liberty. Indeed, it is not for nothing that some defendants actually prefer a jail term to probation, or that most people dread engaging government bureaucracies over even the most rudimentary of tasks such as securing a driver's license or picking up a package at the post office.

*   *   *

IV. "DIFFERENT CONSTITUTIONAL PRINCIPLES": NEW PARADIGMS OF LIBERTY AND RESTRAINT

*   *   *

Most observers of the criminal justice system agree that legislatures, and to some extent executive branch officials, have become too punitive towards criminals and too complacent in regulating invasive policing. But a significant body of work—mainly concerning the proper scope of the Fourth Amendment—disputes whether the current state of criminal justice can be…cured by close judicial oversight.

*   *   *

This controversy has played out even more robustly in the specific context of judicial supervision of new technologies. Typically, the conversation centers on how broadly the Fourth Amendment should regulate claims related to investigative policing. Some scholars urge increased judicial oversight in light of the aggressive assault on privacy that such technologies represent. Others suggest that new technologies constitute particularly poor candidates for such review both as a descriptive and normative matter because courts are poorly positioned to assess emerging issues and lack the flexibility to adapt readily to unanticipated situations.

Rather than rehash the well-trodden paths carved out by these debates, this Section aims to anticipate and counter the primary arguments that might particularly arise in the context of judicial regulation of targeted technological restraints. Specifically, critics might contend that the determination to impose civil regulatory restraints, and the scope of their application, should be left to the legislative branches, which are better situated in terms of accountability, flexibility, and competence. After all, technology has suspended conventional notions of liberty and privacy for every member of society, not just those labeled "dangerous." In a world filled with Google searches and street cameras, as well as publicly available mortgage and professional disciplinary information, the presumptive cloak of anonymity has been lifted from daily life....

But regardless of whether wisdom counsels special attention to the use of invasive technology against the general population, technological regulations that are targeted in nature constitute distinctly strong candidates for judicial attention. General society, however beset by technological intrusions, retains some democratic power to reclaim a measure of its liberty—whether through the wallet or the ballot box. By contrast, targeted technologies specifically isolate particular subgroups, thereby diminishing the probability of effective democratic safeguards.

*   *   *

Some scholars have commented that the capacity of technologies to concentrate their impact constitutes an improvement over the bluntness of the police power when wielded in its physical forms. This line of argument claims that technology allows intrusive policing to focus acutely on suspicious areas or individuals, which in turn decreases the amount or degree of intrusion that the general populace must endure. A checkpoint in the park aimed at identifying sex offenders is inconvenient and unnerving, but most park visitors will not even notice that the park ranger has installed a camera that links to a database of known sex offenders and will sound an alert when one walks into the park. The same can be said for no-fly lists or DNA collection or GPS devices. After all, if technology can identify those persons in the security queue that have suspicious histories or backgrounds, then the rest of the passengers can get through the airport with far fewer insults to their dignity or time-management needs.

But because targeted restraints, by their nature, affect only a discrete and insular minority—typically, convicted or accused criminal offenders, and those misfortunate enough to share those offenders' names or facial structures—they leave the majority of the body politic undisturbed. Thus, even if, as some argue, a collection of "potential criminal suspects" or "potential government targets" might be able to generate some measure of political clout, no equally powerful constituency protects the isolated subgroup. The harm and inconvenience of the technology will truly be visited only upon those few (innocent or guilty) who find themselves repeatedly picked out of the crowd by law enforcement on the basis of a selectively applied technique. That number, inevitably, will be far smaller than the larger political constituency likely necessary to rally against such invasive uses. And the remainder of the population, even if they can imagine falling under government suspicion, may find the very targeted nature of such methods to be proof of their general efficacy and enjoy the benefit that freedom from generally applicable measures provides.

In addition, to the extent that the targeted groups are largely comprised of once convicted criminal offenders, they likely reflect the least politically powerful group in every imaginable respect. Many previously convicted persons have been extirpated quite literally from the body politic through mandatory disenfranchisement statutes. The vast majority were poor when they entered the criminal justice system and are unlikely to have gained financial stature upon exiting. Even the very fact that these technologies can zero in on particular groups may increase the societal stigma they suffer, further diminishing their political salience. It is hard to imagine a constituency eager to coalesce under the banner of the Registered Sex Offenders Political Action Committee. And even if one did, it is harder still to imagine such a group carrying much political sway.

Moreover, even if targeted groups were able to surmount the handicap of their countermajoritarian posture, the unaccountability and invisibility that characterize technological restraints make the exercise of democratic power an all the more unlikely means of cabining their use. Ordinary policing already contains a fair amount of "low visibility discretion" that is difficult to regulate—an officer patrolling the highway chooses which of many speeding cars to stop, or which of many offenders to arrest and charge.

Technological restraints pose even greater obstacles. A person detained is indisputably material; the state's action is difficult to hide or obscure. But individuals under surveillance may not even know that their liberty has been compromised. No alert sounds when a name is entered into a computer-records search, database, or online index. The 70,000 fans at the so-called

Tampa snooperbowl undoubtedly rooted for their teams without feeling any sense of personal intrusion. Even the nineteen innocent fans questioned might not have known why they were singled out, or had much by way of recourse for their troubles. Bluntly stated, it is a lot easier for the government to obscure the existence—much less the contents—of a government database than it is a physical prison. And because technological restraints emanate from so many different sources of state authority, even a vigilant individual may not know where, or how broadly, to look. If the population at large is simply unaware of a measure, it is less capable of organizing politically to regulate it.

It might be argued that this lack of awareness reflects the negligibility of the harm. Yet just because you did not know that your zipper is down does not mean that your privacy was not compromised when everyone saw your underpants. More importantly, although the throngs of fans at the ball game may not feel any ill effects, the nineteen individuals stopped on that occasion—and perhaps stopped every time they attend the game or board a plane or drive on a highway—unquestionably suffer a harm. Yet the ability of technology to isolate them from the masses, and singularly visit the harm on that minority, renders them politically less powerful.

*   *   *

Lastly, it is worth noting that to the extent that new technologies may be difficult to grasp due to their technical nature or fast-changing quality, those concerns are outweighed by the particular expertise of courts in dealing with questions of state power and due process. Although courts may not be the optimal branch for understanding the nuances of a technology's operation, they remain the preferred locus for checking governmental, particularly majority-driven, overreaching and abuse. Whereas deference to legislative and executive judgments on the use and deployment of new technologies might be warranted when such measures apply indiscriminately across the population, such deference is inappropriate when the state acts against the targeted few in the name of the safety of the many.

*   *   *

PEEPING TECHNO-TOMS AND THE FOURTH AMENDMENT: SEEING THROUGH *KYLLO'S* RULES GOVERNING TECHNOLOGICAL SURVEILLANCE

CHRISTOPHER SLOBOGIN

In *Kyllo v. United States*, the Supreme Court struck a blow for the sanctity of the home, in an age when technology threatens to destroy it. This Article wonders whether *Kyllo* is a pyrrhic victory.

Prior to *Kyllo*, the majority of lower courts had held that use of a thermal imaging device to detect heat sources within a house is not a Fourth Amendment search, either because the heat waves detected by such devices are "abandoned" and do not require physical intrusion to discern, or because they are too impersonal to warrant privacy protection. In *Kyllo*, the Supreme Court rejected these rationales, and concluded that the government may not mechanically measure the warmth of the home unless it demonstrates probable cause for doing so. The Court's decision could also be read to say that most other scientifically enhanced investigations of the domicile are searches as well, and thus might indicate a desire to put significant restrictions on *all* technological surveillance of our most private sanctuary.

252

If so, the ruling is a good one. But the Court left at least one loophole in its decision, a loophole that could potentially be quite significant. Its precise holding stated that "[w]here, as here, the Government uses a device *that is not in general public use*, to explore details of the home that would previously have been unknowable without physical intrusion, the surveillance is a 'search.'" As the dissenters in *Kyllo* rightly pointed out, varying Fourth Amendment regulation of technology on the prevalence of that technology is troublesome, because "the threat to privacy will grow, rather than recede, as the use of intrusive equipment becomes more readily available."

Much depends on how the Court defines "general public use." One might be comforted by the majority's insistence (indeed, it was "quite confident") that, despite its availability from over half a dozen national companies, the type of thermal imaging device at issue in *Kyllo* is not in general use. As this Article will document, however, today's marketplace offers a wide array of much cheaper enhancement devices, easily bought over the Internet and from nationwide chains and specialty shops. The march of progress guarantees that this trend will accelerate. Thus, the dissent's caution in *Kyllo* should be taken seriously.

*   *   *

Despite the number of cases mentioning the issue, the general public use concept remains amorphous.... [A] number of courts seem to believe that flashlights and binoculars, and perhaps night scopes as well, are in general public use. The Supreme Court has indicated that airplanes (in navigable airspace) and mapmaking cameras are as well, but that thermal imagers and (probably) beepers are not. But no court has put forth a more general definition of the concept.... [T]he case law provided above suggests three basic definitions, each of which is itself divisible into two or more versions.

The first basic definition focuses on whether the technology in question is "*generally available* to the public"—the language found in *Dow Chemical.* "Generally" means "usually" or "as a rule," while "general" means "applicable to the whole." "Available" means "accessible" or "obtainable," or "ready for immediate use." On these understandings, a generally available item is one that all or virtually all members of the public are able to obtain. Taken literally, this definition would exclude much surveillance technology, except perhaps the cheapest flashlights. It would certainly not encompass mapmaking cameras or low-flying airplanes, suggesting that this is not the definition the Court would endorse.

Moving to a broader definition . . . , general availability could be construed to mean that the item is available to a substantial portion of the public. Under this definition, indicia of general availability might be the number of items manufactured, the cost of the item, and the number of outlets carrying it. More colloquially, this definition could be dubbed the "Wal-Mart test." If the item is available at Wal-Mart, it is likely to be affordable to and accessible by a large segment of the public.

Clearly flashlights are generally available in this sense. They are usually inexpensive (a high-beam version comes as low as $8.00, batteries included), and can be purchased at nationwide stores such as Wal-Mart, K-Mart, and Target, as well as numerous local stores. Binoculars are not as prevalent, but are still relatively cheap, ranging from $9.00 for a pair with a magnification capacity of 4 (4×) to $55.00 for binoculars with 12× power.

*   *   *

What might be somewhat surprising is that Wal-Mart also offers inexpensive versions of highly powerful telescopes and night vision equipment. The Tasco Luminova Telescope costs only $59.87 and has a magnification power of 578. The Night Owl Light Night Vision Monocular costs only $129.87, has infrared capacity, and has a magnification power of 3.1×.

*   *   *

A second, less expansive basic definition of the general public use concept adheres more closely to the words in that phrase: How often does the public *use* a particular type of technology? Generally available items may not be commonly resorted to. For instance, although most of the aforementioned devices are obtainable by a sizeable portion of the public, their use is quite varied; people rely on flashlights all the time, binoculars and zoom lenses somewhat less frequently, and telescopes and night vision equipment less frequently still.

At the same time, all of these items are everyday paraphernalia to certain segments of the population, and are relied upon at least as frequently as low-flying airplanes in carrying out certain types of endeavors. Birdwatchers, sports fans, and hunters make avid use of binoculars. Tourists and loving families focus their zoom lenses on a daily basis. Telescopes are a favorite of stargazers, and night vision devices are popular with hunters. . . .

That observation leads to a third basic definition that is even narrower—general public use *for a particular purpose*. Most of these devices, even if generally available and used by large segments of the public, are not usually used the way police use them. In particular, they are probably not normally employed to look into homes or curtilage.

As the Court demonstrated in [*Florida v.*] *Riley*, there are several versions of this approach as well. A plurality of justices in that case (including Justice Scalia, author of *Kyllo*) adopted what might be called a "positivist" approach, finding the fact that planes could legally fly within 400 feet of the ground dispositive of the issue of whether observation of curtilage from that height was a search. This stance, as the *Riley* dissent pointed out, in essence asserts that "the expectation of privacy is defeated if a single member of the public could conceivably position herself to see into the area in question without doing anything illegal."

The other five Justices took an "empirical" approach to that issue. Justice O'Connor, in a concurring opinion, concluded that if overflights at 400 feet are "rare," then they should be considered searches even though technically in navigable airspace (although she ended up deciding they were *not* rare in this particular area, and thus joined the plurality in finding that no search occurred in *Riley*). The four dissenters in *Riley* fine-tuned the empirical approach further, asking whether overflights at 400 feet for the specific purpose of *observing the contents of residential backyards* are rare, and deciding that they were exceedingly so.

*   *   *

DISCRETIONLESS POLICING:
TECHNOLOGY AND THE FOURTH AMENDMENT

ELIZABETH E. JOH

What if we could eliminate police discretion from traffic stops? What if a computer could accomplish what police officers do, with efficiency and accuracy, and more importantly, without racial prejudice? How would this technology work? Would its use be consistent with the Fourth Amendment? And if constitutional, would the public accept this automated enforcement? Could the war on drugs continue, once traffic stops became discretionless?

These are not just hypothetical questions, at least not for long. This Essay proposes a solution to the problems associated with police discretion in traffic stops that originates neither in constitutional law nor in politics, but in technology. Both the technology and a plan to automate law enforcement exist, yet neither has received serious attention.

In a recent but little-known decision, the Federal Communications Commission established technical standards to make this automation possible. The federal government's Intelligent Transportation Systems initiative proposes a future where all cars use wireless technology to communicate with devices

256

embedded in the road and with other cars. Vehicles would exchange data such as the car's location and speed, as well as problems with the car's mechanics or registration. Currently, policymakers advocate the use of this technology, also known as "dedicated short-range communications" (DSRC), because it will have important safety benefits. Car manufacturers support DSRC because it will provide a means for drivers to purchase goods and services while on the road. Yet this little-known technology demands the attention of criminal procedure scholars, as DSRC could also revolutionize how the police interact with drivers by permitting remote and automatic enforcement of the traffic laws, thereby reducing or eliminating traffic stops by the police.

*   *   *

Largely unchecked by the Court, the problem of police discretion—particularly in the practice of traffic stops—has generated attention from two groups of commentators. Concerned about the impact of police discretion on minority communities, commentators like Tracey Maclin and David Harris have called for the reinterpretation of the Fourth Amendment so that it provides more detailed limitations on when, why, and how the police conduct stops, arrests, and searches.

These scholars join an earlier generation of commentators who have discussed the strains that unbridled police discretion places on a democratic society. These scholars of the police, including Kenneth Culp Davis and Joseph Goldstein, have demanded political and administrative solutions that focus on changing the culture of police organizations. Administrative guidelines that spell out *ex ante* constraints on police discretion and attitudinal changes within the insular world of police culture are essential, they have argued, to actual changes in police behavior on the street.

*   *   *

It may seem far-fetched to suggest that technology could offer a real solution to a problem that has captured the attention of academic lawyers for fifty years. But in April 2005, the United Arab Emirates announced a contract with IBM to install smart-box technology, similar to DSRC systems, in cars sold in that country. Beginning in 2007, United Arab Emirates law will require every car owner to have an in-vehicle smart-box that communicates information about a driver's speed and triggers the automatic issue of a traffic ticket. In addition, automated law enforcement in one form or another is already an accepted practice in Europe, Asia, and even in the United States. The very existence of other programs premised on the idea of automated enforcement counters objections that automated traffic stops are the stuff of fantasy.

Because no one has written about the potential changes to police discretion that could result from new technology, we lack a thorough assessment of DSRC technology, including the relative merits of automated enforcement. Yet the effects of a widespread automated enforcement regime would be dramatic. Traffic stops are often pretextual, a means for discovering evidence of other crimes unrelated to the justification for the initial stop. Thus, if traffic stops were eliminated through widespread automated enforcement, the nature of policing could be drastically different.

*   *   *

To fully understand how an automated system could eliminate the traffic stop, one must possess some familiarity with a federal plan dating back fifteen years. Congress directed the Secretary of Transportation to "promote the widespread use and evaluation of intelligent vehicle-highway systems technology as a component of the Nation's surface transportation systems" by passing the Intermodal Surface Transportation Efficiency Act of 1991. The Department of Transportation selected the Intelligent Transportation Society of America (ITSA), a nonprofit association comprised of local governments and private companies, to serve as its Federal Advisory Committee on the development of intelligent highway technology.

*   *   *

...According to an ITSA Ten Year Vision statement, all new cars would contain factory-installed on-board units connected to the cars' internal sensors and controls. These units would communicate information such as driver location and speed to roadside units embedded in public roadways. Both public agencies (such as local transportation agencies) and private companies (such as gas stations, hotels, and restaurants) would be able to communicate with cars. These onboard units would also communicate with similar units installed in other cars, regardless of manufacturer; they would help to avoid collisions and to increase fuel efficiency by permitting platooning of vehicles, or controlling several vehicles together.

*   *   *

What does this mean for the average driver? Your new car would come equipped with a transponder, or onboard unit, linked to your car's controls. Reducing car accidents is the formal objective of the program, but the incentive to install the necessary equipment on new cars stems from these devices' potential to provide the private sector with a new marketplace. Factory-installed onboard units will permit location-specific advertising, on-demand entertainment, and electronic payment for gas and other consumer services.

Roadside units would be embedded along the roads at regular intervals to receive from passing cars information such as location and speed. A DSRC-enabled car would have the capacity to warn you of sudden moves from other cars; aid in driving around curves; issue an in-vehicle "Amber Alert"; permit rapid clearance across the Mexican or Canadian border; provide instant local traffic data; transmit information about your "electronic license plate"; and request a car with a particular identity to respond. And more importantly for present purposes, a DSRC-enabled car would also permit automated law enforcement of the vehicle code.

*   *   *

Not only is a comprehensive automated enforcement program possible, but we have already had limited experience with its use. In 1993, New York City became the first American city to install photo radar to catch red-light violations. Typically, photo radar works as follows. Sensors embedded in the roadway close to an intersection record the speed of cars traveling over them. If that car exceeds a preset minimum speed while the light is red, a camera at the intersection takes at least one, and sometimes two, pictures to record the car's license plate. Technicians review the photographs for clarity and send the registered owner of the car copies of the photographs and a citation. American cities have been slow to widely adopt a technology that has been available since the 1960s and has been used in Europe since the late 1970s. One recent estimate identified the use of photo radar for red-light enforcement in only eighty cities in twenty states.

Nor is automated enforcement limited to the public sector. A recent case from the Connecticut Supreme Court discussed the speed enforcement policy of American Car Rental, Inc., which installed a GPS device in each of its cars in order to record each car's speed and location. Rental agreements with the company included the following statement: "Vehicles driven in excess of [seventy-nine miles per hour] will be charged a $150 fee per occurrence. All our vehicles are GPS equipped." Whenever the GPS device recorded an 'occurrence' of driving more than seventy-nine miles per hour for two minutes or longer, the device would transmit the car's location and speed to a third-party vendor that would, in turn, send the information to American Car Rental for a fee assessment.

Thus, the use of DSRC to catch speeders, reckless drivers, and tardy registrants is less remarkable for its replacement of humans by machinery than it is for its potential scale.

*   *   *

Critics of programs like the Intelligent Highways Initiative worry that the privacy interests of citizens will be intruded upon. In a basic sense, simply collecting massive amounts of data on driving habits infringes our autonomy or the ability to make decisions and to retain a sphere of private activity free from surveillance. Once that data is amassed, legitimate concerns arise regarding the potential for personal information misuse by the government or private actors, beyond the official purposes of any formal traffic management or policing program.

*   *   *

Privacy is likely only one reason for public rejection. We might also interpret this rejection as a default preference for human enforcement. Ronald Clarke, criminologist and former head of the British Home Office Research and Planning Unit, is an expert on the use of situational crime prevention techniques that include automated enforcement. Clarke is puzzled over this reluctance: "[p]erhaps all these devices offend people's sense of fair play. People have to be given a sporting chance of getting away with crime, especially the ordinary everyday offenses that all of us might commit." The existence of discretion, and therefore the possibility of its abuse, may be a cost people are willing to assume in order to break some traffic laws. Reliance on traffic law enforcement by the police ultimately reduces the certainty that any one person will be caught for violating the law. Yet the prevalence of that preference, which is ultimately a claim to escape enforcement of the law, does not justify its acceptability.

Alternatively, perhaps a legitimate objection would arise not out of people's sense that they deserve a chance to break the law, but rather from their view that there is a meaningful distinction between technical legal violations, and abiding by the purpose for which the laws exist. Traffic laws exist to make illegal unsafe driving, a standard that is perhaps best judged by a person rather than by a machine.

*   *   *

Chapter 8

THE FOURTH AMENDMENT AND THE WAR ON TERROR

INTRODUCTION

After the 9/11 attacks on the World Trade Center and the Pentagon, Congress hastily passed the United and Strengthening America by Providing Appropriate Tools Required to Intercept and Obstruct Terrorism Act of 2001 (aka the USA PATRIOT Act), which significantly expanded the United States government's power to collect private information about innocent Americans in the name of protecting national security. The Bush administration implemented a policy that allowed governmental agents to search without any particularized suspicion the contents of a traveler's laptop, camera, cell phone, or other electronic device when crossing a US border. It used the federal material witness statute to indefinitely detain individuals suspected of being terrorists or of knowing terrorists. It implemented a controversial regulation allowing prison officials to listen in on and record conversations between inmates and their attorneys. It also increased the use of National Security Letters, a device that allows the government to obtain information about terror suspects from Internet providers, phone companies, banks, and credit reporting agencies without a warrant or prior judicial approval. The events of 9/11 gave the Bush administration the impetus and the public support to implement or expand the use of these and other measures of questionable constitutionality. The excerpts in this chapter address several of these measures, illustrating the ways in which the ongoing War on Terror has resulted in serious intrusions on the privacy interests of American citizens.

In "The System of Foreign Intelligence Surveillance Law," Peter P. Swire provides a primer on FISA, the Foreign Intelligence Surveillance Act. Swire explains how FISA, which governs wiretaps for foreign intelligence, came into being and how the procedures of FISA differ from the procedures of Title III, the federal statute that governs domestic wiretaps. Both FISA and Title III require the government to obtain a warrant before engaging in wiretapping activity, but it is much easier to obtain a FISA warrant than a Title III warrant. For example, to obtain a Title III wiretap warrant, the government must demonstrate that it has probable cause to believe the target of the wiretap has committed or is committing a criminal offense. For a FISA warrant, the government only needs to show it has probable cause to believe the target of the wiretap is a foreign power or agent of a foreign power. Swire also explains how the PATRIOT Act impacted foreign intelligence security law. The PATRIOT Act not only made it easier for government officials to obtain FISA warrants, it also significantly expanded the scope of National Security Letters.

In "Protecting the Unpopular from the Unreasonable: Warrantless Monitoring of Attorney Client Communications in Federal Prisons," Teri Dobbins considers the Fourth Amendment implications of a 2001 federal regulation authorizing the monitoring of communications between inmates and their attorneys upon reasonable suspicion that the inmate may use such communications to further or facilitate acts of terrorism. In contrast to most of the critique of this regulation, which has centered on how the monitoring regulation undermines the attorney-client privilege and violates the Sixth Amendment right to counsel, Dobbins argues that the attorney-inmate monitoring regulation also implicates Fourth Amendment concerns.

In "The Detention of Material Witnesses and the Fourth Amendment," Joseph G. Cook examines the use of the federal material witness statute to indefinitely detain possible terrorist suspects. Cook argues that absent probable cause to believe the individual has committed or is committing a crime, such detentions contravene the requirements of the Fourth Amendment.

In "The Cowboy and the Cop: The Saga of Dudley Hiibel, 9/11, and the Vanishing Fourth Amendment," Arnold H. Loewy suggests that 9/11 and the fear of another devastating terror attack explain the Court's 2004 decision in *Hiibel v. Sixth Judicial Court* to uphold the arrest and detention of a citizen for refusing to identify himself to a police officer. Prior to this decision, it was widely believed that an individual could not be punished solely for failing to identify himself to an officer. See, for example, *Brown v. Texas*, 443 U.S. 47, 53 (1978) ("appellant may not be punished for refusing to identify himself"). Included in the Loewy excerpt are Dudley Hiibel's reflections on this incident.

THE SYSTEM OF FOREIGN INTELLIGENCE SURVEILLANCE LAW

Peter P. Swire

*   *   *

Th[e] history of applying the Fourth Amendment and the rule of law to wiretaps is accompanied by a second history, that of using wiretaps and other surveillance tools to protect the national security. Consider the Cold War example of an employee of the Soviet Embassy. What should the standards have been for wiretaps of that employee, who might also be an agent of the KGB? A Title III wiretap would often be impossible to get, because there would be no probable cause that a crime had been or would be committed. Yet this potential or known spy plausibly posed a serious threat to national security. A wiretap might create extremely useful intelligence about the Soviet agent's confederates and actions.

*   *   *

During wartime especially, it is easy to see how the temptation to use "national security" wiretaps against spies and foreign enemies, even on U.S. soil, would be irresistible. The legal basis for such a national security power can be derived from the text of the Constitution. The President is named Commander-in-Chief of the armed forces, and domestic actions against foreign powers may be linked to military and intelligence efforts abroad.... Going beyond the text, the Supreme Court in 1936, in *United States v. Curtiss-Wright Export Corp.*, relied on the structure of the Constitution and the nature of sovereign nations to establish the "plenary and exclusive power of the President as the sole organ of the federal government in the field of international relations."

President Franklin Roosevelt, responding to the Second World War, was the first President to authorize wiretaps on national security grounds. The use of such wiretaps expanded during the Cold War. In 1967, in *Katz*, the Supreme Court declined to extend its holding to cases "involving the national security."...

The Supreme Court finally addressed the lawfulness of national security wiretaps in 1972 in *United States v. United States District Court*, generally known as the "*Keith*" case after the name of the district court judge in the case. The defendant, Plamondon, was charged with the dynamite bombing of an office of the Central Intelligence Agency in Michigan. During pretrial proceedings, the defendants moved to compel the United States to disclose electronic surveillance information that had been obtained without a warrant. The Attorney General submitted an affidavit stating that he had expressly approved the wiretaps, which were used "to protect the nation from attempts of domestic organizations to attack and subvert the existing structure of the Government." The United States objected to disclosure of the surveillance materials, claiming that the surveillance was a reasonable exercise of the President's power (exercised through the Attorney General) to protect the national security. Both the district court and the circuit court held for the defendant.

The Supreme Court unanimously affirmed.... [T]he Court expressly reserved the issues of foreign intelligence surveillance that are now covered by FISA: "[T]he instant case requires no judgment on the scope of the President's surveillance power with respect to the activities of foreign powers, within or without this country."

*   *   *

... The Court invited legislation: "Congress may wish to consider protective standards for... [domestic security] which differ from those already prescribed for specified crimes in Title III." The Court specifically suggested creating a different standard for probable cause and designating a special court to hear the wiretap applications, two invitations taken up by Congress in FISA.

*   *   *

At the level of legal doctrine, FISA was born from the two legal traditions discussed in Part I: the evolving Supreme Court jurisprudence that wiretaps required judicial supervision, and the continuing national security imperative that at least some foreign intelligence wiretaps be authorized. At the level of practical politics, FISA arose from the debate between the intelligence agencies, who sought maximum flexibility to protect national security, and the civil libertarians, who argued that the abuses revealed by the Church Committee should be controlled by new laws and institutions.

The clear focus of FISA, as shown by its title, was on foreign rather than domestic intelligence. The statute authorized wiretaps and other electronic surveillance against "foreign powers." These "foreign powers" certainly included the communist states arrayed against the United States in the Cold War. The definition was broader, however, including any "foreign government or any component thereof, whether or not recognized by the United States." A "foreign power" included a "faction of a foreign nation," or a "foreign-based political organization, not substantially composed of United States persons." Even in 1978, the definition also included "a group engaged in international terrorism or activities in preparation therefor."

*   *   *

The Act drew distinctions between U.S. persons and non-U.S. persons. The former consists essentially of U.S. citizens and permanent residents. Non-U.S. persons could qualify as an "agent of a foreign power" simply by being an officer or employee of a foreign power, or a member of an international terrorist group. The standards for surveillance against U.S. persons were stricter, in line with the Church Committee concerns about excessive surveillance against domestic persons. U.S. persons qualified as an "agent of a foreign power" only if they knowingly engaged in listed activities, such as clandestine intelligence activities for a foreign power, which "involve or may involve a violation of the criminal statutes of the United States."

In FISA, Congress accepted in large measure the invitation in *Keith* to create a new judicial mechanism for overseeing national security surveillance. The new statute used the terms "foreign power" and "agent of a foreign power" employed by the Supreme Court in *Keith*, where the Court specifically said that its holding applied to domestic security wiretaps rather than surveillance of "foreign powers." Instead of creating a special regime for domestic security, however, Congress decided to split surveillance into only two parts—the procedures of Title III, which would apply to ordinary crimes and domestic security wiretaps, and the special procedures of FISA, which would apply only to "agents of a foreign power."

A curious hybrid emerged in FISA between the polar positions of full Title III protections, favored by civil libertarians, and unfettered discretion of the executive to authorize national security surveillance, favored by the intelligence agencies. The statute required the Chief Justice to designate seven (now eleven) district court judges to the new Foreign Intelligence Surveillance Court ("FISC"). These judges had jurisdiction to issue orders approving electronic surveillance upon finding a number of factors, notably that "there is probable cause to believe that the target of the electronic surveillance is a foreign power or an agent of a foreign power." This probable cause standard looks to quite different facts than the Title III standard, which requires "probable cause for belief that an individual is committing, has committed, or is about to commit a particular offense" for wiretaps to be permitted.

FISA orders contain some, but not all, of the other safeguards in Title III. Both regimes require high-level approval within the Department of Justice, with the Attorney General having to give personal approval for FISA applications. Both regimes require minimization procedures to reduce the effects on persons other than the targets of surveillance. Both provide for electronic surveillance for a limited time, with the opportunity to extend the surveillance. Both require details concerning the targets of the surveillance and the nature and location of the facilities placed under surveillance. Both allow "emergency" orders, where the surveillance can begin without judicial approval subject to quick, subsequent approval by a judge.

As for differences, Title III gives discretion to the judge to refuse to issue the order, even where the statutory requirements have been met. Under FISA, however, the judge "shall" issue the order once the statutory findings are met....

The most important difference is that the existence of a Title III wiretap is disclosed to the subject of surveillance after the fact, in line with the Fourth Amendment requirement that there be notice of government searches. By sharp contrast, the FISA process is cloaked in secrecy. Targets of FISA surveillance almost never learn that they have been subject to a wiretap or other observation. The only statutory exception is where evidence from FISA surveillance is used against an individual in a trial or other proceeding. In such instances, the criminal defendant or other person can move to suppress the evidence on the grounds that the information was unlawfully acquired or the surveillance did not comply with the applicable order. Even in this setting the individuals have no right to see the evidence against them. The judge, upon a motion by the Attorney General, reviews the evidence in camera (in the judge's chambers) and ex parte (without assistance of defense counsel).

*   *   *

Finally, the text of the 1978 statute showed that the purpose of the FISA wiretaps was foreign intelligence rather than preventing or prosecuting crimes. The Church Committee and other revelations of the 1970s had shown that the FBI had used the risk of "subversion" and other potential crimes as the justification for investigating a vast array of political and other domestic activity. The 1978 statute therefore specified that the application for a FISA order certify that "the purpose of the surveillance is to obtain foreign intelligence information."

*   *   *

IV. THE PATRIOT ACT, THE NEW GUIDELINES, AND NEW COURT DECISIONS

The attacks of September 11 led to the greatest changes by far in FISA law and practice since its creation in 1978. This Part examines the statutory amendments in the Patriot Act, new Attorney General guidelines on foreign intelligence surveillance and domestic security investigations, and the first published decisions by the FISC and the Foreign Intelligence Surveillance Court of Review ("FISCR").

A. THE PATRIOT ACT

The Uniting and Strengthening America by Providing Appropriate Tools Required to Intercept and Obstruct Terrorism Act of 2001 ("Patriot Act") was proposed by the Bush administration one week after the attacks of September 11 and signed into law on October 26, 2001. Among the numerous changes in the law, the focus here is on three topics: the permission for FISA orders to have only "a significant purpose" of foreign intelligence; the use of FISA orders to get any "tangible object"; and the expansion of national security letters.

1. From "Primary Purpose" to "A Significant Purpose"

The 1978 law required the application for a FISA order to certify that "the purpose of the surveillance is to obtain foreign intelligence information." As discussed above, a number of circuit courts interpreted this language to mean that the "primary purpose" of the order must be to obtain foreign intelligence information. To ensure that the purpose of criminal law enforcement did not predominate, the "wall" was created between law enforcement and foreign intelligence investigations.

The Bush administration proposed that the text should change so that "a purpose" would be for foreign intelligence information. After debate in Congress, the Patriot Act finally provided that "a significant purpose" must exist in order to obtain foreign intelligence information. A separate provision emphasized that Congress wished to promote information sharing between criminal investigations and foreign intelligence investigations....

2. FISA Orders for any "Tangible Object"

Section 215 of the Patriot Act expanded the sweep of FISA orders to compel production of business records and other tangible objects. The original FISA had focused on electronic surveillance and had not created a FISA mechanism for the government to get business records. After the Oklahoma City and first World Trade Center bombings, Congress authorized the use of FISA orders for travel records only.

Section 215 contained two statutory changes that drastically expanded this power. First, the type of records subject to the order went far beyond travel records. Now the search can extend to "any tangible things (including books, records, papers, documents, and other items)." By its terms, the statute apparently would allow a FISA order to trump other laws that usually govern the release of records, including for medical records and other categories of records, that are generally subject to privacy protections.

Second, the legal standard changed for obtaining the order. Previously, the application had to show "specific and articulable facts giving reason to believe that the person to whom the records pertain is a foreign power or an agent of a foreign power." This standard, although less than probable cause, is relatively strict. The Patriot Act eliminated the need for any particularized showing. The application need merely "specify that the records concerned are sought for an authorized investigation . . . to protect against international terrorism or clandestine intelligence activities." What counts as an authorized investigation is within the discretion of the executive branch.

Under this change in the text, FISA orders can now apply to anyone, not only the target of the investigation. Previously, the records or other objects sought had to concern either a foreign power or the agent of a foreign power. Now, the FISA order can require production of records about persons who have nothing to do with a foreign power.

*   *   *

3. Expansion of "National Security Letters"

The Patriot Act significantly expanded the scope of the little-known tool of "National Security Letters" ("NSLs"). These are essentially the foreign intelligence corollary to administrative subpoenas for criminal investigations. Before the Patriot Act, NSLs allowed for access to certain records listed by statute, such as subscriber information for phone companies and Internet Service Providers and basic account information from banks and credit reporting agencies.

The amendments to NSLs track the changes in section 215. Previously, there was the same significant showing required for each record, that "there are specific and articulable facts giving reason to believe that the person or entity to whom the information sought pertains is a foreign power or an agent of a foreign power." The Patriot Act requires only that the records be "relevant" to an authorized investigation, and no longer requires that the target of the request be a foreign power or agent of a foreign power.

The Patriot Act broadened the sorts of investigations that qualify for NSLs for telephone and transactional records. Before, NSLs applied only to an "authorized foreign counter-intelligence operation." Now they apply to "an authorized investigation to protect against international terrorism or clandestine intelligence activities." The Patriot Act also lowered the level of official who could authorize an NSL. Previously, clearance had to come from a position of at least "Deputy Assistant Director." Now, a "Special Agent in Charge" in a bureau field office may authorize an NSL, without any clearance by FBI headquarters.

The expanded scope of NSLs likely deserves significant attention because they operate without the participation of a judge and individuals never receive notice that the records have been sought. Federal officials have stated that NSLs have become more common and been used at least "scores" of times since September 11. Moreover, the Bush administration has sought approval for the CIA and the Pentagon to use NSLs inside of the United States, without the participation of the FBI or the Department of Justice.

*   *   *

PROTECTING THE UNPOPULAR FROM THE UNREASONABLE: WARRANTLESS MONITORING OF ATTORNEY CLIENT COMMUNICATIONS IN FEDERAL PRISONS

TERI DOBBINS

* * *

Entitled "Prevention of Acts of Violence and Terrorism," 28 C.F.R. § 501.3 was promulgated in 1997, amending the existing § 501.... The rule allows the Bureau of Prison (BOP) Director to authorize the warden to implement special administrative measures upon written notice "that there is a substantial risk that a prisoner's communications or contacts with persons could result in death or serious bodily injury to persons, or substantial damage to property that would entail the risk of death or serious bodily injury to persons."

* * *

On October 31, 2001, the Attorney General published an interim rule and request for comments regarding amendments to § 501. One of the amendments was the addition of § 501.3(d).... Section 501.3(d) authorizes the Attorney General to order the Director of the BOP to monitor or review communications between inmates and their attorneys or their attorneys' agents if "reasonable suspicion exists to believe that a particular inmate may use communications with attorneys or their agents to further or facilitate acts of terrorism." According to the text of the rule, the purpose of monitoring is not to gather evidence of past crimes, but to deter inmates from committing future acts that could result in death or serious bodily injury. "Inmate" is defined broadly to include "all persons in the custody of the Federal Bureau of Prisons or Bureau contract facilities." This category includes not only persons charged with or convicted of criminal offenses, but also persons held as "witnesses, detainees, or otherwise." Thus, some of the persons subject to monitoring may not even be suspected or accused of criminal activity.

... [T]he monitoring regulation requires the Director to employ "appropriate procedures" for reviewing the communications for privilege claims and to ensure that "properly privileged materials" are not retained. Additionally, to protect the attorney-client privilege and to avoid compromising the underlying prosecution, a "privilege team" consisting of individuals unassociated with the underlying investigation will be designated to ensure that privileged material is not disclosed to the prosecution team. Unless the head of the privilege team determines that acts of violence or terrorism are imminent, no information gathered from monitoring may be disclosed to anyone without approval from a federal judge.

Finally, the government monitoring is not covert. Unless prior court authorization has been obtained, the Director must provide written notification to the inmate and the attorneys involved before monitoring begins. While the inmate and attorney have notice of the monitoring, the regulation does not provide any mechanism for challenging the determination that an inmate qualifies for monitoring under the standard set out in the regulation, nor does it provide for any judicial oversight of the monitoring or the procedures for protecting the attorney-client privilege.

Many prominent legal, law enforcement, human rights, civil liberty, and religious scholars and organizations submitted comments criticizing the new rule, arguing that it violates inmates' First, Fourth, Fifth, Sixth, and Fourteenth Amendment rights. Much of the analysis in subsequent comments, notes, and articles has focused on inmates' Sixth Amendment right to counsel, implications for the attorney-client privilege, and the chilling effect the rule may have on communications between inmates and their attorneys. Government officials defend the regulation as a valid and constitutional exercise of Executive authority that is necessary to ensure national security. However, the government's arguments in support of the regulation only address Supreme Court precedent regarding the Sixth Amendment rights of inmates. Thus, the presumption that the regulation is constitutional fails to consider whether inmates' Fourth Amendment rights are violated.

*   *   *

Obviously, inmates lose most of their privacy rights while imprisoned.... In *Hudson v. Palmer*, the Supreme Court held that inmates retain no reasonable expectation of privacy in their cells, and the government relies on this holding to support its assertion that inmates retain no Fourth Amendment rights at all. This assertion, however, greatly overstates the holding of *Hudson* and fails to take into account the reasoning behind the holding or the context in which it was decided.

*   *   *

... [T]he *Hudson* Court carefully limited its discussion to the reasonable expectation of inmates *in their cells*. Moreover, the Court's conclusion that no privacy right existed in prison cells was based upon prison officials' need for unfettered access to the cells to search for contraband. The Court did not address inmates' Fourth Amendment rights in relation to searches or seizures for purposes unrelated to institutional security.

*   *   *

Under the test set out in *Hudson*, a Fourth Amendment right to privacy must be established before determining the constitutional validity of a regulation. The proper inquiry is whether society is prepared to recognize a prisoner's expectation of privacy as reasonable when communicating with his or her attorney....

... [M]any state and lower federal courts have held that the right to privacy of communications is essential to the right to effective assistance of counsel. Many state regulations regarding inmate telephone calls, mail, or visits exempt communications with attorneys from the scope of authorized monitoring. Moreover, under BOP regulations, prison officials may inspect and read all correspondence, unless it is labeled "special mail" (which includes attorney-client communications); "special mail" may only be opened and inspected for contraband in the presence of the inmate to or from whom it is sent. Attorney-inmate conversations are also exempt from the routine monitoring of prisoners' telephone calls. Visits by attorneys must take place in an area that allows a "degree of privacy." Finally, "[s]taff may not subject visits between an attorney and an inmate to auditory supervision."

While the right to confidential attorney-inmate communications is usually associated with the Sixth Amendment right to counsel, the Fourth Amendment right to privacy also merits consideration. First, the Sixth Amendment right to counsel only attaches upon the initiation of a criminal prosecution. Consequently, material witnesses, persons arrested but not formally charged, inmates whose convictions are final and whose appeals are exhausted, and other detainees who have no Sixth Amendment right but who are subject to monitoring under the expansive definition of "inmate" under § 501.3(d), would not be able to challenge the regulation on Sixth Amendment grounds. Yet these persons may have as much—or greater—need to communicate in confidence with their attorneys.

The sensitive nature of the communication also makes recognition of a privacy right reasonable. Inmates have a strong interest in obtaining candid legal advice, not only regarding the circumstances that led to their imprisonment, but also respecting to personal issues that may arise while they are incarcerated; they must feel free to discuss potentially embarrassing or even incriminating facts. While the nature of information or activities that an individual seeks to protect is not decisive in determining whether a reasonable expectation of privacy exists, the Supreme Court has indicated that it may be a factor. The largely uniform case law and state and federal regulations exempting attorney-client communications from monitoring reflects recognition of the special and significant nature of these communications and the importance of confidentiality. This widespread acceptance of the confidentiality of such communications demonstrates that society has long recognized the right to private attorney-inmate communications as reasonable.

Society might find the right of privacy unreasonable in the wake of recent terrorist attacks if the government demonstrated that recognizing the right presented a threat to national security. However,... confidential communications between inmates and attorneys pose no greater risk than communications of suspected terrorists outside of the prison context. Both the Supreme Court and Congress have concluded that the threat to national security does not justify abandoning the Fourth Amendment warrant requirement. Moreover, the government has not articulated any reason why obtaining a warrant before conducting the monitoring would hinder the effort to deter inmates from using attorney-client communications to further terrorist plans. Because the recognition of this right does not unduly burden the government, or pose a threat to national security,... the Fourth Amendment proscription against unreasonable searches and seizures should apply to communications between inmates and their attorneys.

*   *   *

THE DETENTION OF MATERIAL WITNESSES
AND THE FOURTH AMENDMENT

Joseph G. Cook

In June 2005, Human Rights Watch and the American Civil Liberties Union published a lengthy report entitled *Witness to Abuse: Human Rights Abuses Under the Material Witness Law Since September 11.* The report began:

> Since the attacks on September 11, 2001, at least seventy men living in the United States—all Muslim but one—have been thrust into a Kafkaesque world of indefinite detention without charges, secret evidence, and baseless accusations of terrorist links. They have found themselves not at Guantá-namo Bay or Abu Ghraib but in America's own federal prison system, victims of the misuse of the federal material witness law in the U.S. government's fight against terrorism.

The law referred to is the federal material witness statute, which authorizes the arrest and detention of an individual whose testimony is material in a criminal proceeding. The statute is not a part of the U.S. Patriot Act, and that fact has probably prevented it from garnering too much attention. Quite to the contrary, it has been around, with but minor changes, for over two hundred years, first appearing in the Judiciary Act of 1789. Its ostensible purpose is to assure the availability of testimony of witnesses who might otherwise elude a subpoena.

* * *

In reality, however, today the law is used primarily for a different purpose, to wit: "to secure the indefinite incarceration of those [the Department of Justice] has wanted to investigate as possible terrorist suspects." Certainly it is open to question whether such use is even authorized by the statute. In any case, the use of the law has been accompanied by a broad range of constitutional abuses which have been cataloged by courts and commentators.

What has been neglected is the underlying assumption of the law, and that will be the focus of my remarks. That is, is the very act of arresting and detaining individuals who are not themselves charged with any criminal activity irreconcilable with the protection of the Fourth Amendment?

One might think that, given a two hundred year window of opportunity, questions regarding the constitutionality of the statute would have been fully explored and its validity beyond peradventure.... Upon close scrutiny, however, the assumption does not appear to be warranted.

The constitutionality of the practice has never been addressed by the Supreme Court, though many courts and commentators appear to think that it has. No lower court has ever elected to grapple with the question, or perhaps no litigants have ever forced any to do so. If we subject the practice of detaining material witnesses to a traditional Fourth Amendment analysis, there is little to be found in the way of supporting precedent. And if, being at a loss for viable precedent, we resort to a device occasionally used by the Supreme Court in cases of first impression—that is, determining those investigative practices recognized by the common law at the time of the American Revolution and labeling them reasonable by virtue of tradition—that too will fail to vindicate the law.

* * *

The Fourth Amendment provides that "[t]he right of the people to be secure in their persons, houses, papers, and effects, against unreasonable searches and seizures, shall not be violated, and no Warrants shall issue, but upon probable cause." It can scarcely be gainsaid that individuals who have been taken into custody and involuntarily detained ostensibly for the purpose of giving testimony, have been arrested. But to support an arrest, as opposed to something less than an arrest, the official making the arrest must have probable cause. Probable cause for an arrest was defined in *Beck v. Ohio* as "whether at that moment the facts and circumstances within their knowledge and of which they had reasonably trustworthy information were sufficient to warrant a prudent man in believing that the petitioner had committed or was committing an offense."... While the presence or absence of probable cause has frequently been a difficult decision, never has it been doubted that to make an arrest there must be reason to believe that the subject *had committed or was committing an offense.* When a material witness is taken into custody, by definition that is not the case. Indeed, one federal court has observed that "individuals detained as material witnesses are rarely charged with crimes" and described the plight of the detained material witness thus:

> With no charges lodged against them, material witnesses are held in custody for periods ranging from several weeks to several months. If the material witness were charged with a crime, he would be entitled to appointment of counsel if he was financially unable to afford one. The material witness is deprived of liberty without an opportunity to consult with counsel or to have his interests represented because he is not charged with a crime. Consequently, individuals that are incarcerated without being charged with criminal activity are afforded less protection than individuals charged with criminal activity.

*   *   *

When confronted with questions of first impression in interpreting the Fourth Amendment, the Supreme Court has on occasion examined the prevailing practices at the time of the ratification of the United States Constitution. The idea here is that the Fourth Amendment enjoins only those searches and seizures which are "unreasonable." If a particular investigative practice was accepted in England at the time of ratification, it might be assumed to be reasonable, or at least not prohibited, by the Fourth Amendment.

*   *   *

The answer, then, to the riddle of the detention of material witnesses might simply be resolved by the revelation that the practice was well-established in England during the colonial era. Indeed, in 1971, the Court of Appeals for the Ninth Circuit said precisely that. In *Bacon v. United States*, the court reassured the readers of its opinion that the detention of material witnesses was hardly extraordinary, because it was "consonant with the long established rule of English Law, in effect when the United States became a nation." To support this statement, the court cited a single English case that was decided in 1612. It would appear to be the only case cited by this or any other court for the long established rule of English Law. The intrepid academic who succeeds in tracking this one down among the dusty tomes in rarely visited library stacks may be excused for saying, "this better be a good one."

The case is styled the *Countess of Shrewsbury's Trial*, and this is her story: at apparently some time in the early part of the seventeenth century, one Lady Arabella Stuart married Sir William Seymour. Arabella was a first cousin of James I. She was a Catholic, and at one point, the Pope had a grand design for an arranged marriage that would put Arabella on the English throne. The plot failed, and James became firmly ensconced as monarch, but he remained apprehensive regarding her children having claim to the throne. To that end, he forbade the marriage of Arabella to William Seymour. They nonetheless were secretly married. In the words of the court reporter, "[b]eing a marriage with one so nearly related in blood to the king, and without his consent, it was deemed an offence [*sic*] against the royal prerogative, on which account lady Arabella and her husband were imprisoned; the former in a private house at Lambeth, the latter in the Tower." They both managed to escape and fled in separate ships to France, King James' men captured Arabella before she reached Calais, and she was returned to the Tower. She died there, never seeing William again.

Mary Talbot, the Countess of Shrewsbury, was Arabella's aunt. She was suspected of abetting this scheme, having prior knowledge of both the wedding and the escape. When called before the Privy Council, however, she refused to divulge any information. As a result, she too ended up in the Tower and was brought before a select council "charged with a high and great contempt of dangerous consequence." ...

The Countess of Shrewsbury proffered two arguments in her defense: (1) "she had made a rash vow that she would not declare anything in particular touching the said points; and for that (as she said) it was better to obey God than man," and (2) "[s]he stood upon her privilege of nobility." The court found both defenses unavailing, holding that "the countess by her allegiance was bound, without being demanded, to reveal to the king what she knows concerning the premises, upon which great mischief may happen to the king and the realm."

As is readily apparent, the *Shrewsbury* decision provides no support for the notion that the English common law recognized a power to detain material witnesses. The Countess of Shrewsbury was not a material witness; rather, she was a party "charged with a high and great contempt." While the charge against her arose out of her refusal to testify, the substantive charge of abetting the illegal marriage and escape of Lady Arabella arose prior to the time she was taken into custody.

For at least a half century prior to the trial of the Countess of Shrewsbury, the law of England authorized compelling the testimony of witnesses in criminal and civil cases. The Second Act of Phillip and Mary in 1555 empowered justices to bind over witnesses to give evidence against defendants in felony cases. And in 1562, the Statute of Elizabeth provided that in civil cases, any person who refused to testify after being served with process would be subject to a ten pound fine as well as damages for the harm caused to the aggrieved party. Under neither statute, however, was there any recognition of a power to detain witnesses in anticipation of their giving evidence.

*   *   *

... [T]oday the material witness statute is rarely used in other than terrorist-related investigations.... But the fact that the power is rarely used is far from reassuring. For if we accept the unchallenged assumption that the law is constitutional, it means upon a proper showing of risk, either (a) material witnesses in all cases may be detained indefinitely should federal prosecutors choose to use their power more liberally, or (b) the only parties at risk are material witnesses that match the profile of previously identified terrorists.

If the first reading is correct—if prosecutors have the constitutional right to detain any material witness upon no more of a showing than the prosecutor's averment that the witness will likely not honor a subpoena—then surely the practice deserves constitutional scrutiny. If, on the other hand, the law is only used as a weapon against terrorism, and only individuals who fall within a class of suspected terrorists are vulnerable, then there are different reasons to voice constitutional concern.

Over a half century ago, this country subjected a significant number of its citizens to involuntary internment for no reason other than their being of Japanese heritage. While that action was sustained by the Supreme Court, it is not a celebrated episode in American history.

*   *   *

THE COWBOY AND THE COP:
THE SAGA OF DUDLEY HIIBEL, 9/11,
AND THE VANISHING FOURTH AMENDMENT

ARNOLD H. LOEWY

Americans have had a longstanding traditional right to anonymity. The anonymous pamphleteer, for example, in addition to being a part of folklore, is engaged in a constitutionally protected activity. The right to wander aimlessly in the nighttime is also constitutionally protected. And, prior to June 21, 2004, the Supreme Court had never so much as hinted that the state could punish a person for refusal to identify himself in the absence of probable cause to arrest. In *Hiibel v. Sixth Judicial Court*, however, the Court held that a rural rancher/cowboy, lawfully parked by the side of the road, could be deemed a criminal simply for refusing to identify himself to a police officer, notwithstanding that he was guilty of no other crime.

In this essay, I shall explore how we came to reach such a legal climate; and, in the course thereof, ultimately focus on whether Dudley Hiibel was a victim of 9/11. And, if he was, are we all less free because of it?

*   *   *

II. WHAT HAPPENED

For Deputy Sheriff Lee Dove, the encounter began with a phone call from a known and reliable source. A man identified as Mr. Riddley had called to tell the police that he had seen a man and woman driving in a red and silver GM pickup truck on Grass Valley Road. The couple had been arguing, and the man, who was wearing a black cowboy hat, had hit the woman. Deputy Dove drove to the scene and spoke to Mr. Riddley, who confirmed his report. Deputy Dove then followed Grass Valley Road and saw a red and silver GM pickup truck parked by the side of the road. A woman was sitting in the passenger seat, and a man wearing a black cowboy hat was standing by the passenger side door smoking a cigarette. Deputy Dove stepped out of his car to investigate.

As far as Dudley Hiibel knew, the officer striding towards him was on routine patrol, perhaps concerned that his truck was parked too closely to the road. At the same time that Deputy Dove had been talking to Mr. Riddley, Hiibel and his daughter had been driving down the road arguing about a boy in town. Mr. Hiibel didn't like the boy, but his daughter Mimi had been seeing him against her father's wishes. Tempers were high and at one point Mimi, while driving the truck, struck her father on the shoulder out of frustration. Hiibel asked his daughter to pull the truck over. Once they were parked, he got out and lit up a cigarette to calm his nerves. He began speaking to his daughter again, when they were interrupted by the wail of a police siren. Unaware of the officer's purpose, and still concerned about his daughter in the truck, Dudley Hiibel cautiously greeted the officer walking towards him.

Fortunately, Deputy Dove's squad car was equipped with a video camera that captured the confrontation between Hiibel and Dove, and recorded Hiibel's ultimate arrest.... [The officer proceeded to arrest Hiibel after Hiibel refused to provide him with any identification.]

*   *   *

There undoubtedly are cases where obtaining the identity of a suspect would be relevant to dispelling or confirming a suspicion. For example, if a woman calls the police to say: "There is a man lurking in the bushes near my apartment. I'm afraid it's my ex-boyfriend, Albert Jones. I have a restraining order against him. I can't go out and look. He might kill me." Under those circumstances, ascertaining the man's name would be reasonably related to dispelling or confirming suspicion. Similarly, if a man is lurking outside of a schoolyard, ascertaining the man's name to check against sex offender lists would be reasonably related to dispelling suspicion. In cases like the ones just hypothesized, I am willing to assume *arguendo* that there would be no Fourth Amendment objection to arresting someone for failure to respond to an *appropriately explained* request for identification.

In this case, the reasonable suspicion was predicated upon an alleged assault on a female. Having found Hiibel by the side of the road and a young woman in the truck, one would have thought that the first step would be to ascertain the well-being of the female, not the name of the male. [Deputy Dove] could have observed the female to see if she had any injuries. He could have asked her if she had been attacked, and if either her affirmative response or the manner of her negative response led Deputy Dove to believe that she had been assaulted, he could have arrested her father. Had the officer done that, he would have learned that young Mimi Hiibel had not been assaulted and the whole matter would have been resolved.

Proper police citizen interaction is important. A brief detention on the basis of reasonable suspicion is an exception to the general rule of probable cause that we approved in *Terry v. Ohio*. We have always insisted, however, that the detention be no more intrusive than necessary. Besides being counterproductive to ascertaining the well-being of Mimi Hiibel, Officer Dove's demand for identification surely intruded on Dudley Hiibel's sense of security, privacy, and personal autonomy far more than any good that the deputy might have hoped to attain.

*   *   *

IV. RAMIFICATIONS OF THE CASE

In deciding *Hiibel*, the Supreme Court made no reference to 9/11. The Nevada Supreme Court in reaching the same conclusion, however, was not so subtle. As that court put it:

Most importantly, we are at war against enemies who operate with concealed identities and the dangers we face as a nation are unparalleled. Terrorism is "changing the way we live and the way we act and the way we think." During the recent past, this country suffered the tragic deaths of more than 3,000 unsuspecting men, women, and children at the hands of terrorists; seventeen innocent people in six different states were randomly gunned down by snipers; and our citizens have suffered illness and death from exposure to mail contaminated with Anthrax.... To deny officers the ability to request identification from suspicious persons creates a situation where an officer could approach a wanted terrorist or sniper but be unable to identify him or her if the person's behavior doesn't rise to the level of probable cause necessary for an arrest.

Although a tad more subtle, the United States Supreme Court view of the case is no less deadly to personal security. The Court, despite saying that the request for identification must be reasonably related to the stop, left little doubt there would never (or hardly ever) be a case involving reasonable suspicion in which identification would not be required.

*　　*　　*

What is perhaps most disturbing about *Hiibel*, particularly from the insights gained by watching the videotape of the incident, is that the case is more about police power than it is about victim or community safety. In that regard, it is first cousin to *Atwater v. Lago Vista*, a case decided just a few months before 9/11. In that case, Bart Turek, a policeman who pretended to be concerned with the safety of Atwater's unbelted children, arrested their mother, denied her the opportunity to make arrangements for her children, and drove Atwater to the police station in handcuffs and without fastening her seatbelt in the police car.

Similarly, in *Hiibel*, Lee Dove, supposedly concerned with the safety of young Mimi Hiibel, arrested her father despite her protests to stop. When Mimi exited the truck to try to assist her father, she was thrown to the ground, face first, and handcuffed by one of deputy Dove's colleagues.

*　　*　　*

V. HIIBEL IN HIS OWN WORDS

I conclude this essay with an editorial by Dudley Hiibel from the *Los Angeles Times*.

A lot of people want to know why I went all the way to the Supreme Court rather than give my name to a policeman. "What's so important about that?" they ask. "What's the big principle at stake?" And last week, when the Supreme Court ruled against me, maybe some thought I was foolish to have done it. But I still think I did the right thing and that there were some issues that had to be decided.

The story began on May 21, 2000, when I was on a rural road near my ranch in Winnemucca, Nev. My daughter and I had gotten into an argument. She was driving, and I was the passenger. We stopped by the side of the road, parked legally, and we continued our argument. I figured we would finish it out and then cool off for a moment.

That's when I heard sirens, and all of a sudden a police car drove up. A deputy walked up to me and demanded my "papers." I asked him what the problem was. "Why do you guys have me surrounded?" I asked, because by now there were two or three more police cars. He refused to explain why he was there or why he wanted my papers. Eleven times he demanded my identification. I refused to give it to him each time, and he finally handcuffed me and took me to jail. The cops threw my daughter on the ground, cuffed her hands behind her and demanded her name as well, but by that time I was on my way to the county jail. I got there at midafternoon and stayed overnight.

I hadn't been argumentative; I wasn't picking a fight. Basically, when Deputy Dove demanded my papers—and he didn't ask for them, he demanded them—I didn't say, "Hey cop, I'm not going to give you nothing." I just asked why he wanted them. "What have I done?" I asked. If he'd explained what he was doing there, perhaps it could have been settled on the spot. But his position was that he wanted the papers first.

Here's why this was so important to me: I don't believe that the authorities in the United States of America are supposed to walk up to you and ask for your papers. I thought that wasn't lawful. Apparently I was wrong, but I thought that that was part of what we were guaranteed under the Constitution. We're supposed to be free men, able to walk freely in our own country—not hampered, not stopped at checkpoints. That's part of what makes this country different from other places. That's what I was taught.

And it's not just because it's in the Constitution. It's something that you just kind of know. It's kind of obvious. If you haven't committed a crime, you shouldn't be harassed by the police. If they suspect you of something, I don't see why they shouldn't explain it. I wasn't violent. And it was proven later in court that I hadn't committed any crimes.

These days, it's like we're all guilty until proven innocent. You walk into an airport and everybody's a suspect. Like the way people were treated in Soviet Russia, in Red China, in Castro's Cuba.

We don't want the United States to become that.

*   *   *

Frankly, I believe that Dudley Hiibel's assessment of the law was superior to that of the five Supreme Court justices that ruled against him. It is sad commentary that a simple rancher/cowboy with an eighth grade education understands the intricacies of the Constitution better than the five elite lawyers that constituted a majority of the Supreme Court that ruled against him.

*   *   *

Chapter 9

NEW DIRECTIONS FOR THE FOURTH AMENDMENT

INTRODUCTION

As we have seen in the preceding chapters, much has been offered in the way of critique of the Supreme Court's Fourth Amendment jurisprudence. While critique is important and useful, it is equally important to think in terms of solutions. The excerpts in this chapter offer different perspectives on what should be done to improve the Court's Fourth Amendment jurisprudence.

In the first excerpt, "The Return of Reasonableness: Saving the Fourth Amendment from the Supreme Court," Melanie D. Wilson argues that juries should decide questions of citizen reasonableness, i.e., Fourth Amendment issues requiring a determination of how reasonable citizens think and behave, while the Court should decide questions of police reasonableness or questions requiring a determination of whether the police acted reasonably. Under Wilson's proposal, juries would decide whether a "seizure" within the meaning of the Fourth Amendment has taken place, as this question requires a determination as to whether the reasonable person in the suspect's shoes would have felt free to leave or terminate the encounter with the police. Juries would also decide whether a "search" within the meaning of the Fourth Amendment has taken place, as this question involves a determination as to whether the defendant's expectation of privacy was one that a reasonable citizen would have held. Conversely, courts would decide whether a police officer reasonably relied on a search warrant later deemed invalid for purposes of the *Leon* good faith exception to the exclusionary rule, as this question involves a determination as to whether the police officer acted reasonably. Wilson's proposal responds to concerns raised by Thomas K. Clancy and Janice Nadler in chapter 3. Both Clancy and Nadler noted that in determining whether a "seizure" has taken place, the Supreme Court often focuses on the reasonableness of the police conduct even though under its test for a seizure, it should ask whether the reasonable person in the suspect's shoes would have felt free to leave or terminate the encounter with the police.

In "'Everyman''s Fourth Amendment: Privacy or Mutual Trust between Government and Citizen?," Scott E. Sundby suggests that the privacy metaphor that dominates our current understanding of the Fourth Amendment should be supplemented with a government-citizen trust metaphor because privacy or the "right to be let alone" no longer fully captures the values animating the Fourth Amendment. Sundby argues that since the primary constitutional value underlying the Fourth Amendment is that of "trust" between the government and the citizen, a government-citizen trust metaphor should replace the privacy metaphor in Fourth Amendment jurisprudence.

In "Human Dignity under the Fourth Amendment," John D. Castiglione, like Sundby, opines that the current privacy-centric model of the Fourth Amendment fails to recognize other core constitutional values underlying the Fourth Amendment. Castiglione argues that one of these core values, the value of human dignity, should be recognized along with privacy as a central principle of the Fourth Amendment. He proposes a new test that examines whether the governmental action was degrading, dehumanizing, or otherwise offensive to the individual's sense of dignity to measure the validity of a search or seizure.

In "Respect and the Fourth Amendment," Andrew E. Taslitz argues that "respect" should be at the center of all Fourth Amendment reasoning. One strategy Taslitz offers to achieve a respect-based Fourth Amendment jurisprudence is listening to the voices of the oppressed. Taslitz's proposal seeks to address the racial equality concerns expressed in the excerpts by Devon W. Carbado, Anthony C. Thompson, Tracey Maclin, and Frank Rudy Cooper.

In the last excerpt, "Reasonableness and Objectivity: A Feminist Discourse of the Fourth Amendment," Dana Raigrodski offers a feminist critique of the Fourth Amendment. Raigrodski observes that reasonableness standards tend to mask the fact that what the powerful think is reasonable is often considered oppressive to those without power. She argues that the concept of reasonableness should be discarded in search-and-seizure law and replaced with a methodology of narratives and a focus on anti-subordination and empowerment principles.

THE RETURN OF REASONABLENESS: SAVING THE FOURTH AMENDMENT FROM THE SUPREME COURT

MELANIE D. WILSON

The term "reasonable" means rational, "[n]ot excessive or extreme," "not demanding too much." Behaving reasonably, therefore, requires conduct "[w]ithin the bounds of common sense." The acts of a reasonable person are "not absurd"; they are "not ridiculous." Reasonable people act "by fair or sensible standards of judgment; rightly or justifiably."

Although the Fourth Amendment centers on "reasonableness," the Court's Fourth Amendment jurisprudence has been anything but. A prominent legal scholar once described the Court's jurisprudence as "an embarrassment."

*　　*　　*

Maybe "embarrassment" is too harsh. But, when the Court assesses "reasonableness," the floor protection guaranteed by the Fourth Amendment, the Court has certainly rendered some inconsistent, seemingly result-oriented,

293

common-sense-defying opinions that have, in effect, undermined the primary purpose of the Amendment—to protect the people from undue government intrusions on privacy and liberty.

This Article contends that the Court's most perplexing Fourth Amendment outcomes occur in one category of Fourth Amendment cases and that an additional faulty habit of the Court is exacerbating the Court's problematic results. More precisely, the integrity of the Court's cases suffers when Supreme Court Justices assess issues of Fourth Amendment reasonableness by critiquing the "reasonable" beliefs and actions of ordinary citizens ("citizen reasonableness")—issues that juries should decide. In addition, the Court sometimes oversteps its traditional, law-declaring role to decide issues of pure fact.

*   *   *

This Article urges a re-evaluation of who should conduct Fourth Amendment reasonableness assessments and contends that juries of reasonable citizens, not Supreme Court Justices, should decide issues of citizen reasonableness. Thus, the Supreme Court will take its first step toward returning reasonableness to its Fourth Amendment jurisprudence when it: (1) Allows juries to decide those "mixed" questions of Fourth Amendment law that require an evaluation of how reasonable citizens think and behave, and (2) Enforces a fact/law dichotomy in which the Court restricts its assessment of Fourth Amendment facts to a clear-error, deferential review.

To promote the proposed approach, the Supreme Court should divide Fourth Amendment issues into distinct groups and assign whole groups to judges or juries, depending on which body is best-suited to decide the entire group. Using its current balancing formula, the Court should continue to decide those types of issues that require the declaration of general principles of law and those that turn on broad policy judgments about the protections the Fourth Amendment does and does not offer. It should also decide those issues requiring an evaluation of how reasonable law enforcement officers act given specific facts and circumstances. But the Court should defer to citizen juries on issues of how reasonable citizens think and behave, and to fact-finding bodies on issues of fact and on questions that hinge on the credibility of witnesses. Sometimes, the fact-finding body will be a judge (as it currently is in all Fourth Amendment cases); other times, a jury should be impaneled to evaluate fact-laden issues.

Even though judges currently decide all Fourth Amendment suppression issues, there are persuasive arguments for permitting juries to decide *at least* some Fourth Amendment questions. The reasons are particularly strong for allowing juries of reasonable citizens to assess the actions and beliefs of other "reasonable" citizens.

Allowing juries to decide citizen reasonableness may result in more substantive Fourth Amendment protection for the American people by reducing the number of cases in which the beliefs of seemingly reasonable people are declared to be unreasonable. If, for instance, juries prove to be more likely to find that a reasonable person in a suspect's circumstances would feel obligated to answer police questions or constrained to reject a law enforcement officer's requests to search his or her person or belongings, then the number of Fourth Amendment rights-protecting cases will increase, and the Fourth Amendment will provide greater protection for the individual. But even if juries comprised of ordinary citizens raise or maintain the standards for citizen reasonableness, the Court's process will improve. At a minimum, allowing juries to decide these issues will promote a respect for the Court's cases by: (1) Reducing the appearance that the Court's Fourth Amendment decisions are result-oriented; (2) Increasing the transparency and democracy of the process by including "the people" in Fourth-Amendment-rights-protection; and (3) Lending some integrity to all rulings that label citizen conduct or expectations as "unreasonable."

Nay-sayers to this proposed change in process are sure to criticize the proposal as undermining predictability for law enforcement officers, who must fulfill a duty of crime prevention and resolution, while trying to comply with the Fourth Amendment. But predictability is not mandated by the Fourth Amendment. Although predictability of Fourth Amendment rules is, admittedly, a worthy goal, the Constitution does not suggest that predictability trumps individual rights. Furthermore, as the Court's past decisions illustrate, except when the Court declares broad, bright-line rules identifying the reasonableness floor, no matter who evaluates reasonableness, the process involves subjectivity and an inherent unpredictability, because it demands an assessment of the unique circumstances of each case. Therefore, there may be no significant increase in the unpredictable outcomes when fact finders (including juries) are substituted for appellate judges.

Furthermore, the proposed change in process will not inhibit the Supreme Court from continuing to provide extensive guidance to the police by announcing bright-line, black-letter rules of law declaring the floor protections the Fourth Amendment guarantees. Such straight-forward rules will continue to provide predictability and uniformity in Fourth Amendment cases that do not rest on highly fact-specific situations or hinge on the perspectives of ordinary people. Finally, because the proposal argues that the Court should continue to assess, de novo, issues of law enforcement reasonableness, and issues turning on how reasonable officers behave in response to specific factual catalysts, the Court will continue to provide bright-line rules in many cases. The proposal will impact only the small percentage of cases that assess citizen behaviors and beliefs, and it is those cases that deserve a change in process because they currently defy logic and common sense.

*   *   *

"EVERYMAN" 'S FOURTH AMENDMENT: PRIVACY OR MUTUAL TRUST BETWEEN GOVERNMENT AND CITIZEN?

SCOTT E. SUNDBY

The Supreme Court's recent Fourth Amendment decisions have drawn increasingly sharp criticism from the legal academy. Article after article documents the Court's transgressions: how it has riddled the Warrant Clause with exceptions, has suffocated individual privacy through an all-encompassing reasonableness standard, and has extended unprecedented powers to law enforcement agencies. If ever a united cry of warning has been made that a basic civil liberty was in danger, this chorus of law review laments is it.

Yet a curious thing has happened. Apart from this chorus of academics, an occasional civil liberties lawyer, and a disenchanted judicial dissenter or two, the warning largely has gone unheard and unheeded by both the judiciary and the public at large. The politician on the stump is far more likely to stir a crowd's passions by calling for an expanded "war on crime" than by suggesting that greater restrictions on law enforcement activities are necessary to preserve what, in the public's mind, are the rights of accused criminals. More and more, the scholarly critics appear to be an isolated band of constitutional purists, out of touch with reality, trying to form a protective circle around the dying ember of the Fourth Amendment based on the forlorn hope that, if jealously guarded, some day a new theoretical and political wind might again fan it to life.

Perhaps, though, the problem is in part with the critiques of the Court's Fourth Amendment decisions themselves. Generally, critics have assumed that the factors which the Court uses to measure Fourth Amendment reasonableness—privacy, intrusiveness, and government need—are the proper ones to be weighed in deciding whether a warrant is required or what level of suspicion must justify a search or seizure. Consequently, most arguments have coalesced along the lines that the Court has not properly measured the individual's expectations of privacy, that it has underemphasized the Warrant Clause's requirements of a warrant based on probable cause, or that it has struck the wrong balance of individual and government interests in deciding that a particular intrusion was "reasonable." Not surprisingly, therefore, proposed solutions have tended to focus on a more skilled and sensitive use of these factors rather than a disagreement with the factors themselves.

The inability of these Fourth Amendment critiques to strike a responsive judicial or popular chord suggests, however, that their analyses are missing a more deeply rooted and fundamental problem by asking the wrong questions. What if the problem is not with judges improperly doing their Fourth Amendment sums but with the factors themselves? Might reliance upon privacy as the standard weight of the Fourth Amendment no longer provide, by itself, an adequate measure for assessing the propriety of government intrusions? Is making privacy the centerpiece of the debate over the "reasonableness" of a specific intrusion skewing the very values the Amendment is designed to protect?

*   *   *

This Article makes an initial effort to reframe the Fourth Amendment debate by exploring how the Court's current metaphor for conceptualizing Fourth Amendment values, Justice Brandeis's famous image of "the right to be let alone," no longer fully captures the values that are at stake.

*   *   *

... I argue for a new metaphor for the Fourth Amendment to complement "the right to be let alone." Drawing upon the values underlying the Constitution and the Bill of Rights, I suggest that the animating principle which has been ignored in the current Fourth Amendment debate is the idea of reciprocal government-citizen trust.

* * *

II. PRIVACY'S FAILURE AS GUARDIAN OF THE FOURTH AMENDMENT

* * *

A. PRIVACY IN A NON-PRIVATE WORLD

... [A] Fourth Amendment based upon expectations of privacy must contend with the changing nature of modern society. The very notion of a right to be left alone seems a bit tattered once placed in the context of contemporary life. Justice Brandeis spoke of the Fourth Amendment as guarding against unjustifiable intrusions upon the private life of the individual in part out of a concern for encroaching technology. Even Justice Brandeis, though, could not have fully envisioned the world of the 1990s, where the difference between public and private largely has become blurred. Technological and communication advances mean that much of everyday life is now recorded by someone somewhere, whether it be credit records, banking records, phone records, tax records, or even what videos we rent. We may want to be left alone, but we realistically do not expect it to happen in any complete sense....

The fact that it has become increasingly difficult to find a Walden Pond ... in today's world does not mean that privacy no longer has a role within the Fourth Amendment; indeed, it may support all the more an argument for a stronger Amendment to protect what enclaves of privacy are left. But this requires thinking of privacy in general, abstract value terms, such that everyone, including the Court, would agree that "privacy" is a cherished principle. However, under the Court's current Fourth Amendment formulaic approach, privacy is not invoked as an overarching *value* but rather is used as a specific *fact* to assess whether and how the Fourth Amendment should apply to a given intrusion. Such an approach asks, for example, whether the individual has a "reasonable expectation of privacy" in a particular activity, and, if so, whether the government's need outweighs the scope of the privacy intrusion. Privacy is thus treated as a quantifiable fact that can be used to help resolve concrete legal disputes.

When used as a factual measure, reliance upon privacy as the centerpiece of Fourth Amendment rights actually creates the potential for less overall privacy protection. This is true most simply because as governmental and nongovernmental intrusions on privacy expand, the scope of what one reasonably expects to be private correspondingly becomes truncated. In other words, because the Court is not asking whether bank or phone records *should* be kept private (thus invoking privacy as a value), but, rather, whether we as a *factual* matter expect others to see and use those records (thus viewing privacy as a measurable fact), Fourth Amendment protections will shrink as our everyday expectations of privacy also diminish.

*   *   *

The problem of how we use privacy to measure Fourth Amendment rights is compounded by technological advances that have enabled the government to invade privacy in a less physically intrusive manner. The Norman Rockwell scene of Officer Friendly patrolling Main Street while he whistles and twirls a nightstick has been replaced by drug-sniffing dogs, urinalysis spectrometers, unmanned drones, heat sensors, DNA testing, helicopter flyovers, and electronically tracked beepers....

Certainly, such technological and resource-efficient techniques are laudable to the extent they allow an *already* justified search to be conducted in the least intrusive fashion possible. The use of advanced techniques in this way serves privacy interests because a legitimate Fourth Amendment search that otherwise would be conducted at a greater intrusiveness level is in fact carried out at a lower level of intrusion. For example, where a legitimate need to search for weapons exists, a metal detector will promote the privacy interest by achieving the government's objective without subjecting the individual to a patdown and an opening of packages.

The increasing tendency, however, is to use the lesser intrusion on privacy as part of the *justification* for a government search that otherwise would not be allowed. As a result, the Fourth Amendment's balancing factors of privacy and the government's need for the intrusion become viewed as dependent variables on a sliding scale: minimizing the level of the privacy intrusion can help compensate for a weaker government justification, such as one lacking individualized suspicion. Used in this analytical fashion, the government's ability to intrude in a less physically intrusive manner does not promote privacy interests but actually undermines the overall right to be free from government surveillance by expanding the scope of acceptable intrusions. A physical search of a person for evidence of drug use while on the job, which normally would require individualized suspicion, now becomes permissible if the government uses minimally intrusive means (at least in a physical sense), such as blood or urinalysis tests.

By making privacy the central factor in the Fourth Amendment's equation, therefore, the Court unwittingly introduced a factor that, over the long term, resulted in an overall decline in the Amendment's protections. This situation will only worsen as the inevitable march of government regulation further blurs the notion of what is private and as technological advances enable the government to invade privacy in more pervasive, but physically less intrusive, ways.

*   *   *

III. A NEW FOURTH AMENDMENT METAPHOR: GOVERNMENT-CITIZEN TRUST

*   *   *

A. THE POWER OF THE METAPHOR

A student of the Court's constitutional decisionmaking quickly becomes acquainted with balancing tests in all their various shapes and sizes: strict and rational; two-part, three-part, and four-part; unitary and sliding. Such tests do provide some guidance to those needing to determine the constitutionality of their actions.... Yet, because the very process of weighing competing interests requires evaluative judgments, plenty of room remains for disagreement even where all agree on the stated test....

Despite the legal community's predilection for trying to capture a constitutional principle through a carefully formulated test, occasionally a metaphor or animating image emerges that captures the underlying essence of a constitutional value far better than the legal test. One of the most notable examples is Justice Holmes's characterization of the First Amendment's Free Speech Clause as resting upon the belief that "the ultimate good desired is better reached by free trade in ideas—that the best test of truth is the power of the thought to get itself accepted in the competition of the market." Without the captivating image of the marketplace of ideas, one might question whether Justice Holmes's proffered legal test, written in dissent, would have gained the acceptance that it later did from the Court.

* * *

As noted earlier, the Fourth Amendment has had its own guiding image, that of the "right to be let alone—the most comprehensive of rights and the right most valued by civilized men." As with the marketplace of ideas, this "right to be let alone" also has had a marked impact on the development of constitutional law, extending its influence not only over the Fourth Amendment but also aiding in the eventual recognition of a distinct constitutional "right of privacy." And, like the marketplace metaphor, the values represented by the "right to be let alone" are powerfully embedded within American society: images of individualism; the home as one's castle; and the desire for freedom from government interference that led the colonists to seek the New World.

Developments such as growing government regulation and expanding technological capacity, however, have robbed the "right to be let alone" of much of its power to control the legal discourse concerning the Fourth Amendment.... Thus, although privacy undoubtedly remains an essential American value, the concept no longer fully captures the Fourth Amendment's role as a meaningful regulator of government-citizen interactions. What is needed is a look at what values are at stake beyond physical privacy interests and a way of expressing these values that impresses upon the public why seemingly mundane and almost distasteful Fourth Amendment issues, such as whether the Amendment protects garbage bags or urine specimens, hold importance for how the United States and its Constitution function.

* * *

B. Trust as a Constitutional Value

...I would characterize the jeopardized constitutional value underlying the Fourth Amendment as that of "trust" between the government and the citizenry. This vision of the Fourth Amendment's purpose is founded upon the idea that integral to the Constitution and our societal view of government is a reciprocal trust between the government and its citizens. Government action draws its legitimacy from the trust that the electorate places in its representatives by choosing them to govern. This mandate from the citizenry legitimatizes government action, however, only if the citizenry's decision itself is an informed and free choice such that the government can claim that it has the true consent of the governed. To achieve this legitimatizing mandate, therefore, the government itself must act so that it does not imperil the citizenry's ability to give its consent in an informed and free manner.

* * *

Even a rudimentary comparison of democratic to totalitarian and anarchist states demonstrates the central role that government-citizen trust plays in a free society. Totalitarian regimes maintain power not through the consent of the governed but by physical, economic, and psychological control over the populace. Such governments exercise control through a variety of means, but among the most essential is the use of the police power to reinforce the message that the government is superior and in control of the individual. Measures such as identification checkpoints, random searches, the monitoring of communications, and the widespread use of informants not only are means of keeping track of the citizenry, but also act as continuous symbolic reminders that the citizenry is dominated by the government. Far from fostering trust, the government's actions convey a message of distrust in order to perpetuate control of the citizenry.

Likewise, societies besieged by civil unrest provide examples of the importance that the trust be reciprocal. While many factors may cause unrest, certainly one of the most prevalent is distrust of the government's willingness to listen to the dissidents' voices and respect their interests. When such distrust occurs, the disenchanted group will view the government as illegitimate and be inclined to look to means outside the formal political process to have its voice heard. In the best scenario, such actions will be peaceful acts of civil disobedience that will produce meaningful change; in the worst case, the dis-enfranchised will turn to terrorism and acts of violence. Indeed, the process may become circular as acts of protest and rebellion provoke oppressive actions by a distrustful government. These measures, in turn, create greater resentment and distrust of the government among the populace and further fuel its discontent and unrest.

The above examples are not meant to suggest that the United States is on the verge of slipping into a cycle of totalitarianism and anarchy. They do suggest, however, that a crucial part of American democracy's staying power is the role of reciprocal government-citizen trust in fostering the confidence among all individuals that they have the opportunities and capabilities to participate meaningfully in society. Individuals and groups who feel that the government is not recognizing their concerns and beliefs may otherwise perceive the government as lacking legitimacy, resulting in an increased sense of alienation and lack of confidence that the government will respond seriously to their needs. The sustainability of our constitutional system of government is thus largely dependent upon ensuring that this reciprocal trust is maintained.

* * *

C. The Metaphor of Trust as the Fourth Amendment's Guiding Principle

Proposing the idea of government-citizen trust as a central value for the Fourth Amendment has several immediate up-front liabilities. First, the notion of trust sounds, and is in many ways, so simple, so nonlegalistic, and so nonphilosophical, that it risks being dismissed as not sufficiently grounded in legal-political theory.

* * *

Advocating government-citizen trust as a guiding metaphor of the Fourth Amendment also is vulnerable to the criticism that it reflects an unrealistic world view: the concept of trust seems to offer little assistance to the police officer confronted late at night with a dangerous-looking individual or to a neighborhood overrun with drug dealers....

One must keep in mind, however, the metaphor's purpose in this context.

Using trust as one of the Fourth Amendment's driving principles is not meant to be a specific rule of police behavior to be carried around with the officer's *Miranda* card. Rather, the metaphor helps frame the debate over Fourth Amendment issues in a way that keeps decisions from devolving into what appear to be only disagreements over factual privacy issues, such as the frequency of use of navigational airspace at different altitudes. By casting the issues in a broader context of the relationship between government and citizen, the implications of a particular ruling can be ferreted out.

This broadening of perspective is especially crucial because Fourth Amendment issues increasingly do not concern unexpected police-suspect street encounters where the police need fast and ready rules, but involve searches and seizures based on a preexisting legislative or administrative plan. Employee drug-testing, sobriety checkpoints, immigration roadblocks, "factory surveys," flyovers, inventory searches, and safety inspections are all examples of ongoing government programs based on reviewable rules and standards, rather than of unanticipated police-individual encounters. These types of government intrusions create a particularly fertile opportunity for a reviewing court to articulate Fourth Amendment principles that are not shaped by exigency concerns, but, instead, allow a reasoned assessment of an ongoing governmental scheme of intrusions....

It is the need for the Fourth Amendment to respond to these "initiatory intrusions"—those situations where the government is initiating the intrusion rather than responding to some suspicious behavior by the individual (i.e., a "responsive intrusion")—that most persuasively supports adoption of the trust metaphor.... Ultimately, the message that must be conveyed is that the Fourth Amendment is not just for the criminally accused anymore, but is a civil right that affects us all.

*   *   *

HUMAN DIGNITY UNDER THE FOURTH AMENDMENT

JOHN D. CASTIGLIONE

The reasonableness requirement of the Fourth Amendment is just about the most unhelpful guidepost one could have concocted, given the burdens that have been placed upon it as the cornerstone of American criminal procedure and law enforcement. Setting aside questions as to whether the generalized-reasonableness construction of the Fourth Amendment comports with original understanding, "reasonableness" has emerged as the bottom-line constitutional requirement when the government subjects an individual to a search or seizure of person or property. However, as any first-year law student taking a torts class can tell you, reasonableness as an analytical concept is maddeningly frustrating and often little more than a shorthanded reference for "What would *I* do in this situation?" This squishy-at-best guidepost seems especially ill-suited for crafting workable standards governing the behavior of law enforcement officers, whose lives and careers depend daily on making split-second decisions regarding the scope of their authority, and who benefit from clear, bright-line rules articulated with consistency by courts.

Unfortunately, until some brave group of souls gets around to amending the Fourth Amendment, reasonableness is all we have.... At the very highest level, the Warren Court "revolution" and the resulting Burger and Rehnquist "counterrevolutions" have, with varying degrees of jurisprudential and intellectual consistency, made continual attempts to strike an appropriate balance between liberty and security under the reasonableness requirement....

It has become increasingly clear, though, that reasonableness jurisprudence, governed by the totality of the circumstances "test," is not currently up to the challenge of providing a coherent methodology for the creation of consistent decisions reflective of the underlying philosophical and moral structure of the Fourth Amendment and the Constitution. Increasingly, courts have allowed their analysis of reasonableness to devolve into little more than an awkward balancing exercise between the needs of law enforcement and the interests of privacy. At first glance, this privacy/law enforcement dichotomy seems quite appropriate; the Fourth Amendment has been primarily understood for decades now as a bulwark against unreasonable privacy invasions by the government in the course of its law enforcement functions. It therefore seems entirely natural to balance privacy, however defined, against the government's interest in effective law enforcement and social control. And, indeed, it is an appropriate inquiry to undertake when passing on the constitutionality of government action in most search-and-seizure contexts.

This privacy-centric analysis, however, is incomplete. Privacy, an exceedingly broad, multi-faceted concept nevertheless does not encompass a number of core constitutional values that should be understood to underlie the Fourth Amendment. Chief among these values is human dignity. As courts' decisions have moved towards an almost exclusive focus on privacy as the counterbalance to the government's law enforcement interest, the government's interests have increasingly prevailed and the sphere of protection afforded to the individual has shrunk. Simply put, it has become increasingly clear that privacy as a concept has proved itself an insufficient analytical tool to support an even moderately robust interpretation of the Fourth Amendment. Privacy alone is unequal to the task of providing a doctrinal framework that supports a truly protective Fourth Amendment.

If a more sound jurisprudence is to emerge, a value distinct from privacy must be articulated and incorporated into the reasonableness analysis. In this Article, I propose that human dignity, as defined, should stand alongside privacy as a primary animating principle of the Fourth Amendment. I seek to pair privacy, which, as noted, has become the dominant value behind the reasonableness requirement, with dignity, which is an even more fundamental value that underlies not only the Fourth Amendment, but arguably the entire constitutional structure. While dignity as a concept has always existed around the periphery of constitutional search-and-seizure jurisprudence, and has intermittently been cited by the Supreme Court as a consideration in the reasonableness analysis, it has been severely underdeveloped both in the case law and in the academic literature. I seek to bring dignity to the fore as a usable constitutional value and interpretive device.

*   *   *

The Supreme Court has hinted at dignity's place as a Fourth Amendment value, but has alternately conflated the dignitary interest with the privacy interest, or ignored the dignitary interest altogether. While there is significant overlap (and, in some cases, concurrence) between the two concepts, they are distinct values, and should be treated as such. As an intuitive matter, one can have no privacy at all—either as an expectation or an objective fact—and still maintain a legitimate expectation of being treated with dignity. Even if one has no privacy, liberty, or property, or the legitimate expectation of the same, such as is the case with a prisoner, there remains a core human right to be free of government action that unreasonably or unnecessarily strips one of his dignity or intrinsic humanity.... Thus, courts' current focus on privacy as the sole counterbalance to the state's law enforcement interest is inadequate because it fails to protect (both as a doctrinal matter and increasingly in practice) against dignitary impositions, and courts must now move to formally factor dignity into the reasonableness equation.

*   *   *

... The modern conception of human dignity can be traced back to classical Roman thought, where Cicero referred to *dignitas* as a concept regarding human beings as having worth and an expectation of respect by virtue of being human. Importantly, the recognition of human worth and entitlement to some measure of respect arose independently of any particular social status. This entitlement to worth or respect, Cicero argued, is a consequence of the "superior minds" of humans—superior, at least, to that of beasts. Dignity arises in man, Cicero claimed, as a consequence of man's ability to reason, both practically and morally.... This reason-based conception of individual worth evolved through the Middle Ages, when a theologically based conception of dignity began to emerge. This conception emphasized the notion that man has dignity (by having worth and being deserving of respect, in accordance with Cicero's model) not only—or not necessarily—because he can reason, but because he is made in the image of God....

The late eighteenth century brought a new vision of human dignity, when Immanuel Kant articulated what is considered to be one of the more cogent explanations of the meaning of dignity in the modern era, as well as offering a test for determining when it has been offended. Kant, like Cicero, believed that human beings have dignity because they have reason, but formulated reason as the ability of humans to appreciate the implications or "universality" of their actions. Kant's well-known categorical imperative instructs, in its first formulation, that individuals should "act only according to principles which can be conceived and willed as a universal law." From this principle Kant derived his second formulation, which provides that individuals should "[a]ct in such a way that you treat humanity, whether in your own person or in the person of any other, always at the same time as an end and never simply as a means." Accordingly, a violation of that precept is a violation of human dignity, because every individual has a right to be treated as an end, not as a means. Dignity, therefore, can be conceived as the inherent right of all men to be treated by others in accordance with the categorical imperative. Failure to be so treated is an offense against dignity.

Today, all of those conceptions of dignity survive and are accepted, informing our notions of what *dignity* means. If one were to consult the dictionary, *dignity* today is formally defined as "[t]he quality of being worthy or honourable; worthiness, worth, nobleness, excellence." This definition is largely in accord with the three long-standing conceptions of dignity outlined earlier, yet still amorphous in its own right.

Some in the legal field have attempted to bring clarity to the proceedings. Professor R. George Wright, in an engaging recent work exploring the foundations of the "dignity of the person" from a philosophical and general constitutional case law perspective, goes about the task of defining dignity somewhat in reverse. Because dignity as a concept is, to some extent, inherently ethereal, Wright argues that defining what dignity stands *in contrast to* is informative in determining what it actually *is*. As he sees it, dignity stands in contrast to "brutality, cruelty...humiliation, uncivilized or barbarous behavior, harsh treatment…" and so on. Others have similarly negatively triangulated the definition of *dignity*, noting that the concept of "degradation" offers important definitional lessons. This view posits a "subjective degradation" in which one's dignity can be offended when one psychologically feels degraded.

*   *   *

III. TOWARD A WORKABLE INCORPORATION OF DIGNITY INTO THE REASONABLENESS TEST

*   *   *

Dignity should…become a recognized, fully integrated element of the reasonableness analysis. Simply put, searches and seizures that infringe on an individual's reasonable expectation of being treated with dignity, independent of any violation of any other protected interest, are unreasonable and in violation of the Fourth Amendment….

A. TOWARD A WORKABLE STANDARD

The basic formulation is simple: whether a search or seizure is reasonable is determined by assessing, on the one hand, the degree to which it intrudes upon an individual's dignity and, on the other hand, the degree to which the search or seizure, and the manner in which it is conducted, is needed for the promotion of legitimate governmental interests. Searches or seizures that demean, degrade, or humiliate the suspect (or otherwise offend notions of the dignity of the person), and which cannot be justified given the law enforcement interest at stake, are unreasonable, leading to remedies that normally arise from an unreasonable search or seizure. Courts should make two inquiries: (1) was the search or seizure itself—or the manner in which it was conducted—degrading, dehumanizing, or otherwise offensive to the individual's legitimate sense of dignity, and if so, (2) should that imposition on the individual's dignitary interest be tolerated in light of the government's interest in executing that search and seizure? If the answer to inquiry (1) is yes and the answer to inquiry (2) is no, the search or seizure is invalid under the Fourth Amendment.

Of course, an evaluation of a dignitary imposition by the government need not, and should not, be exclusive of an evaluation of the imposition on an established privacy interest, as the open-ended textual command of reasonableness (and the Court's totality test) makes clear. Courts can and should evaluate both, if applicable to the situation. Privacy should retain its place at the center of Fourth Amendment jurisprudence, standing alongside dignity and fulfilling the Supreme Court's mandate in cases like *Schmerber* that "[t]he overriding function of the Fourth Amendment is to protect personal privacy *and* dignity against unwarranted intrusion by the State." Under this model, courts would still evaluate the imposition of the government's actions on the suspect's privacy while having a method for evaluating the dignitary interest that is lost when analysis focuses solely on privacy. Searches that intrude on both the suspect's privacy and dignitary interest would be especially susceptible to invalidation. Searches that intrude on both interests, but perhaps not enough on either interest in isolation to warrant invalidation, could be a candidate for invalidation based on the combined harm.

*   *   *

RESPECT AND THE FOURTH AMENDMENT

ANDREW E. TASLITZ

One question prompted this article: "Why do many minority communities experience rage at certain police search and seizure practices involving their communities' members?" My apparently obvious answer: because the police act in ways that make minority communities feel disrespected.... History, philosophy, and social science converge in establishing that "respect" should... be at the center of all Fourth Amendment reasoning. What "respect" is, how it is conceived of by minority versus majority communities, and what psychological and social processes lead to its loss are, however, not so obvious. Nor has it yet become clear to the United States Supreme Court what role respect-based concerns should play in Fourth Amendment analysis.... Understanding the Court's current approach and its failures, and defending a respect-enhancing alternative, first requires an analysis of the dominant "mere technicality" vision of the Fourth Amendment.

* * *

... Consider this scenario:

> Two police officers, Cagney and Lacey, pay off a local stool pigeon for infor-
> mation about a planned cocaine sale. The stoolie's information is vague, and
> he refuses to reveal his sources. Nevertheless, based on this tip, Cagney and
> Lacey guess that a cocaine sale will happen that night at a Water Street ware-
> house and set up a stakeout. Unable to see much, they choose to break in.
> Inside, they find not only a massive quantity of cocaine but a large shipment
> of illegal firearms ready to hit the street. Their elation at a job well done is
> quickly ended when a judge suppresses the evidence. Because the search was
> done without a warrant or probable cause, the trial judge barred the jury
> from hearing or seeing anything about the drugs and weapons confiscated by
> the detectives. Lacking evidence, the prosecution was forced to withdraw the
> case, and another dangerous criminal walked free.

Th[e] image of left-wing judges allowing criminals to exploit the Fourth
Amendment and other legal technicalities has long been standard fare in
movies, television shows, and newspaper stories. The media feeds the impression of a massive, increasingly violent crime problem. That problem is por-
trayed as exacerbated by the helpless system's flooding of the streets with
guilty men freed by wily lawyers.

*　　*　　*

... [T]he Court too has generally accepted the view of the Fourth Amendment as a mere technicality.... [T]he general trend is to narrow the scope of
Fourth Amendment rights and, even when such rights are recognized, to
narrow still further when the exclusionary remedy will be available to enforce
the Amendment.

The burden of this narrowing vision of Fourth Amendment rights has
often fallen hardest on racial and ethnic minorities. The Court purports to
endorse a colorblind search and seizure jurisprudence. Ignoring race, however, is often precisely what promotes racial disparities.

To use the most obvious example, an officer who stops a car going one
mile over the speed limit has probable cause to believe that the law has been
violated. If the officer only stops those speeders who are African American, or
Hispanic American, or Asian American, that seems wrong. It unsettles American notions of equal treatment. Yet if, as the Court suggests, we cannot con-

sider the officer's racial attitudes and assumptions, or perhaps not even whether his conduct has a disparate racial impact, this "racial profiling" is tolerated by the state. The Court's position on profiling and the role of race in search and seizure decisions is a bit more complex and subtle than my claim here that they entirely ignore race. But the bottom line point would be unchanged by exploring those complexities: a colorblind search and seizure jurisprudence often results in racial injustice.

* * *

"Respect" is in part about status or esteem. Each person feels respected when he is treated as significant and of equal worth with every other person. Groups too struggle for equal status.

But respect is also about inclusion, about being considered full members of the wider political community. When African Americans in Jim Crow America could not sit at white lunch counters, they felt excluded from the American community. Yet, what is rarely recognized is that Jim Crow laws went to the heart of the Fourth Amendment by regulating where certain citizens could choose to work, live, eat, and play. Similarly, today, when officers employ racial profiling to stop young African American males walking down the street, the officers insult and degrade the young men and their racial groups, making them feel less than full members of the American polity.

* * *

... [A] substantive vision of the Fourth Amendment's value to our republic must replace the near-sighted view of mere technicalities. This article seeks to articulate such a vision, one rooted in the substantive value of respect.

* * *

II. SEARCHING FOR RESPECT

*   *   *

D. REDEFINING RESPECT AS TREATING FITTINGLY

*   *   *

2. Fittingness

Respect as fittingness is the idea that each person is entitled to be treated in accordance with his status concerning some specified attribute. Any lesser treatment is insulting. The status is objective: It either exists or it does not. Thus a trustworthy co-worker is treated unfittingly if other co-workers act as if he is not trustworthy. That both he and his co-workers honestly believe that he is untrustworthy does not alter the fact that he has been treated unfittingly.

Human rights theorists generally agree that in some respect all humans are alike, thus all sharing the same status and requiring treatment befitting that status. Theorists debate what attribute of sameness all humans share. Some think that it is being made in "the image of God," others that it is the *capacity* to achieve moral goodness, and still others (the Kantians) that it is rationality and autonomy—humans' nature as self-directing beings legislating their own life plans. Whatever the quality that we all share, that quality entails certain rights or entitlements without which our status as humans is ignored. Freedom of conscience, privacy, the right to own property earned by the sweat of our brow, and freedom of movement are among the rights commonly deemed to belong to every person simply by nature of her humanity. Furthermore, many fittingness theorists agree that these sorts of entitlements necessarily imply diversity in life choices. Respect must therefore be shown for the sorts of differences that are central to personal identity. Many of these differences are rooted in our identification with historically important social groups, each person's total set of overlapping connections to such groups helping to define who he uniquely is. That individual-group connection requires fitting treatment for both.

3. Fittingness and Belongingness

But how can we determine in an individual case whether we have "treated" someone fittingly? That is a question I will answer in Part III; I first want to examine one aspect of fitting treatment: encouraging a sense of "belongingness."

To treat someone as a whole—as uniquely complete in himself—is status-enhancing, expressing the idea that each human is of equal and infinite worth. Simultaneously treating a person as a part or member of a valued broader whole—as someone essential to making society what it is—is also status-enhancing. The idea of "partnership" best expresses this ideal: each of us is a whole unto ourselves yet a valuable partner committed to, and essential for, the greater good.

A different way to make this same point is to view fitting treatment as treatment that is not humiliating—that does not act as if we are outside the family of man. All men are entitled to membership in *some* political society, albeit not necessarily in any particular one. Members of a political society who are treated as not full members—as second-class citizens—usually face that fate because they are viewed as less than fully human. That perceived sub-humanity is usually rooted in their membership in an oppressed sub-group. Exclusion from full citizenship rights is therefore humiliating and thus unfitting. State-enforced disrespect consequently is doubly insulting: first, by treating its victims as unworthy of better treatment in and of themselves; second, by excluding them from full membership in the polity.

*   *   *

What is true in statutory civil rights law is true as well of the constitutional law governing searches and seizures. Racial profiling of African Americans, for example, humiliates the person stopped, who is treated as less than fully and equally human because of his membership in a historically oppressed group. But whites stopped on fabricated motor vehicle violations to meet ticketing quotas are also insulted. To infringe upon the right of free movement without adequate reason is to treat a person as unworthy of having that right, a right necessarily entailed by his simple humanity.

III. PRACTICES, PRINCIPLES, AND HISTORY

*   *   *

A. Social and Historical Practices Are Bases for Intuitions Useful in Developing and Justifying Principles

... [L]earning from the experiences and attitudes of the subjugated helps society to see its failings more clearly. This is the "method of listening," which requires decision makers to move back and forth between hearing the voices of the oppressed and comparing their experiences and perspectives to current governing principles[.]

*   *   *

One strategy for effective listening is to hear with the aid of the device of "subperson-hood." ... [S]ometimes overtly, sometimes covertly, majorities behave in ways that exclude minorities from the category of full "persons" entitled to equal treatment. Physical "stigmata" such as skin color, an accent, or an odd way of dress trigger a dominant group's moral blindness, serving as "marks of Cain upon people's very humanity." Bearers of stigmata are "seen as human beings, but as severely flawed human beings—in other words, as subhuman." Respect for persons is usually justified by their presumed rationality and autonomy. But subpersons are subconsciously viewed by, or at least treated by, majorities ("persons") as neither fully rational nor fully capable of guiding their own destinies.

*   *   *

In the Fourth Amendment area, the elements of subpersonhood are evident everywhere. Consent searches and quality of life policing are used disproportionately against African Americans. How the "reasonable person" would behave or feel during interactions with the police is in effect judged from the perspective of the middle-class white person expecting police protection rather than the poor person familiar with police abuse. Police racial animus is deemed irrelevant to Fourth Amendment reasoning. While animus is still relevant to proving a Fourteenth Amendment equal protection violation, the standards of proof even to obtain discovery in such cases are so high as to render relief highly unlikely. Poor suspects, again disproportionately racial minorities, rely on underpaid lawyers in overcrowded courts to uncover police wrongdoing and combat police abuse.

* * *

The subpersonhood idea does more, however, than highlight systemic inequalities. It is a lens through which stories can be told to build empathy among receptive members of the majority. That empathy does more than encourage equal treatment. It enables the dominant group to understand the true nature of the interests at stake. Those aligned with the power of the majority at one time and place may be its victims under other circumstances. A legal doctrine protective of the less privileged can in other circumstances help the more privileged.

* * *

V. WHAT PRACTICAL DIFFERENCE WILL A RESPECT-BASED SEARCH AND SEIZURE JURISPRUDENCE MAKE?

My use of the word "respect" may be troubling to some readers. In everyday usage, the word often implies simple courtesy. An image is called to mind of an officer speaking in gentle tones, listening attentively to a driver's explanation of why he ran a red light, then issuing the ticket anyway. The officer listened and spoke "respectfully," but the results of his interaction with the driver were unchanged.

That is not worrisome if the officer had every right to stop the driver. But if the officer lied about the color of the light to meet some self-imposed ticketing quota, his conduct would still be wrong. Its wrongness would be unaltered even if the officer convinced the driver that the light was indeed red, the driver therefore feeling that he was treated fairly.

Respectful listening and speaking in the sense used in this example are part of what a respect-based constitutional philosophy embraces. Such behavior in fact is simply good policing, enhancing the community's willingness to support police actions. But respectful treatment requires more. The mendacious officer in the altered hypothetical acts disrespectfully despite his courtesy. He treats the driver as a mere "means," not an end in himself, effectively punishing the driver in a way that he did not deserve.

Current jurisprudence would, of course, condemn the above officer's conduct if his lies were discovered. But in many other situations, a respect-based jurisprudence will lead to different results than under current law.... [A] respect-based approach has implications for every current search and seizure doctrine.

*   *   *

First, a respect-based approach will alter the nature of fact-finding at suppression hearings and in magistrates' decisions on warrant applications. Judges thus must often decide whether there was reasonable suspicion for police to stop a pedestrian whom the officers believed to be involved in a crime. But "reasonable suspicion"—like "negligence" in a tort trial or "consent" in a rape trial—is not some indisputable truth existing "out there." ...

... [W]e must decide whether, given the information available to the police, their suspicion of the pedestrian was "reasonable." Yet that question turns on a series of value-based judgments about what inferences can fairly be drawn, and with what degree of confidence, from the information available. If minority and majority communities on average draw very different conclusions from the same observations, whose perspective the courts recognize alters the outcome. As one illustration, assume that police see a young African American male in a poor, predominantly African American neighborhood "fleeing" when police arrive on the scene. The white middle class majority might see such flight as revealing the suspect's consciousness of guilt. The African American community likely sees the youth's flight as more consistent with self-preservation, fleeing because he wants to avoid the risk of an unfair and unpleasant confrontation with the police. Current law generally favors the consciousness of guilt argument, but a respect-based jurisprudence, absent more individualized evidence, favors the self-preservation inference.

Second, by infusing equality norms into the Fourth Amendment, a respect-based jurisprudence makes inquiry into discriminatory police motives and racially disparate police actions relevant at suppression hearings.... Racial profiling claims are not, therefore, relegated to hard-to-prove equal-protection-based civil class actions. Rather, they are also central Fourth

Amendment concerns of the *criminal* justice system. Furthermore, because racially disparate impact theories should be embraced, evidence of certain widespread police practices, rather than only of the conduct of the individual officers involved in a specific complaint, becomes highly relevant. As noted earlier, current law by contrast prohibits inquiry into subjective police officer motivations under the Fourth Amendment and is ambiguous about the relevance of disparate impact. Much case law also often limits evidence of police misconduct to the officers' actions in the individual case, making patterns of police conduct difficult to prove.

Third, for novel cases, the Court balances the depth of the state's intrusion on the individual against the state's justifications for its actions to determine what is reasonable. Usually the Court engages in "categorical balancing," crafting a new rule to determine reasonableness in future similar cases. This balancing currently involves a thumb on the police side of the scale. The Court frequently considers widely-defined social benefits of police action but only its costs to the individual suspect. When the Court does consider broader social costs, it often (albeit not always) gives them short shrift. It also defines those costs narrowly, often ignoring the impact of its decisions on racial unity, labor discipline, and healthy human relationships. Police concerns are weighty; broader citizenry subgroup concerns slight. A respect-based jurisprudence would routinely consider all the social costs of police action, including the impact on communities of color. That would not necessarily alter outcomes in all cases because state actions under current law might meet the requirements of respectful treatment. But results may be changed in some instances.

Notably, remember that in *Terry v. Ohio*, ... the Supreme Court first permitted police stop-and-frisks on mere reasonable suspicion rather than probable cause. The Court acknowledged, in passing only, its awareness of the "wholesale harassment by certain elements of the police community, of which minority groups, particularly Negroes, frequently complain...." The Court elaborated, in a footnote, that field interrogations "are a major source of friction between the police and minority groups." Additionally, the Court acknowledged that the exacerbation of police-community tensions would be "particularly true in situations where the 'stop and frisk' of youths or minority group members is 'motivated by the officers' perceived need to maintain the power image of the beat officer, an aim sometimes accomplished by humiliating anyone who attempts to undermine police control of the streets.'"

... [D]espite this rare recognition of the risks to minority community respect, the Court adopted the *Terry* stop-and-frisk on mere reasonable suspicion rule, summarily concluding that such police harassment would not be stopped by applying the exclusionary rule.

*   *   *

…[A] respect-based jurisprudence would give the humiliation concerns noted by the Court greater weight. Despite its ambiguity, *Terry* is fairly read as the Court washing its hands of such concerns with humiliation. At a minimum, a willingness to dirty its hands could have led the Court to narrow the scope of the *Terry* rule. Instead, the rule and its unguided balancing approach have expanded, making police intrusions based on guesses and stereotypes all that much easier.…

Fourth, a respect-based jurisprudence emphasizes that all three branches of government are bound by the Fourth Amendment. *Terry*'s acknowledgment of other remedies than the exclusionary rule may implicitly have embraced a judgment that other branches were better equipped to address minority group concerns. If so, that is a judgment that the Court should have defended. The Court has an obligation to create incentives for other branches to meet their constitutional obligations. Bowing entirely out of setting adequate minimum standards for respectful police behavior does not serve that goal. At a minimum, the Court should have interceded with an express willingness to lower its vigilance if other branches proved up to the task.

*   *   *

Fifth, because a respect-based jurisprudence is very concerned with current social practices and attitudes, it makes far more extensive use of social science than is true today. Such social science is not always decisive, but it is frequently relevant. Social science could enlighten efforts to understand minority versus majority group experiences, inform judgments about which governmental branches can best function in their own particular ways, and reveal likely or unexpected effects of police actions. At times, reliance on social science would readily alter results, as Justice Stevens argued in his recent dissent in *Illinois v. Wardlow*. There, Justice Stevens concluded, empirical data suggested that African American males fleeing from the police in a high crime neighborhood were more likely to do so from fear of the police rather than as recognition of guilt. Accordingly,...Stevens would have found no reasonable suspicion where a *Terry* stop was based solely on a suspect's flight in a crime-ridden community.

*   *   *

Additionally, a respect-based jurisprudence involves the Court in history more deeply than is now the case. As noted earlier, the history of slavery and Reconstruction, not merely of the 1791 ratification of the Bill of Rights, becomes critical. That history supports the emphasis on respect, sheds light on some specific issues, identifies paradigm cases, and aids in balancing. But understanding the evolving nature of our commitments and the ways in which, and reasons for, our failures to meet them requires immersion in more modern history as well. The Japanese-American internment is once again a primary example, thus becoming relevant to understanding modern racial profiling of Hispanic and African Americans. In particular, the study of the internment reveals the critical social functions of freedom of movement, helping to combat minimization of this value in reasonableness balancing. The commitments of a people to respect its members are meaningless if abstracted from relevant history.

Finally, although I have repeatedly talked about minority group historical experiences and minority attitudes, many Fourth Amendment questions will not turn on issues of race. Nevertheless, the experiences of the most vulnerable among us can help to inform judgments about whether search and seizure practices that burden all equally adequately demonstrate respect for human value. Moreover, the history of African Americans led to the Fourteenth Amendment and thus is important to whites as well as to racial and ethnic minorities. In any event, the value of respect is important to all and is a too-often-neglected Fourth Amendment value, as the analysis of the arrest of the driver who did not wear her seatbelt in the *Atwater* case, discussed earlier in this article, illustrates....A respect-based approach...hold[s] out the hope of more careful, fully informed decisions aspiring to the best of American ideals.

*   *   *

REASONABLENESS AND OBJECTIVITY:
A FEMINIST DISCOURSE OF THE FOURTH AMENDMENT

DANA RAIGRODSKI

Reasonableness is traditionally regarded as an objective standard reflecting a neutral and communal agreement beyond the particular subjective viewpoints of individuals. Because of its appeal [to] objectivity, reasonableness has gained a prominent position in almost every area of American law, including search and seizure law.... The effectiveness of the reasonableness principle in achieving objectivity...depends upon its fundamental neutrality and its detachment from the subjective ideals of any individual. Feminists have thus re-examined reasonableness as part of a critique of objectivity.

Objectivity is a fundamental precept of Anglo-American jurisprudence. Patricia Williams observes how the opposition of objectivity to subjectivity constructs our theoretical legal understanding. Our legal thought and rhetoric are characterized by the existence of "transcendent, a-contextual, universal legal truths" that are conveyed by objective, unmediated voices such as judges. "The more serious problem of this essentialized world view is a worrisome tendency to disparage anything that is nontranscendent (temporal, historical), contextual

323

(socially constructed), or non-universal (specific) as 'emotional,' 'literary,' 'personal,' or just Not True." The result is, as Letti Volpp points out, that our jurisprudence fails to recognize the inherent subjectivity of legal standards and masks the oppressive force of the law against subordinated communities.

Williams and Volpp are not alone in pointing out the subjectivity of objectivity. As part of a persistent feminist investigation of the relationship between power and knowledge, many feminist scholars have demonstrated how particular views of the world dominate our discourse, "how our 'knowledge' is far less diverse than our people." Central to these critiques is skepticism about claims of objectivity and neutrality, and about statements that purport to have universal applicability. The point is that frequently what passes for the whole truth is instead a representation of events from the perspective of those who possess the power to have their version of reality accepted.

*   *   *

The gendered hierarchy of the objective-subjective dichotomy and the resulting invalidation of subjectivity is manifest in the way each of the prongs of the *Katz* test is articulated and applied as well as in the way the two prongs relate to each other.... In *Katz* itself, Justice Harlan's requirement that an expectation of privacy be one that society is prepared to recognize as reasonable correlates with the majority's holding that the government violated the privacy that the defendant justifiably relied on. Subsequent cases applying the test explained that the expectation must be objectively reasonable to be legitimate. Both in the search context and in the standing context the standard was restated so that reasonable is supplanted by legitimate, and both terms are employed interchangeably. Hence: objective = reasonable = legitimate = justified.

Like objectivity, notions of reasonableness, legitimacy, and justification occupy the strong male sides of common dichotomies in our legal and social discourse. Consequently, in a hidden and implicit manner, subjective expectations of privacy are dismissed and devalued, as are the weaker female sides of these dichotomies with which they are associated. Hence: subjective = unreasonable = illegitimate = unjustified.

*   *   *

The manner in which the two prongs of the *Katz* test relate to each other, normatively and as applied, further perpetuates the axiomatic supposition about the objectivity of reasonableness and the unreasonableness of subjectivity. Normatively, the first prong of the *Katz* test supposedly reaffirms the value of individual subjectivity, by assigning it a positive role in the determination of the scope of the constitutional protection. However, it is doctrinally inferior to the second objective prong. The test expresses a normative hierarchy between its two prongs, in which the individual's subjective expectations of privacy are subjugated to the objective expectations of privacy that are recognized by society. The test is essentially an objective one: whether the expectation is one that society is prepared to recognize as reasonable. If the subjective expectation deviates from that which the Court constructs as an objectively reasonable perspective, then it is invalidated and undeserving of constitutional protection.

*   *   *

2. THE SCHIZOPHRENIC TREATMENT OF SUBJECTIVITY: EMPOWERING THE POLICE

The Court's treatment of subjectivity is inconsistent. Sometimes its reasoning or holdings affirm and value subjectivity, and in other instances they degrade and invalidate subjectivity. Rather than being a coincidental inconsistency, this schism in the treatment of subjectivity is itself an expression of male power and serves to perpetuate male domination.

*   *   *

When it comes to police officers, the split treatment of subjectivity is clearly visible. On the one hand, "bad" subjective state of mind of the police is deemed irrelevant to the constitutional inquiry, based on the traditional rationale that personal subjective viewpoints have no place in an otherwise objective jurisprudence. On the other hand, the Court explicitly treasures the unique subjective experiences of police officers in fighting crime and law enforcement, and otherwise gives weight to the officer's "good" subjective state of mind in several contexts. The *Terry* Court even explicitly positioned the two against each other when it stated that "in determining whether the officer acted reasonably in such circumstances, due weight must be given, not to his inchoate and un-particularized suspicion or hunch, but to the specific reasonable inferences which he is entitled to draw from the facts in light of his experience."

*   *   *

IV. Discarding the Pretense of Reasonableness and Objectivity

As a feminist, my concern is not with the affirmation itself of the actual personal experiences and perceptions of individual officers. Law would be more just if the actual experiences and viewpoints of us all, especially of those of us who have traditionally been silenced and excluded from the legal discourse, were to shape our jurisprudence, inside and outside of the Fourth Amendment. For that to happen, however, the law must accept the actual perspectives of all as equally valuable rather than upholding or degrading particular perspectives in a manner that consistently empowers the government and subordinates the individual, especially those who are already socially oppressed.

Is it possible for feminist or other outsider constructions of reality to attain the status of objectivity within a legal framework that recognizes multiple realities? Martha Chamallas thinks the answer depends on whether objectivity will come to mean a construction of reality deserving legal recognition and protection rather than a neutral assessment devoid of perspective. I propose that we take a step further towards transforming our discourse and jurisprudence. Rather than trying to attain the status of objectivity within a discourse based on the division of objectivity from subjectivity, we can strive to discard the male epistemology of objectivity and the dichotomies it entails. We need to "discard the habit of equating our most noble aspirations with objectivity and neutrality" and adopt a concrete experience-based multi-perspectival epistemology and methodology. This alternative epistemology is not to be mistaken for replacing male objectivity with female subjectivity. The point is not that subjectivity is superior to objectivity or that passion is superior to reason. Rather, it is only through the wholesale rejection of the polarization of the dualistic pairs that we can create "the possibility of wholeness."

Within that newly envisioned feminist jurisprudence, should we also discard the concept of reasonableness or should we retain and redefine it? Like objectivity, the concept of reasonableness carries with it an immense symbolic power that can legitimate outsider claims. On the other hand, like objectivity, the risk is that even when used by the disempowered, reasonableness will continue to hide power hierarchies and thereby legitimate fundamentally oppressive structures. Especially if the new formulations of reasonableness are presented as neutral themselves, the redefined construct will merely reinforce and legitimate an unequal status quo. The failure, so far, of battered women's self-defense work in transforming the concept of reasonableness, and the emergence of gender- and race-specific reasonableness sub-standards, demonstrate how grave that risk is. It also seems futile and even harmful to attempt a transformation of the concept of reasonableness when it is so closely tied to the idea of objectivity and cannot allow for such a transformation.

Within Fourth Amendment jurisprudence in particular, reasonableness and objectivity have proven unable to address the core problems of citizen-government relations in a meaningful and just manner. Neither the overarching umbrella of reasonableness nor any specific reasonableness-based standards account for the power hierarchy that exists between the government, particularly the police, and the citizenry. Nor can any reasonableness standard meaningfully constrain oppressive power or address the harms of subordination. To the contrary, the notions of reasonableness and objectivity perpetuate such oppressive hierarchies. Therefore, it is especially important to displace the notion of reasonableness and the ideology of objectivity within search and seizure law.

Fourth Amendment jurisprudence should instead be restructured to account for government power and its abuse as means of controlling and subordinating the citizenry. Such a constitutional regime that is concerned with power and with hierarchical relations of domination will examine the behavior of the police officer and of the individual in light of the power hierarchies between them. This paradigmatic shift requires abandoning reasonableness-based standards altogether. Instead, I suggest we embrace the values of anti-subordination and empowerment to guide us in resolving power struggles within the context of the Fourth Amendment.

Refocusing the Fourth Amendment on oppressive power and subordination will require a new legal discourse, one explicitly committed to seeking out multiple perspectives other than our own instead of perpetuating an ideology of false objectivity and elitist reasonableness. This transformation is called for by the substantive core of the Fourth Amendment, by the general feminist critique of objectivity, by the commitment of feminists to voice the experiences of the oppressed other, and by the need to build on these experiences as a source of unique knowledge in the struggle against our subordination.

A commitment to anti-subordination and empowerment requires us to abandon the pretense of abstract objectivity and universal knowledge and adopt a multi-perspectival way of knowing informed by the detailed particularities of our lives.... As Ann Scales observes, if the purpose of law is indeed to decide the moral crux of the matter in real human situations, "[I]t would seem obvious that law's duty is to enhance, rather than to ignore, the rich diversity of life. Yet this purpose is not obvious; it is obscured by the myth of objectivity which opens up law's destructive potential."

*   *   *

Feminist epistemology values the multiplicity of perspectives and realities. It takes multiplicity to be constitutive of reality; it sees different perspectives as systematically related to each other and to other relations, such as exploited and exploiter; and it regards different perspectives as emergent and always changing. Feminist legal scholars have developed several versions of such multi-perspectival jurisprudence, but one message, captured by Martha Minow, unites them: "Only through the variety of relationships constructed by many people seeing from different perspectives can truth be known and community be created."

Judges, lawyers, and police officers must rethink how we come to know what we know. Particularly within the context of the Fourth Amendment, we must contemplate how and what we know about harm and injurious behavior. We must be more attentive to the lives of other people and the forces they operate within. Moreover, we must learn to view the world from more than a single, reflexive position. Patricia Williams has described this practice as the "ambivalent, multivalent way of seeing that is... at the heart of what is called critical theory, feminist theory, and the so-called minority critique." It is the "fluid positioning that sees back and forth across boundary," and which has been the "daily experience of people of color and of women."

Others advocate multiple consciousness as a jurisprudential method that ties together consciousness-shifting with a search for the pathway to a just world. In consciousness-shifting, Mari Matsuda refers to the ability to see that the law reflects a particular viewpoint, to operate within that view, and at the same time to shift out of it for purposes of critique, analysis, and strategy. Such multiple consciousness is not a mere random ability to see all points of view, but a deliberate choice to see the world from the standpoint of the oppressed. We can all choose to know the concrete lived details of others by reading, studying, and listening. The jurisprudence of outsiders teaches us that these details and the emotions they evoke are important as we set out on the road to justice.

For some, like Martha Minow, acknowledging our own inability to escape our perspective and seeking out multiple viewpoints is specifically the path to justice. As Martha Minow declares:

> Justice is engendered when judges admit the limitations of their own viewpoints, when judges reach beyond those limits by trying to see from contrasting perspectives, and when people seek to exercise power to nurture differences.... As we make audible, in official arenas, the struggles over which version of reality will secure power, we disrupt the silence of one perspective, imposed as if universal.

Minow thus calls on judges to identify vantage points, to learn how to adopt contrasting vantage points, and to decide which vantage points to embrace in given circumstances. She urges the judiciary to make a perpetual commitment to seek out unstated assumptions and typically unheard points of view. Rather than rules and fixed standards, we need struggles over descriptions of reality. Law should be "an opportunity to endow rival vantage points with the reality that power enables, to redescribe and remake the meanings of the world that has treated only some vantage points as legitimate."

*   *   *

It is not easy to understand those whose experiences and values are very different from our own. It takes practice, emotional maturity, and humility to make a habit of looking through the perspectives of others, advocates Minow. It takes an even greater effort to be moved by them. We need to open our minds to the possibility that a reality other than our own may matter. Indeed, the very effort to imagine another perspective could sensitize us to the possibility of a variety of perspectives, and could allow us to open our minds to accept more than one, two, or even three truths in any given situation.

*   *   *

To aid judges, lawyers, police officers, and the public in familiarizing ourselves with the perspectives of others, I suggest that we explicitly adopt a methodology of narratives. We should incorporate first person narratives into judicial opinions, police training, and media coverage of Fourth Amendment issues. Up until now, attempts to "imagine" other perspectives within traditional doctrinal structures like a reasonable person or officer standard have resulted in a narrow, one-dimensional, elitist, and oppressive perspective. In contrast, we should make room for concrete personal accounts of the parties involved. To some extent, personal accounts of police officers are already included in the law, as exemplified by the Court's deference to officers' accounts in forming reasonable suspicion and probable cause. But even an officer's voice is often filtered through the hypothetical lenses of the reasonable officer, and her first person testimony is relegated to a footnote rather than being a focal point of the Court's opinion.

* * *

Therefore, courts should allow all the facts to be presented by the parties; they should encourage the speech of the 'legally inarticulate' and include it within the universe of social realities that the law comprehends. Rather than having judges and lawyers re-tell the citizen or officer's story in the voice and from the perspective of an outside third person, the law should presume that each experience can be best described by the individual who experienced it. In this way, the legal system will empower individuals—citizens and officers alike— not only by responding to their experiences but also by giving them a space to speak their own words. This may allow all the parties to feel counted within the legal system and provide the recognition and validation that are important goals of many of those seeking legal relief and of many police officers.

* * *

In sum, the legal discourse of the Fourth Amendment can become empowering to the individual by letting the person's unmediated voice be spoken, and by listening to his or her story. However, for the directive to listen to be a meaningful normative guide rather than empty rhetoric, we should view our commitment to voice multiplicity and diversity as part of an expanded commitment to the true sharing of social power. Like Nancy Ehrenreich, I see multi-perspectivity as a substantive commitment. First, it requires a dedication to making decisions based on genuine attempts at understanding the perspectives and social circumstances of others, to making choices with care and humility. Second, it requires a willingness to reach results that actually produce the sharing of power with the powerless. We must be willing to accept the hard choices—and losses—that a true redistribution of power would entail.

APPENDICES

CONSTITUTION OF THE UNITED STATES OF AMERICA

Preamble

We, the people of the United States, in order to form a more perfect union, establish justice, insure domestic tranquility, provide for the common defense, promote the general welfare, and secure the blessings of liberty to ourselves and our posterity, do ordain and establish this Constitution for the United States of America.

Article I

Section I

1. All legislative powers herein granted shall be vested in a Congress of the United States, which shall consist of a Senate and House of Representatives.

Section II

1. The House of Representatives shall be composed of members chosen every second year by the people of the several States; and the electors in each

State shall have the qualifications requisite for electors of the most numerous branch of the State Legislature.

2. No person shall be a Representative who shall not have attained to the age of twenty-five years, and been seven years a citizen of the United States, and who shall not, when elected, be an inhabitant of that State in which he shall be chosen.

3. Representatives and direct taxes shall be apportioned among the several States which may be included within this Union, according to their respective numbers, which shall be determined by adding to the whole number of free persons, including those bound to service for a term of years, and excluding Indians not taxed, three-fifths of all other persons. The actual enumeration shall be made within three years after the first meeting of the Congress of the United States, and within every subsequent term of ten years, in such manner as they shall by law direct. The number of Representatives shall not exceed one for every thirty thousand, but each State shall have at least one Representative; and until such enumeration shall be made, the State of New Hampshire shall be entitled to choose three; Massachusetts, eight; Rhode Island and Providence Plantations, one; Connecticut, five; New York, six; New Jersey, four; Pennsylvania, eight; Delaware, one; Maryland, six; Virginia, ten; North Carolina, five; South Carolina, five, and Georgia, three.

4. When vacancies happen in the representation from any State, the executive authority thereof shall issue writs of election to fill such vacancies.

5. The House of Representatives shall choose their speaker and other officers; and shall have the sole power of impeachment.

Section III

1. The Senate of the United States shall be composed of two Senators from each State, chosen by the Legislature thereof for six years; and each Senator shall have one vote.

2. Immediately after they shall be assembled in consequence of the first election, they shall be divided as equally as may be into three classes. The

seats of the Senators of the first class shall be vacated at the expiration of the second year, of the second class at the expiration of the fourth year, and of the third class at the expiration of the sixth year, so that one third may be chosen every second year; and if vacancies happen by resignation, or otherwise, during the recess of the Legislature of any State, the executive thereof may make temporary appointments until the next meeting of the Legislature, which shall then fill such vacancies.

3. No person shall be a Senator who shall not have attained to the age of thirty years, and been nine years a citizen of the United States, and who shall not, when elected, be an inhabitant of that State for which he shall be chosen.

4. The Vice-President of the United States shall be President of the Senate, but shall have no vote unless they be equally divided.

5. The Senate shall choose their other officers, and also a President pro tempore, in the absence of the Vice-President, or when he shall exercise the office of President of the United States.

6. The Senate shall have the sole power to try all impeachments. When sitting for that purpose, they shall all be on oath or affirmation. When the President of the United States is tried, the chief-justice shall preside: and no person shall be convicted without the concurrence of two thirds of the members present.

7. Judgment in cases of impeachment shall not extend further than to removal from office, and disqualification to hold and enjoy any office of honor, trust, or profit under the United States; but the party convicted shall nevertheless be liable and subject to indictment, trial, judgment, and punishment, according to law.

Section IV

1. The times, places and manner of holding elections for Senators and Representatives shall be prescribed in each State by the Legislature thereof; but the Congress may at any time by law make of alter such regulations, except as to the place of choosing Senators.

Section V

1. Each House shall be the judge of the election, returns, and qualifications of its own members, and a majority of each shall constitute a quorum to do business; but a smaller number may adjourn from day to day, and may be authorized to compel the attendance of absent members, in such manner and under such penalties as each House may provide.

2. Each House may determine the rule of its proceedings, punish its members for disorderly behavior, and, with the concurrence of two thirds, expel a member.

3. Each House shall keep a journal of its proceedings, and from time to time publish the same, excepting such parts as may in their judgment require secrecy; and the yeas and nays of the members of either House on any questions shall, at the desire of one fifth of those present, be entered on the journal.

4. Neither House, during the session of Congress, shall, without the consent of the other, adjourn for more than three days, nor to any other place than that in which the two houses shall be sitting.

Section VI

1. The Senators and Representatives shall receive a compensation for their services, to be ascertained by law, and paid out of the treasury of the United States. They shall, in all cases, except treason, felony, and breach of the peace, be privileged from arrest during their attendance at the sessions of their respective houses, and in going to and returning from same; and for any speech or debate in either house, they shall not be questioned in any other place.

2. No Senator or Representative shall, during the time for which he was elected, be appointed to any civil office under the authority of the United States which shall have been created, or the emoluments whereof shall have been increased during such time; and no person holding any office under the United States shall be a member of either House during his continuance in office.

Section VII

1. All bills for raising revenue shall originate in the House of Representatives, but the Senate may propose or concur with amendments, as on other bills.

2. Every bill which shall have passed the House of Representatives and the Senate shall, before it become a law, be presented to the President of the United States; if he approve, he shall sign it, but if not, he shall return it, with his objections, to that House in which it shall have originated, who shall enter the objections at large on their journal, and proceed to reconsider it. If after such reconsideration two thirds of that House shall agree to pass the bill, it shall be sent, together with the objections, to the other House, by which it shall likewise be reconsidered; and if approved by two thirds of that House it shall become a law. But in all such cases the votes of both Houses shall be determined by yeas and nays, and the names of the persons voting for and against the bill shall be entered on the journal of each House respectively. If any bill shall not be returned by the President within ten days (Sundays excepted) after it shall have been presented to him, the same shall be a law in like manner as if he had signed it, unless the Congress by their adjournment, prevent its return; in which case it shall not be a law.

3. Every order, resolution, or vote to which the concurrence of the Senate and House of Representatives may be necessary (except on a question of adjournment) shall be presented to the President of the United States; and before the same shall take effect shall be approved by him, or being disapproved by him, shall be repassed by two thirds of the Senate and the House of Representatives, according to the rules and limitations prescribed in the case of a bill.

Section VIII

1. The Congress shall have power to lay and collect taxes, duties, imposts, and excises, to pay the debts and provide for the common defense and general welfare of the United States; but all duties, imposts, and excises shall be uniform throughout the United States.

2. To borrow money on the credit of the United States.

3. To regulate commerce with foreign nations, and among the several States, and with the Indian tribes.

4. To establish an uniform rule of naturalization and uniform laws on the subject of bankruptcies throughout the United States.

5. To coin money, regulate the value thereof, and of foreign coin, and fix the standard of weights and measures.

6. To provide for the punishment of counterfeiting the securities and current coin of the United States.

7. To establish post offices and post roads.

8. To promote the progress of science and useful arts, by securing for limited times to authors and inventors the exclusive rights to their respective writings and discoveries.

9. To constitute tribunals inferior to the Supreme Court.

10. To define and punish piracies and felonies committed on the high seas, and offenses against the law of nations.

11. To declare war, grant letters of marque and reprisal, and make rules concerning captures on land and water.

12. To raise and support armies, but no appropriation of money to that use shall be for a longer term than two years.

13. To provide and maintain a navy.

14. To make rules for the government and regulation of the land and naval forces.

15. To provide for calling forth the militia to execute the laws of the Union, suppress insurrections, and repel invasions.

16. To provide for organizing, arming, and disciplining the militia, and for governing such part of them as may be employed in the service of the United States, reserving to the States respectively the appointment of the officers, and the authority of training the militia according to the discipline prescribed by Congress.

17. To exercise exclusive legislation in all cases whatsoever over such district (not exceeding ten miles square) as may, by cession of particular States and the acceptance of Congress, become the seat of Government of the United States, and to exercise like authority over all places purchased by the consent of the Legislature of the State in which the same shall be, for the erection of forts, magazines, arsenals, dry docks, and other needful buildings.

18. To make all laws which shall be necessary and proper for carrying into execution the foregoing powers, and all other powers vested by this Constitution in the Government of the United States, or in any department or officer thereof.

Section IX

1. The migration or importation of such persons as any of the States now existing shall think proper to admit shall not be prohibited by the Congress prior to the year one thousand eight hundred and eight, but a tax or duty may be imposed on such importation, not exceeding ten dollars for each person.

2. The privilege of the writ of habeas corpus shall not be suspended, unless when in cases of rebellion or invasion the public safety may require it.

3. No bill of attainder or ex post facto law shall be passed.

4. No capitation or other direct tax shall be laid, unless in proportion to the census or enumeration hereinbefore directed to be taken.

5. No tax or duty shall be laid on articles exported from any State.

6. No preference shall be given by any regulation of commerce or revenue to the ports of one State over those of another, nor shall vessels bound to or from one State be obliged to enter, clear, or pay duties in another.

7. No money shall be drawn from the Treasury but in consequence of appropriations made by law; and a regular statement and account of the receipts and expenditures of all public money shall be published from time to time.

8. No title of nobility shall be granted by the United States. And no person holding any office of profit or trust under them shall, without the consent of the Congress, accept of any present, emolument, office, or title of any kind whatever from any king, prince, or foreign state.

Section X

1. No state shall enter into any treaty, alliance, or confederation, grant letters of marque and reprisal, coin money, emit bills of credit, make anything but gold and silver coin a tender in payment of debts, pass any bill of attainder, ex post facto law, or law impairing the obligation of contracts, or grant any title of nobility.

2. No State shall, without the consent of the Congress, lay any impost or duties on imports or exports, except what may be absolutely necessary for executing its inspection laws, and the net produce of all duties and imposts, laid by any State on imports or exports, shall be for the use of the Treasury of the United States; and all such laws shall be subject to the revision and control of the Congress.

3. No State shall, without the consent of Congress, lay any duty of tonnage, keep troops or ships of war in time of peace, enter into any agreement or compact with another State, or with a foreign power, or engage in war, unless actually invaded, or in such imminent danger as will not admit of delay.

Article II

Section I

1. The Executive power shall be vested in a President of the United States of America. He shall hold his office during the term of four years, and, together with the Vice-President, chosen for the same term, be elected as follows:

2. Each State shall appoint, in such manner as the Legislature thereof may direct, a number of electors, equal to the whole number of Senators and Representatives to which the State may be entitled in the Congress; but no Senator or Representative or person holding an office of trust or profit under the United States shall be appointed an elector.

3. [The electors shall meet in their respective States and vote by ballot for two persons, of whom one at least shall not be an inhabitant of the same State with themselves. And they shall make a list of all the persons voted for, and of the number of votes for each, which list they shall sign and certify and transmit, sealed, to the seat of the government of the United States, directed to the President of the Senate. The President of the Senate shall, in the presence of the Senate and House of Representatives, open all the certificates, and the votes shall then be counted. The person having the greatest number of votes shall be the President, if such number be a majority of the whole number of electors appointed, and if there be more than one who have such majority, and have an equal number of votes, then the House of Representatives shall immediately choose by ballot one of them for President; and if no person have a majority, then from the five highest on the list the said House shall in like manner choose the President. But in choosing the President, the vote shall be taken by States, the representation from each State having one vote. A quorum, for this purpose, shall consist of a member or members from two thirds of the States, and a majority of all the States shall be necessary to a choice. In every case, after the choice of the President, the person having the greatest number of votes of the electors shall be the Vice-President. But if there should remain two or more who have equal votes, the Senate shall choose from them by ballot the Vice-President.]*

---

*This clause is superseded by Article XII.

4. The Congress may determine the time of choosing the electors and the day on which they shall give their votes, which day shall be the same throughout the United States.

5. No person except a natural born citizen, or a citizen of the United States at the time of the adoption of this Constitution, shall be eligible to the office of President; neither shall any person be eligible to that office who shall not have attained to the age of thirty-five years and been fourteen years a resident within the United States.

6. In case of the removal of the President from office, or of his death, resignation, or inability to discharge the powers and duties of the said office, the same shall devolve on the Vice-President, and the Congress may by law provide for the case of removal, death, resignation, or inability, both of the President and Vice-President, declaring what officer shall then act as President, and such officer shall act accordingly until the disability be removed or a President shall be elected.

7. The President shall, at stated times, receive for his services a compensation, which shall neither be increased nor diminished during the period for which he shall have been elected, and he shall not receive within that period any other emolument from the United States, or any of them.

8. Before he enter on the execution of his office he shall take the following oath or affirmation: "I do solemnly swear (or affirm) that I will faithfully execute the office of President of the United States, and will, to the best of my ability, preserve, protect, and defend the Constitution of the United States."

Section II

1. The President shall be Commander-in-Chief of the Army and Navy of the United States, and of the militia of the several States when called into the actual service of the United States; he may require the opinion, in writing, of the principal officer in each of the executive departments upon any subject relating to the duties of their respective offices, and he shall have power to grant reprieves and pardons for offenses against the United States except in cases of impeachment.

2. He shall have power, by and with the advice and consent of the Senate, to make treaties, provided two thirds of the Senators present concur; and he shall nominate, and by and with the advice and consent of the Senate shall appoint ambassadors, other public ministers and consuls, judges of the Supreme Court, and all other officers of the United States whose appointments are not herein otherwise provided for, and which shall be established by law; but the Congress may by law vest the appointment of such inferior officers as they think proper in the President alone, in the courts of law, or in the heads of departments.

3. The President shall have power to fill up all vacancies that may happen during the recess of the Senate by granting commissions, which shall expire at the end of their next session.

Section III

He shall from time to time give to the Congress information of the state of the Union, and recommend to their consideration such measure as he shall judge necessary and expedient; he may, on extraordinary occasions, convene both Houses, or either of them, and in case of disagreement between them with respect to the time of adjournment, he may adjourn them to such time as he shall think proper; he shall receive ambassadors and other public ministers; he shall take care that the laws be faithfully executed, and shall commission all the officers of the United States.

Section IV

The President, Vice-President, and all civil officers of the United States shall be removed from office on impeachment for and conviction of treason, bribery, or other high crimes and misdemeanors.

ARTICLE III

Section I

The judicial power of the United States shall be vested in one Supreme Court, and in such inferior courts as the Congress may from time to time ordain and establish. The judges, both of the Supreme and inferior courts, shall hold their offices during good behavior, and shall at stated times receive for their services a compensation which shall not be diminished during their continuance in office.

Section II

1. The judicial power shall extend to all cases in law and equity arising under this Constitution, the laws of the United States, and treaties made, or which shall be made, under their authority; to all cases affecting ambassadors, other public ministers, and consuls; to all cases of admiralty and maritime jurisdiction; to controversies to which the United States shall be a party; to controversies between two or more States, between a State and citizens of another State, between citizens of different States, between citizens of the same State claiming lands under grants of different States, and between a State, or the citizens thereof, and foreign States, citizens, or subjects.

2. In all cases affecting ambassadors, other public ministers, and consuls, and those in which a State shall be party, the Supreme Court shall have original jurisdiction. In all the other cases before mentioned the Supreme Court shall have appellate jurisdiction both as to law and fact, with such exceptions and under such regulations as the Congress shall make.

3. The trial of all crimes, except in cases of impeachment, shall be by jury, and such trial shall be held in the State where the said crimes shall have been committed; but when not committed within any State the trial shall be at such place or places as the Congress may by law have directed.

Section III

1. Treason against the United States shall consist only in levying war against them, or in adhering to their enemies, giving them aid and comfort. No person shall be convicted of treason unless on the testimony of two witnesses to the same overt act, or on confession in open court.

2. The Congress shall have power to declare the punishment of treason, but no attainder of treason shall work corruption of blood or forfeiture except during the life of the person attained.

ARTICLE IV

Section I

Full faith and credit shall be given in each State to the public acts, records, and judicial proceedings of every other State. And the Congress may by general laws prescribe the manner in which such acts, records and proceedings shall be proved, and the effect thereof.

Section II

1. The citizens of each State shall be entitled to all privileges and immunities of citizens in the several States.

2. A person charged in any State with treason, felony, or other crime, who shall flee from justice, and be found in another State, shall on demand of the Executive authority of the State from which he fled, be delivered up, to be removed to the State having jurisdiction of the crime.

3. No person held to service or labor in one State, under the laws thereof, escaping into another shall, in consequence of any law or regulation therein, be discharged from such service or labor, but shall be delivered up on claim of the party to whom such service or labor may be due.

Section III

1. New States may be admitted by the Congress into this Union; but no new State shall be formed or erected within the jurisdiction of any other State, nor any State be formed by the junction of two or more States, or parts of States, without the consent of the Legislatures of the States concerned, as well as of the Congress.

2. The Congress shall have power to dispose of and make all needful rules and regulations respecting the territory or other property belonging to the United States; and nothing in this Constitution shall be so construed as to prejudice any claims of the United States, or of any particular State.

Section IV

The United States shall guarantee to every State in this Union a republican form of government, and shall protect each of them against invasion, and, on application of the Legislature, or of the Executive (when the Legislature cannot be convened), against domestic violence.

ARTICLE V

The Congress, whenever two thirds of both Houses shall deem it necessary, shall propose amendments to this Constitution, or, on the application of the Legislatures of two thirds of the several States, shall call a convention for proposing amendments, which, in either case, shall be valid to all intents and purposes, as part of this Constitution, when ratified by the Legislatures of three fourths of the several States, or by conventions in three fourths thereof, as the one or the other mode of ratification may be proposed by the Congress; provided that no amendment which may be made prior to the year one thousand eight hundred and eight shall in any manner affect the first and fourth clauses in the Ninth Section of the First Article; and that no State, without its consent, shall be deprived of its equal suffrage in the Senate.

ARTICLE VI

1. All debts contracted and engagements entered into before the adoption of this Constitution shall be as valid against the United States under this Constitution as under the Confederation.

2. This Constitution and the laws of the United States which shall be made in pursuance thereof and all treaties made, or which shall be made, under the authority of the United States, shall be the supreme law of the land, and the judges in every State shall be bound thereby, anything in the Constitution of laws of any State to the contrary notwithstanding.

3. The Senators and Representatives before mentioned, and the members of the several State Legislatures, and all executive and judicial officers, both of the United States and of the several States, shall be bound by oath or affirmation to support this Constitution; but no religious test shall ever be

required as a qualification to any office or public trust under the United States.

ARTICLE VII

The ratification of the Conventions of nine States shall be sufficient for the establishment of this Constitution between the States so ratifying the same.

THE AMENDMENTS TO THE CONSTITUTION*

The Conventions of a number of the States having, at the time of adopting the Constitution, expressed a desire, in order to prevent misconstruction or abuse of its powers, that further declaratory and restrictive clauses should be added, and as extending the ground of public confidence in the Government will best insure the beneficent ends of its institution;

Resolved, by the Senate and House of Representatives of the United States of America, in Congress assembled, two-thirds of both Houses concurring, that the following articles be proposed to the Legislatures of the several States, as amendments to the Constitution of the United States; all or any of which articles, when ratified by three-fourths of the said Legislatures, to be valid to all intents and purposes as part of the said Constitution, namely:

AMENDMENT I

Congress shall make no law respecting an establishment of religion, or prohibiting the free exercise thereof; or abridging the freedom of speech, or of the press; or the right of the people peaceably to assemble, and to petition the Government for a redress of grievances.

---

*The Bill of Rights consists of the first ten amendments to the Constitution.

AMENDMENT II

A well regulated Militia, being necessary to the security of a free State, the right of the people to keep and bear Arms, shall not be infringed.

AMENDMENT III

No Soldier shall, in time of peace be quartered in any house, without the consent of the Owner, nor in time of war, but in a manner to be prescribed by law.

AMENDMENT IV

The right of the people to be secure in their persons, houses, papers, and effects, against unreasonable searches and seizures, shall not be violated, and no Warrants shall issue, but upon probable cause, supported by Oath or affirmation, and particularly describing the place to be searched, and the persons or things to be seized.

AMENDMENT V

No person shall be held to answer for a capital, or otherwise infamous crime, unless on a presentment or indictment of a Grand Jury, except in cases arising in the land or naval forces, or in the Militia, when in actual service in time of War or public danger; nor shall any person be subject for the same offense to be twice put in jeopardy of life or limb; nor shall be compelled in any criminal case to be a witness against himself, nor be deprived of life, liberty, or property, without due process of law; nor shall private property be taken for public use, without just compensation.

AMENDMENT VI

In all criminal prosecutions, the accused shall enjoy the right to a speedy and public trial, by an impartial jury of the State and district wherein the crime shall have been committed, which district shall have been previously ascertained by law, and to be informed of the nature and cause of the accusation; to be confronted with the witnesses against him; to have compulsory process for obtaining witnesses in his favor, and to have the Assistance of Counsel for his defence.

AMENDMENT VII

In Suits at common law, where the value in controversy shall exceed twenty dollars, the right of trial by jury shall be preserved, and no fact tried by a jury, shall be otherwise re-examined in any Court of the United States, than according to the rules of the common law.

AMENDMENT VIII

Excessive bail shall not be required, nor excessive fines imposed, nor cruel and unusual punishments inflicted.

AMENDMENT IX

The enumeration in the Constitution, of certain rights, shall not be construed to deny or disparage others retained by the people.

AMENDMENT X

The powers not delegated to the United States by the Constitution, nor prohibited by it to the States, are reserved to the States respectively, or to the people.

AMENDMENT XI

The Judicial power of the United States shall not be construed to extend to any suit in law or equity, commenced or prosecuted against one of the United States by Citizens of another State, or by Citizens or Subjects of any Foreign State.

AMENDMENT XII

The Electors shall meet in their respective states, and vote by ballot for President and Vice-President, one of whom, at least, shall not be an inhabitant of the same state with themselves; they shall name in their ballots the person voted for as President, and in distinct ballots the person voted for as Vice-President, and they shall make distinct lists of all persons voted for as President, and of all persons voted for as Vice-President and of the number of votes for each, which lists they shall sign and certify, and transmit sealed to the seat of the government of the United States, directed to the President of the Senate; The President of the Senate shall, in the presence of the Senate and House of Representatives, open all the certificates and the votes shall then be counted; The person having the greatest Number of votes for President, shall be the President, if such number be a majority of the whole number of Electors appointed; and if no person have such majority, then from the persons having the highest numbers not exceeding three on the list of those voted for as President, the House of Representatives shall choose immediately, by ballot, the President. But in choosing the President, the votes shall be taken by states, the representation from each state having one vote; a quorum for this purpose shall consist of a member or members from two-thirds of the states, and a majority of all the states shall be necessary to a choice. And if the House of Representatives shall not choose a President whenever the right of choice shall devolve upon them, before the fourth day of March next following, then the Vice-President shall act as President, as in the case of the death or other constitutional disability of the President. The person having the greatest number of votes as Vice-President, shall be the Vice-President, if such number be a majority of the whole number of Electors appointed, and if no person have a majority, then from the two highest numbers on the list, the Senate shall choose the Vice-President; a quorum for the purpose shall consist of two-thirds of the whole number of Senators, and a majority of the whole number shall be necessary to a choice. But no person constitutionally ineligible to the office of President shall be eligible to that of Vice-President of the United States.

AMENDMENT XIII

1. Neither slavery nor involuntary servitude, except as a punishment for crime whereof the party shall have been duly convicted, shall exist within the United States, or any place subject to their jurisdiction.

2. Congress shall have power to enforce this article by appropriate legislation.

Amendment XIV

1. All persons born or naturalized in the United States, and subject to the jurisdiction thereof, are citizens of the United States and of the State wherein they reside. No State shall make or enforce any law which shall abridge the privileges or immunities of citizens of the United States; nor shall any State deprive any person of life, liberty, or property, without due process of law; nor deny to any person within its jurisdiction the equal protection of the laws.

2. Representatives shall be apportioned among the several States according to their respective numbers, counting the whole number of persons in each State, excluding Indians not taxed. But when the right to vote at any election for the choice of electors for President and Vice-President of the United States, Representatives in Congress, the Executive and Judicial officers of a State, or the members of the Legislature thereof, is denied to any of the male inhabitants of such State, being twenty-one years of age, and citizens of the United States, or in any way abridged, except for participation in rebellion, or other crime, the basis of representation therein shall be reduced in the proportion which the number of such male citizens shall bear to the whole number of male citizens twenty-one years of age in such State.

3. No person shall be a Senator or Representative in Congress, or elector of President and Vice-President, or hold any office, civil or military, under the United States, or under any State, who, having previously taken an oath, as a member of Congress, or as an officer of the United States, or as a member of any State legislature, or as an executive or judicial officer of any State, to support the Constitution of the United States, shall have engaged in insurrection or rebellion against the same, or given aid or comfort to the enemies thereof. But Congress may by a vote of two-thirds of each House, remove such disability.

4. The validity of the public debt of the United States, authorized by law, including debts incurred for payment of pensions and bounties for services in suppressing insurrection or rebellion, shall not be questioned. But neither the United States nor any State shall assume or pay any debt or obligation incurred in aid of insurrection or rebellion against the United States, or any claim for the loss or emancipation of any slave; but all such debts, obligations and claims shall be held illegal and void.

5. The Congress shall have power to enforce, by appropriate legislation, the provisions of this article.

AMENDMENT XV

1. The right of citizens of the United States to vote shall not be denied or abridged by the United States or by any State on account of race, color, or previous condition of servitude.

2. The Congress shall have power to enforce this article by appropriate legislation.

AMENDMENT XVI

The Congress shall have power to lay and collect taxes on incomes, from whatever source derived, without apportionment among the several States, and without regard to any census or enumeration.

AMENDMENT XVII

The Senate of the United States shall be composed of two Senators from each State, elected by the people thereof, for six years; and each Senator shall have one vote. The electors in each State shall have the qualifications requisite for electors of the most numerous branch of the State legislatures. When vacancies happen in the representation of any State in the Senate, the executive authority of such State shall issue writs of election to fill such vacancies: Provided, That the legislature of any State may empower the executive thereof to make temporary appointments until the people fill the vacancies by election as the legislature may direct. This amendment shall not be so construed as to affect the election or term of any Senator chosen before it becomes valid as part of the Constitution.

AMENDMENT XVIII

1. After one year from the ratification of this article the manufacture, sale, or transportation of intoxicating liquors within, the importation thereof into, or the exportation thereof from the United States and all territory subject to the jurisdiction thereof for beverage purposes is hereby prohibited.

2. The Congress and the several States shall have concurrent power to enforce this article by appropriate legislation.

3. This article shall be inoperative unless it shall have been ratified as an

amendment to the Constitution by the legislatures of the several States, as provided in the Constitution, within seven years from the date of the submission hereof to the States by the Congress.

AMENDMENT XIX

The right of citizens of the United States to vote shall not be denied or abridged by the United States or by any State on account of sex. Congress shall have power to enforce this article by appropriate legislation.

AMENDMENT XX

1. The terms of the President and Vice President shall end at noon on the 20th day of January, and the terms of Senators and Representatives at noon on the 3d day of January, of the years in which such terms would have ended if this article had not been ratified; and the terms of their successors shall then begin.

2. The Congress shall assemble at least once in every year, and such meeting shall begin at noon on the 3d day of January, unless they shall by law appoint a different day.

3. If, at the time fixed for the beginning of the term of the President, the President elect shall have died, the Vice President elect shall become President. If a President shall not have been chosen before the time fixed for the beginning of his term, or if the President elect shall have failed to qualify, then the Vice President elect shall act as President until a President shall have qualified; and the Congress may by law provide for the case wherein neither a President elect nor a Vice President elect shall have qualified, declaring who shall then act as President, or the manner in which one who is to act shall be selected, and such person shall act accordingly until a President or Vice President shall have qualified.

4. The Congress may by law provide for the case of the death of any of the persons from whom the House of Representatives may choose a President whenever the right of choice shall have devolved upon them, and for the case of the death of any of the persons from whom the Senate may choose a Vice President whenever the right of choice shall have devolved upon them.

5. Sections 1 and 2 shall take effect on the 15th day of October following the ratification of this article.

6. This article shall be inoperative unless it shall have been ratified as an amendment to the Constitution by the legislatures of three-fourths of the several States within seven years from the date of its submission.

Amendment XXI

1. The eighteenth article of amendment to the Constitution of the United States is hereby repealed.

2. The transportation or importation into any State, Territory, or possession of the United States for delivery or use therein of intoxicating liquors, in violation of the laws thereof, is hereby prohibited.

3. The article shall be inoperative unless it shall have been ratified as an amendment to the Constitution by conventions in the several States, as provided in the Constitution, within seven years from the date of the submission hereof to the States by the Congress.

Amendment XXII

1. No person shall be elected to the office of the President more than twice, and no person who has held the office of President, or acted as President, for more than two years of a term to which some other person was elected President shall be elected to the office of the President more than once. But this Article shall not apply to any person holding the office of President, when this Article was proposed by the Congress, and shall not prevent any person who may be holding the office of President, or acting as President, during the term within which this Article becomes operative from holding the office of President or acting as President during the remainder of such term.

2. This article shall be inoperative unless it shall have been ratified as an amendment to the Constitution by the legislatures of three-fourths of the several States within seven years from the date of its submission to the States by the Congress.

Amendment XXIII

1. The District constituting the seat of Government of the United States shall appoint in such manner as the Congress may direct: A number of electors of President and Vice President equal to the whole number of Senators

and Representatives in Congress to which the District would be entitled if it were a State, but in no event more than the least populous State; they shall be in addition to those appointed by the States, but they shall be considered, for the purposes of the election of President and Vice President, to be electors appointed by a State; and they shall meet in the District and perform such duties as provided by the twelfth article of amendment.

2. The Congress shall have power to enforce this article by appropriate legislation.

Amendment XXIV

1. The right of citizens of the United States to vote in any primary or other election for President or Vice President, for electors for President or Vice President, or for Senator or Representative in Congress, shall not be denied or abridged by the United States or any State by reason of failure to pay any poll tax or other tax.

2. The Congress shall have power to enforce this article by appropriate legislation.

Amendment XXV

1. In case of the removal of the President from office or of his death or resignation, the Vice President shall become President.

2. Whenever there is a vacancy in the office of the Vice President, the President shall nominate a Vice President who shall take office upon confirmation by a majority vote of both Houses of Congress.

3. Whenever the President transmits to the President pro tempore of the Senate and the Speaker of the House of Representatives his written declaration that he is unable to discharge the powers and duties of his office, and until he transmits to them a written declaration to the contrary, such powers and duties shall be discharged by the Vice President as Acting President.

4. Whenever the Vice President and a majority of either the principal officers of the executive departments or of such other body as Congress may by law provide, transmit to the President pro tempore of the Senate and the Speaker of the House of Representatives their written declaration that the President is unable to discharge the powers and duties of his office, the Vice President shall immediately assume the powers and duties of the office as

Acting President. Thereafter, when the President transmits to the President pro tempore of the Senate and the Speaker of the House of Representatives his written declaration that no inability exists, he shall resume the powers and duties of his office unless the Vice President and a majority of either the principal officers of the executive department or of such other body as Congress may by law provide, transmit within four days to the President pro tempore of the Senate and the Speaker of the House of Representatives their written declaration that the President is unable to discharge the powers and duties of his office. Thereupon Congress shall decide the issue, assembling within forty eight hours for that purpose if not in session. If the Congress, within twenty one days after receipt of the latter written declaration, or, if Congress is not in session, within twenty one days after Congress is required to assemble, determines by two thirds vote of both Houses that the President is unable to discharge the powers and duties of his office, the Vice President shall continue to discharge the same as Acting President; otherwise, the President shall resume the powers and duties of his office.

Amendment XXVI

1. The right of citizens of the United States, who are eighteen years of age or older, to vote shall not be denied or abridged by the United States or by any State on account of age.

2. The Congress shall have power to enforce this article by appropriate legislation.

Amendment XXVII

No law, varying the compensation for the services of the Senators and Representatives, shall take effect, until an election of Representatives shall have intervened.

SOURCES AND PERMISSIONS

CHAPTER 1

"FOURTH AMENDMENT FIRST PRINCIPLES"

Harvard Law Review 107, no. 4 (1994): 757, 757–59, 761–62, 770–75. *Harvard Law Review* 107, no. 757 (1994) by Akhil Reed Amar (the "Material"). All rights reserved. Published by permission of the author c/o Writers Representatives LLC, New York, NY 10011.

"RECOVERING THE ORIGINAL FOURTH AMENDMENT"

Michigan Law Review 98, no. 3 (1999): 547, 559–60, 573–78, 582–90. Reprinted by permission of Thomas Y. Davies.

THE FOURTH AMENDMENT: ORIGINS AND ORIGINAL MEANING 602–1791

New York: Oxford University Press, 2009, pp. 1, 773–78, 781. Reprinted by permission of William J. Cuddihy and Oxford University Press.

"Second Thoughts about First Principles"

Harvard Law Review 107, no. 4 (1994): 820, 821–24, 830–33, 836–41. Courtesy of Carol S. Steiker.

"Perspectives on the Fourth Amendment"

Minnesota Law Review 58 (1974): 349, 395–400. *Perspectives on the Fourth Amendment* is the text of the Oliver Wendell Holmes Lectures delivered by Professor Anthony G. Amsterdam at the University of Minnesota Law School on January 22, 23, and 24, 1974. Courtesy of Anthony G. Amsterdam and the *Minnesota Law Review.*

"The Fourth Amendment and Common Law"

Columbia Law Review 100, no. 7 (2000): 1739, 1739–43, 1757–61, 1770–75, 1794. Reprinted by permission of David A. Slansky and the *Columbia Law Review.*

CHAPTER 2

"Katz and the Origins of the 'Reasonable Expectation of Privacy' Test"

McGeorge Law Review 40, no. 1 (2009): 1, 4–10, 12. Reprinted courtesy of Peter Winn and *McGeorge Law Review.*

"Four Models of Fourth Amendment Protection"

Stanford Law Review 60, no. 2 (2007): 503, 504–509, 511–17, 519–20. Reprinted by permission of Orin S. Kerr and *Stanford Law Review.*

"The Distribution of Fourth Amendment Privacy"

The George Washington Law Review 67, no. 5 (1999): 1265, 1268–73. Courtesy of William J. Stuntz and *The George Washington Law Review.*

"WHAT IS A SEARCH? TWO CONCEPTUAL FLAWS IN
FOURTH AMENDMENT DOCTRINE AND SOME HINTS OF A REMEDY"

Stanford Law Review 55, no. 1 (2002): 119, 122–23, 126–29, 132–38. Reprinted by permission of Sherry F. Colb and *Stanford Law Review*.

"DIGITAL DOSSIERS AND THE DISSIPATION
OF FOURTH AMENDMENT PRIVACY"

Southern California Law Review 75, no. 5 (2002): 1083, 1089–95, 1134–35, 1137–38. Reprinted with the permission of Daniel J. Solove and the *Southern California Law Review*.

"THE SUPREME COURT, CRIMINAL PROCEDURE, AND JUDICIAL INTEGRITY"

American Criminal Law Review 40, no. 1 (2003): 133, 141–42. Reprinted with permission of Stephen A. Saltzburg and the publisher, *American Criminal Law Review* © 2003.

"OPEN FIELDS IN THE INNER CITY: APPLICATION OF THE
CURTILAGE DOCTRINE TO URBAN AND SUBURBAN AREAS"

George Mason University Civil Rights Law Journal 15, no. 2 (2005): 297, 310–12m 314m 316–19. Reprinted by permission of Carrie Leonetti and the *George Mason University Civil Rights Law Journal* .

CHAPTER 3

"THE SUPREME COURT'S SEARCH FOR A DEFINITION OF A SEIZURE:
WHAT IS A 'SEIZURE' OF A PERSON WITHIN THE
MEANING OF THE FOURTH AMENDMENT?"

American Criminal Law Review 27, no. 4 (1990): 619, 625–26, 633–37, 639–40. Reprinted with permission of Thomas K. Clancy and the publisher, *American Criminal Law Review* © 1990.

"(E)RACING THE FOURTH AMENDMENT"

Michigan Law Review 100, no. 5 (2002): 946, 947–50, 952–64, 974–78, 980–82, 984–86. Courtesy of Devon W. Carbado.

"'Black and Blue Encounters'—Some Preliminary Thoughts about Fourth Amendment Seizures: Should Race Matter?"

Valparaiso University Law Review 26, no. 1 (1991): 243, 248–50, 268–76, 278–79. Courtesy of Tracey Maclin and the *Valparaiso University Law Review*.

"No Need to Shout: Bus Sweeps and the Psychology of Coercion"

Supreme Court Review, 2002: 153, 157–60, 162–63, 165, 173–77, 179–83, 185–90. Reprinted by permission of Janice Nadler and the University of Chicago Press.

CHAPTER 4

"*Terry v. Ohio* at Thirty-Five: A Revisionist View"

Mississippi Law Journal 74, no. 2 (2004): 423, 430–33, 485–87, 490, 492–97. Courtesy of Lewis R. Katz and the *Mississippi Law Journal*.

"Stopping the Usual Suspects: Race and the Fourth Amendment"

New York University Law Review 74, no. 4 (1999): 956, 962–64, 966–72, 987–89. Courtesy of Anthony C. Thompson and the *New York University Law Review*.

"*Terry v. Ohio*, The Warren Court, and the Fourth Amendment: A Law Clerk's Perspective"

St. John's Law Review 72, nos. 3–4 (1998): 891, 891–95. First published in vol. 72 of *St. John's Law Review*. Courtesy of Earl C. Dudley Jr. and the *St. John's Law Review*.

"Let's Not Bury *Terry*: A Call for Rejuvenation of the Proportionality Principle"

St. John's Law Review 72, nos. 3–4 (1998): 1053, 1053–57, 1081–85. Courtesy of Christopher Slobogin, Milton Underwood Professor of Law; Vanderbilt University Law School; and the *St. John's Law Review*. First published in vol. 72 of the *St. John's Law Review*. The author slightly modified the proposals described in this article in his book *Privacy at Risk: The New Government Surveillance and the Fourth Amendment*, chap. 2 (2007).

CHAPTER 5

"'DRIVING WHILE BLACK' AND ALL OTHER TRAFFIC OFFENSES: THE SUPREME COURT AND PRETEXTUAL TRAFFIC STOPS"

Journal of Criminal Law and Criminology 87, no. 2 (1997): 544, 544–47, 560–68. David A. Harris is the copyright holder, and this article is reprinted by his permission.

"'WALKING WHILE BLACK': ENCOUNTERS WITH THE POLICE ON MY STREET"

Legal Times, November 10, 1997, p. 23. Used by permission of Paul Butler and the *Legal Times*.

"CULTURAL CONTEXT MATTERS: *TERRY'S* 'SEESAW EFFECT'"

Oklahoma Law Review 56, no. 4 (2003): 833, 862–68. Permission granted by Frank Rudy Cooper.

"PROFILING TERROR"

Ohio State Journal of Criminal Law 1, no. 1 (2003): 45, 46–59, 76–80. Courtesy of Sharon L. Davies.

CHAPTER 6

"THE ROAD TO *MAPP V. OHIO* AND BEYOND: THE ORIGINS, DEVELOPMENT AND FUTURE OF THE EXCLUSIONARY RULE IN SEARCH-AND-SEIZURE CASES"

Columbia Law Review 83, no. 6 (1983): 1365, 1366–68, 1372–75, 1380, 1384–89. Reprinted by permission of the *Columbia Law Review*.

"THE EXCLUSIONARY RULE ON THE SCAFFOLD: BUT WAS IT A FAIR TRIAL?"

American Criminal Law Review 22, no. 2 (1984): 85, 85–90, 97–98, 105–10, 112–15. © 2010 by the American Bar Association. Reprinted with permission. All rights

"THE END OF THE EXCLUSIONARY RULE, AMONG OTHER THINGS: THE ROBERTS COURT TAKES ON THE FOURTH AMENDMENT"

Cato Supreme Court Review, 2006: 283, 295–303, 307–309. Reprinted by permission of David A. Moran, Clinical Professor of Law and Co-Director, Michigan Innocence Clinic; University of Michigan Law School; and the *Cato Supreme Court Law Review*.

"THE EXCLUSIONARY RULE"

Harvard Journal of Law & Public Policy 26, no. 1 (2003): 111, 111–17. Guido Calabresi, "The Exclusionary Rule," *Harvard Journal of Law and Public Policy* 26, no. 1 (2003): 111, 111–17. Reprinted with permission.

CHAPTER 7

"THE FOURTH AMENDMENT AND NEW TECHNOLOGIES: CONSTITUTIONAL MYTHS AND THE CASE FOR CAUTION"

Michigan Law Review 102, no. 5 (2004): 801, 865–75, 882–87. Courtesy of Orin S. Kerr and the *Michigan Law Review*.

"A WORLD WITHOUT PRIVACY: WHY PROPERTY DOES NOT DEFINE THE LIMITS OF THE RIGHT AGAINST UNREASONABLE SEARCHES AND SEIZURES"

Michigan Law Review 102, no. 5 (2004): 889, 889–91, 900–903. Courtesy of Sherry F. Colb and the *Michigan Law Review*.

"PARADIGMS OF RESTRAINT"

Duke Law Journal 57, no. 5 (2005): 1321, 1323–27, 1364–69, 1372, 1393–1400. Courtesy of Erin Murphy.

"Peeping Techno-Toms and the Fourth Amendment: Seeing Through *Kyllo*'s Rules Governing Technological Surveillance"

Minnesota Law Review 86, no. 6 (2002): 1393, 1393–94, 1402–1406. Courtesy of Christopher Slobogin and the *Minnesota Law Review*.

"Discretionless Policing: Technology and the Fourth Amendment"

California Law Review 95, no. 1 (2007): 199, 199–202, 216–21, 224–26, 230–31. Courtesy of Elizabeth E. Joh. © 2007 by the *California Law Review, Inc.* Reprinted from *California Law Review* 95, no. 1, by permission of the *California Law Review, Inc.*

CHAPTER 8

"The System of Foreign Intelligence Surveillance Law"

The George Washington Law Review 72, no. 6 (2004): 1306, 1312–15, 1320–23, 1325, 1330–33. Courtesy of Peter P. Swire and *The George Washington Law Review*.

"Protecting the Unpopular from the Unreasonable: Warrantless Monitoring of Attorney Client Communications in Federal Prisons"

Catholic University Law Review 53, no. 2 (2004): 295, 299, 301–304, 331, 333–34, 336–39. Courtesy of Teri Dobbins and the *Catholic University Law Review*.

"The Detention of Material Witnesses and the Fourth Amendment"

Mississippi Law Journal 76, no. 2 (2006): 585, 585–88, 603–609, 612. Courtesy of the *Mississippi Law Journal*.

"The Cowboy and the Cop: The Saga of Dudley Hiibel, 9/11, and the Vanishing Fourth Amendment"

Pennsylvania State Law Review 109, no. 4 (2005): 929, 929–30, 937–38, 940–45. Courtesy of Arnold H. Loewy and the *Pennsylvania State Law Review*.

CHAPTER 9

"THE RETURN OF REASONABLENESS: SAVING THE FOURTH AMENDMENT FROM THE SUPREME COURT"

Case Western Reserve Law Review 59, no. 1 (2008): 1, 1–3, 6–9. Courtesy of Melanie D. Wilson and by permission of the *Case Western Reserve Law Review.*

"'EVERYMAN' 'S FOURTH AMENDMENT: PRIVACY OR MUTUAL TRUST BETWEEN GOVERNMENT AND CITIZEN?"

Columbia Law Review 94, no. 6 (1994): 1751, 1751–54, 1758–63, 1771–75, 1777–79, 1785–87. Courtesy of Scott E. Sundby and by permission of the *Columbia Law Review.*

"HUMAN DIGNITY UNDER THE FOURTH AMENDMENT"

Wisconsin Law Review, no. 4 (2008): 655, 656–61, 675–79, 694–96. Copyright 2008 by the Board of Regents of the University of Wisconsin System; reprinted by permission of the *Wisconsin Law Review* and John D. Castiglione.

"RESPECT AND THE FOURTH AMENDMENT"

Journal of Criminal Law and Criminology 94, no. 1 (2003): 15, 15–17, 20–22, 27–29, 33, 47–51, 53–54, 56–57, 88–98. Courtesy of Andrew E. Taslitz and the *Journal of Criminal Law and Criminology.* Reprinted by special permission of Northwestern University School of Law, *Journal of Criminal Law and Criminology.* The ideas expressed in this article are expanded upon in Andrew E. Taslitz, *Reconstructing the Fourth Amendment: A History of Search and Seizure, 1789–1868* (2006).

"REASONABLENESS AND OBJECTIVITY: A FEMINIST DISCOURSE OF THE FOURTH AMENDMENT"

Texas Journal of Women and the Law 17, no. 2 (2008): 153, 190–91, 196–99, 213–18, 220–21. Courtesy of Dana Raigrodski.